SILENCED

Caitlin Press Inc.
8100 Alderwood Road,
Halfmoon Bay, BC V0N 1Y1
www.caitlin-press.com

Text and cover design by Vici Johnstone
Cover photo courtesy Sheldon Boles
Printed in Canada

Caitlin Press Inc. acknowledges financial support from the Government of
Canada and the Canada Council for the Arts, and from the Province of British
Columbia through the British Columbia Arts Council and the Book Publisher's
Tax Credit.

Library and Archives Canada Cataloguing in Publication

Reilly Schmidt, Bonnie, 1955-, author
    Silenced : the untold story of the fight for equality in the
RCMP / Bonnie Reilly Schmidt.

Includes bibliographical references and index.
ISBN 978-1-927575-89-5 (paperback)

    1. Policewomen—Canada—History. 2. Equality—Canada—History.
3. Royal Canadian Mounted Police—History. I. Title.

HV8023.R44 2015   363.2082   C2015-903565-1

SILENCED

THE UNTOLD STORY OF THE FIGHT
FOR EQUALITY IN THE RCMP

BONNIE REILLY SCHMIDT

CAITLIN PRESS

To the women of
Troop 17 (1974/75).

And to Candace Smith,
for the courage to come back.

CONTENTS

ACKNOWLEDGEMENTS

I owe an enormous debt of gratitude to many people who believed that the history of women in the RCMP was a story that needed to be told. First and foremost, I am indebted to the women and men who agreed to be interviewed for this research. Not only were they generous with their time but they were extremely helpful in sharing their memories, photographs, letters, histories, books, and news clippings with me. I especially wish to acknowledge the women of the RCMP who consented to be interviewed, many of whom were still working in the police force at the time. All of them took a chance on an unknown historian whom they trusted with their stories and their anonymity. I have the utmost respect for them as women and as police officers. Without them, the personal side of the history of female Mounties would remain untold.

Reliving painful memories with a stranger was sometimes difficult, especially for those women who were struggling with post-traumatic stress disorder. Thank you seems an inadequate expression of gratitude, but it is my hope that their stories will contribute to a more open dialogue about mental illness in the RCMP and across the first responder community in Canada.

Many others in the RCMP, serving and retired, deserve a special note of thanks. Commissioner Beverley Busson offered her support during the early stages of this project and graciously granted me permission to interview members of the RCMP across Canada in 2007. I could not have asked for a better cheerleader. In addition, Karen Adams, Sheldon Boles, Jane Hall, Ric Hall, Cheryl Joyce, Don Klancher, Fraser MacRae, Margaret Shorter, Fred Stark, and Bev Zaparozan were instrumental in providing historical information, photographs, studies, and documents, or in connecting me with their colleagues. I would also like to acknowledge the help I received from the Vancouver division of the RCMP Veterans Women's Auxiliary, particularly Dorothy Martinson, who connected me with other "Unpaid Mounties." Special thanks are also due to my "Special O" girlfriends—still friends after all these years.

A number of people outside of the RCMP made important contributions. I would especially like to thank Doris Toole, not only for her time and photographs, but for filling in the many details that were missing from the history of the first troop of female Mounties to enter the training academy in 1974. Shannon Cunningham at the RCMP's Historical Collections Unit in Regina was extremely helpful. Shannon spent the better part of a workday with me, explaining the significance of the women's uniform and allowing me to photograph a number of items from their collection. Sandy Ramos, the former historian for the RCMP in Ottawa, offered invaluable insights into the importance of the history of the police force at home and abroad. Thanks are also due to the librarians at Library and Archives Canada in Ottawa as well as at Simon Fraser University.

I consider myself very fortunate to have been guided by a number of wonderful historians who inspired me during my academic career. The influence of my senior Ph.D. advisor at Simon Fraser University, Dr. Willeen Keough, can be found in the pages that follow. I would also like to thank Nawal Musleh Motut, Anne Toews, Sylvie Murray, Jack and Nicole Gaston, and Alisa Webb for their interest and encouragement. Thanks are also due to the Social Sciences and Humanities Research Council of Canada for providing funding for this research through a doctoral scholarship, and to Simon Fraser University for several research and travel grants.

My publisher, Vici Johnstone, is an amazing and endlessly energetic woman who was enthusiastic about the book from the start and has patiently walked me through the many details of publishing a manuscript and negotiating the world of publishing in Canada. Thanks are also due to my editor Kathleen Fraser, Andrea Routley, and the entire Caitlin team. I especially want to thank poet and author Kate Braid, who not only inspires me as a writer but was instrumental in connecting me with Caitlin Press. In sisterhood, Kate.

A number of friends remained enthusiastic and interested no matter how often I talked about the RCMP over the years, especially

Gail Purdy, Crista Santos, and Judi Russell. Thank you for reminding me at key points in time that it was the journey, and not necessarily the end result, that really mattered. My dad, Howard Reilly, loved me enough to believe that I could write a book at this stage in life despite the naysayers, although I'm sure he wondered at times if I'd ever finish. The same is true of Twyla and Peter, who supported me during the several years it took to finish this project. This book is dedicated to the memory of Agnes Schmidt who passed away while patiently waiting for me to finish. This book is also dedicated to my grandson Karsten and my granddaughter Naomi, who are fortunate enough to live in a world where female police officers are no longer an anomaly. Finally, my husband, Vic, probably knows more about women and the RCMP than he ever hoped to imagine. Without his advice, encouragement, and support, this book would not be possible. He's the light of my life.

Beati pacifica. Pro gloria domini.

LIST OF ABBREVIATIONS AND ACRONYMS

A/Commr.	Assistant Commissioner
AM	Administration Manual (RCMP)
C/M	Civilian Member
CBC	Canadian Broadcasting Corporation
CEDC	Clothing and Equipment Design Committee
CEWC	Committee for Equality of Women in Canada
CO	Commanding Officer
Col.	Colonel
Commr.	Commissioner
CP	Canadian Press
CPIC	Canadian Police Information Centre
Cpl.	Corporal
CSIS	Canadian Security Intelligence Service
Cst.	Constable
D/Commr.	Deputy Commissioner
DSRR	Division Staff Relations Representatives
EEA	Employment Equity Act (Canada) 1986
FLQ	Front de libération du Québec
CFUW	Canadian Federation of University Women
GD	General Duty
GI	General Investigations
HCU	Historical Collections Unit (RCMP)
Insp.	Inspector
LAC	Library and Archives Canada (formerly Public Archives Canada)
Maj.	Major

NCO	Non-Commissioned Officer (the rank of corporal, sergeant, or staff sergeant)
OIC	Officer-in-Charge (usually, the rank of inspector or higher)
OPP	Ontario Provincial Police
PAC	Public Archives Canada (now Library and Archives Canada)
PARE	Physical Abilities Requirement Evaluation
PTSD	Post-Traumatic Stress Disorder
R/M	Regular Member
RCSW	Royal Commission on the Status of Women in Canada
RFT	Recruit Field Training Program
RIC	Royal Irish Constabulary
S/Cst.	Special Constable
S/Sgt.	Staff Sergeant
Sgt.	Sergeant
SS	Security Service
Supt.	Superintendent
UDM	Uniform and Dress Manual
UN	United Nations

NOMENCLATURE

The RCMP has undergone two name changes since its inception:

North-West Mounted Police (NWMP)
1873–1904
    The North-West Mounted Police was founded in 1873. Since the original mandate of the force was to police the North-West Territories, its name reflected the regional scope of its authority.

Royal North-West Mounted Police (RNWMP)
1904–1919
    In 1904, the status "Royal" was conferred on the NWMP by King Edward VII in recognition of the military contributions made by members of the police force to the Empire during the Anglo-South African War (1899–1902).

Royal Canadian Mounted Police (RCMP)
1919–present
    The present name of the force, the Royal Canadian Mounted Police, came with the amalgamation of the RNWMP and the Dominion Police. Prior to 1919, the country was divided into two parts and policed by two separate police forces. The RNWMP's jurisdiction covered all of the territory west of what is now known as Thunder Bay, Ontario. The Dominion Police, a small federal police force formed in 1868 to perform protective duties in Ottawa and investigate federal offences, were responsible for policing all of eastern Canada. In November 1919, in the wake of the Winnipeg general strike and on the advice of RNWMP Commr. A.B. Perry, both police forces were amalgamated by an act of Parliament to form the RCMP, giving Canada a centralized police force responsible for federal law enforcement.

AUTHOR'S NOTE

Oral histories are one of the major sources for this study. Historians have limited access to official RCMP documents about women in the police force, and I was no exception. Despite attempts to obtain documentation under the Access to Information Act, I was denied access to many of the files I requested for this research.

In the absence of official documents, the oral histories of people who have worked for the RCMP became invaluable resources in compiling this history.

The names of the people who are quoted in the following chapters are pseudonyms that I have created. The exceptions are cases where names have become a matter of public record, such as when recorded in autobiographical or historical material or identified in the media, or cases in which the narrators have agreed to be identified.

The names of the colleagues and commanding officers of those who were interviewed have also been changed or omitted to protect their anonymity and that of the narrators. I have also changed or invented the locations of the detachments and regions of the country in the retelling of certain events.

Any pseudonyms that are similar to, or the same as, the names of people who are currently working or who have worked in the past for the RCMP are purely coincidental.

INTRODUCTION

It's taken more than 100 years, but the Mounties have finally got their women.

—*Toronto Star*, 1974

Constable Beverley MacDonald was a twenty-three-year-old RCMP rookie just out of training when she arrived at her first posting in Salmon Arm, British Columbia, in 1975. Salmon Arm was a small, working-class farming and logging community located in the interior of the province. Most of the RCMP officers posted at the detachment were young, single men with just a few years of service. MacDonald, who was one of the first thirty-two women to be hired by the RCMP, recalled that members of the community felt special to have been chosen as one of the first towns in Canada to be assigned a female Mountie. Many of Salmon Arm's citizens had never seen a female police officer before.

Although people in the community were generally supportive of the idea of women in the RCMP, they were also curious about whether a woman could do the work. While on routine patrol in town one day, MacDonald noticed that her police cruiser had a flat tire. Pulling over in front of the Shuswap Inn Pub, she radioed in to the detachment to say she would be out of the vehicle to change the tire. Just out of training and in good physical condition, MacDonald had little difficulty in replacing the flat. When she finished, she was greeted by a round of applause from the patrons of the pub who had been watching her through the window. She also heard members of the detachment, who were hiding in nearby bushes, cheering her on.[1] Stories such as

---

1 Commissioner Beverley Busson, speech at Langley, BC, November 1, 2007. Also in Bonnie Reilly Schmidt, "Women in Red Serge: Thirty-Five Years Later," *The Quarterly* 74, no. 4 (Fall 2009), 4.

MacDonald's demonstrate the importance of recording the history of women in the RCMP. Their narratives offer an alternative and more inclusive approach to the historical record of the police force, one that tells us much about changing societal values and shifting attitudes toward gender.

The narratives of the first women to join the RCMP in the 1970s and 1980s have only recently begun to receive some public attention. Historical accounts of the police force continue to be dominated by men in much the same way as they have since the nineteenth century. In 1873, following the formation of the North-West Mounted Police, journalists began to write stories of Mounties tracking whiskey smugglers, capturing outlaws, and keeping the peace between settlers and Aboriginal people. It was not long before memoirs written by former members of the police force, featuring tales of danger and adventure on the wild Canadian prairie, captured the imagination of popular readers. Throughout the twentieth century, the image of the RCMP continued to be shaped by the print media, popular histories, dime novels, and even comic strips. Hollywood soon capitalized on the public's ongoing interest in the men of the RCMP, producing over 240 Mountie movies that portrayed them as dashing and handsome heroes, protagonists who always saved the day. For its part, the RCMP did not discourage the idealization of its image. Such an image generated respect and trust, values that were essential to maintaining lawful authority in the communities Mounties policed.

Given this history, it is not surprising that most Canadians continued to think of the men of the RCMP in heroic terms as late as the 1970s. Policing was generally thought of as a manly pursuit and few Canadians, including RCMP officers, could conceive of female Mounties. Of course, women have been active in the work of the RCMP, both in paid and unpaid capacities, for most of its history. But their absence from the historical record has led to assumptions that the RCMP and police work has always been the explicit province of men.

Silenced: The Untold Story of the Fight for Equality in the RCMP, offers an alternative perspective of the history of the police force. Based on forty-three interviews with male and female police officers, including some of the first women to be hired by the RCMP, it recounts how between 1974 and 1990 the first women challenged assumptions about police work as an exclusively male occupation. Their narratives reveal that despite a great deal of resistance and some pretty incredible odds, the women of the RCMP managed to assert their equality as police officers on their own terms. Although the first women to join the RCMP did not think of themselves as feminists who were breaking ground for women's rights, their work as Mounties nevertheless signified women's changing role in Canadian society.

Why did the RCMP wait 101 years to hire women? Despite the fact that women had worked in policing in municipal departments across Canada since 1912, the RCMP's journey toward hiring the first female Mounties was long and complex. There were two key reasons for the delay. The first, and most important, had to do with the preservation of the masculine image of the police force and, as a corollary, the country. The RCMP enjoyed a privileged position as Canada's federal police force, a status not held by any other police department. The force's long paramilitary history was intimately connected to Canadian nationhood, and by the 1970s the figure of the manly Mountie in his red serge tunic was firmly entrenched as an iconic symbol of Canada, both at home and abroad. It was an image of the country that the federal government was reluctant to alter, and one that the RCMP's commanding officers were very keen to maintain.

The second reason had more to do with inexperience. Quite simply, the RCMP did not know in what capacity women could most effectively be utilized. The force's refusal to hire women earlier in the century handicapped their decision-making process seventy years later. Although the NWMP briefly hired women to act as matrons and gold inspectors during the Yukon gold rush, they were not engaged in patrol or enforcement activities in the same way women working for municipal police departments had been throughout the century. When commanding officers began to consider hiring women in 1970, a number of questions emerged. Could the RCMP use women to work in more traditional policing roles—as matrons or to do social service work with female offenders and children? Should they be hired strictly for traffic or bylaw enforcement work, freeing up male officers to investigate more serious crimes? Or should their work be confined to plainclothes investigations, an area where they were already proving successful? Most importantly, were women capable of performing as uniformed personnel with full police powers? These questions may have been more easily answered if the RCMP had had a point of reference from earlier decades on which to base their decision.

Despite the delay, when the decision was finally made in 1974 to hire women on an equal basis with men, the RCMP officially promoted itself as a gender-neutral organization. Female Mounties earned the same rate of pay, underwent the same training, and were invested with full police powers. Unofficially, however, questions about whether women were equal to, or different from, male police officers were often at the centre of much of the discrimination they encountered within the organization. Male members of the RCMP understood brawn and physical size as essential to effective law enforcement. In contrast, women possessed a number of inescapable "natural" conditions, such as a smaller stature and lesser physical strength. According to many of their detractors, these physical characteristics only emphasized their biological inferiority and therefore their unsuitability to the work.

Were the women of the RCMP, then, equal to or different from male police officers? Many of the first female Mounties struggled with the pressure of having to choose one or the other category to define themselves. Within RCMP culture, if they considered themselves to be equal to men, they were branded as unfeminine and manly, a "women's libber" who hated men. If they considered themselves to be different from men, they were characterized as poor substitutes for "real" police officers and unable to perform the work. It was a no-win situation for female Mounties, who would always fail to live up to male standards of policing no matter which category they chose. Few within or outside the RCMP had considered the possibility that women could be both equal to and different from their male colleagues.

Finally, there is one additional reason the RCMP waited so long to hire female police officers. The men of the RCMP, like those in most other private and public industries and institutions in Canada in the 1960s and 1970s, viewed advances being made by women in society as coming at the cost of men. Many Canadians did not see how increased rights for women benefited society as a whole. Men and women were still thought of in dichotomous terms and their roles were understood as existing in opposition, rather than in tandem. The maintenance of power became an important issue within the RCMP where many men strove to maintain control of the police force rather than relinquish any part of their monopoly. At least from a gendered point of view, it was obvious that the RCMP was an organization that was not representative of the communities they were policing.

It was against this historical backdrop that 292 young women from across Canada applied to join the RCMP in 1974. Thirty-two, representing every province, were chosen to form the first female troop in the history of the RCMP, Troop 17 (1974/75). For most of the women, becoming a Mountie meant job security, interesting work, a chance to help others, and the opportunity to don the famous RCMP uniform and represent their country. None realized that being a woman and a Mountie would present them with a number of unique challenges that they were expected to negotiate to be considered good police officers. Their fight for equality as members of the RCMP was only just beginning.

PROLOGUE

Maybe we should focus on the things that make us the same instead of different. Maybe, after 21 years, we should just let it rest.

—Supt. Beverley Busson
Pony Express, 1995

In 1989, Baltej Singh Dhillon was the first practising Sikh to be hired as a member of the RCMP. Dhillon was told that as a member of the RCMP he would have to shave his beard, cut his hair, and cease wearing his turban. He asked the RCMP to make an exception, arguing that wearing a turban was his religious duty as a Sikh and that being asked to remove it was a violation of his religious rights under Canada's Charter of Rights and Freedoms. In April 1989, RCMP commissioner Norman Inkster recommended to the federal government that the prohibition against the wearing of turbans by members of the RCMP be lifted. The commissioner's recommendation and Dhillon's request were forwarded to the federal Cabinet for consideration.[1] Dhillon's request sparked a heated national debate about immigration, multiculturalism, and Canadian identity. He received hate mail and death threats while in training at the RCMP's academy. The mayor of one town asked the RCMP not to post Dhillon to his community.[2]

Many Canadians viewed the RCMP's Stetson hat as central to the iconic image of the police force. The public strongly resisted any alteration of that image. Some 150,000 Canadians signed a petition,

---

1   "Sikh Mounties Permitted to Wear Turbans," *The National*, CBC Television, originally aired March 15, 1990, http://www.cbc.ca/archives/entry/1990-sikh-mounties-permitted-to-wear-turbans.

2   Larissa Cahute, "First Canadian Sikh Member of the RCMP Describes His 'Struggle,'" *Vancouver Desi*, June 24, 2013, http://www.vancouverdesi.com/news/nridiaspora/exhibit-sikh-heritage-museum-tells-of-turbans-troubles-times-in-b-c/466404.

delivered to Parliament, urging the federal government not to amend the *RCMP Act* to permit officers to wear turbans.[3] In the end, the government did not agree with the protests. On March 15, 1990, Solicitor General Pierre Cadieux announced that Cabinet had passed an order-in-council authorizing an amendment to the RCMP Act to allow members of the RCMP to wear turbans.

The emotional debate surrounding Stetsons and turbans overshadowed another significant development that day regarding the RCMP uniform, one that received far less attention from the media. Cadieux also announced that for the first time, female members of the RCMP would be authorized to wear the same review order dress uniform as their male counterparts.[4] For many female Mounties, it was an unexpected turn of events after sixteen years of lobbying the police force to make the change. Many of the first women to join the police force had viewed the policy regarding two different dress uniforms for men and women as a significant distinction. Marianne Robson, a member of the first troop, felt that the difference in dress uniforms before 1990 "showed that they didn't really want us there. They wanted to make sure that we were always different."[5] While some female Mounties wanted to maintain the feminized version of the uniform, others saw the change as a symbolic step toward their full equality as members of the RCMP. Until that point, the two distinct uniforms had been a visual inequality that communicated difference and called into question women's legitimacy as equal representatives of state authority.[6]

Following the government's announcement, a short bulletin advising of the change was sent to all RCMP detachments and departments

---

3   Navneet Sidhu, "Baltej Singh Dhillon: Making History: A Sikh Canadian Hero," 2012, http://www.canadiansikhheritage.ca/files/baltej%20singh%20dhillon.pdf (accessed January 6, 2013; now defunct).

4   The order-in-council stated, "All members shall wear the same significant uniform of the RCMP." Bulletin, "Unisex Review Order—Female Members," RCMP file UDM 53, February 28, 1991 (revised April 12, 1991). Access to Information file GA-3951-3-03134/08.

5   Marianne Robson, interview with author, July 29, 2008.

6   Thank you to Yvonne Gall for the idea of visual inequality. Yvonne Gall, producer "First Ladies of the RCMP: The History of Women in the Force," *The Current with Anna Maria Tremonti*, CBC Radio, November 30, 2011.

for inclusion in the *Uniform and Dress Manual*. Female police officers were instructed to place their orders for review order items as "initial issue."[7] The memo's terse words belied the significance of the policy change to the women who had been waiting to wear the same RCMP uniform worn by the men. Robson recalled the emotions she felt as she tried on her new uniform for the first time: "I remember in 1990 ... picking up my Stetson ... and taking it home and putting it on. And saying it took me sixteen years to get here. Sixteen long years, but I've got it now. Still got it. So that was a hard battle."[8] Placing the Stetson hat on her head for the first time symbolized the end of a long and difficult struggle for recognition as an equal member of the RCMP. For Robson and many women working in the RCMP, the differences between male and female Mounties were finally beginning to blur.

---

7   Bulletin, "Unisex Review Order—Female Members."

8   Marianne Robson, interview with author, July 29, 2008.

THE RIDERS OF
THE PLAINS

Horses were sacrificed for the arrest, but the M.P.s are worse than bloodhounds when they scent the track of a smuggler, and they fetch their men every time.

—John J. Healey

Fort Benton Record (Montana), 1877

Perhaps no other national image so perfectly symbolizes the degree to which women were positioned as unequal members in Canadian society as the figure of the dashing Mountie. Since the nineteenth century, the Mountie has served as both an iconic symbol of Canada and an ideal representation of Canadian manhood. With his imposing physique, tailored red tunic, riding boots, and Stetson hat, few images better invoked ideal masculinity than the virile hero astride his horse. The Mountie was not only a gendered representation of Canada, but a racialized one. As a representative of the state, the Mountie symbolized the dominance of white men over civilized society. Indeed, for much of its history, the RCMP was composed solely of men of Anglo-Celtic birth or descent.[1] Aboriginal people, women, and ethnic and cultural minorities were not considered suitable as regular members of the police force for the better part of one hundred years. Policies such as these tell us a lot about the assumptions and traditions from a previous century that shaped the foundational beliefs of the police force, beliefs that persisted long after the arrival of women in 1974.

---

1   Steve Hewitt, *Riding to the Rescue: The Transformation of the RCMP in Alberta and Saskatchewan, 1914–1939* (Toronto: University of Toronto Press, 2006), 30. Also in Keith Walden, *Visions of Order: The Canadian Mounties in Symbol and Myth* (Toronto: Butterworth & Co., 1982), 30.

THE FORMATION OF THE POLICE FORCE

The North-West Mounted Police (NWMP) was the brainchild of Prime Minister Sir John A. Macdonald. As early as 1869, Macdonald envisioned a mounted force that would serve both a civil and a military function in the newly acquired North-West Territories. The police force was essential to attracting white settlers and economic investment to the region, and its presence was meant to communicate that the more than fifty thousand Aboriginal people living on the land were peacefully assimilated.[2] American whiskey traders had long been involved in selling illegal alcohol to the Aboriginal population north of the border, contributing to increased alcoholism and unrest. The Canadian government was anxious to end the whiskey trade, and an armed police force was viewed as a way to enforce liquor prohibition. Macdonald was inspired by the Royal Irish Constabulary (RIC), the Empire's largest and most professional police force at the time. Organized to control civil strife and social unrest in Ireland using men from the local population, the RIC served as a model for many of the Empire's colonial forces.[3] Macdonald planned to build a similar paramilitary force.

But the formation of the police force encountered a number of economic and political delays until a crisis threatened to dismantle the government's plans. In 1873, anarchy on the prairies appeared imminent when ten white hunters from Montana crossed the border into Saskatchewan and murdered thirty-six members of an Assiniboine tribe they suspected of stealing their horses. The event, known as the Cypress Hills Massacre, spurred the government into action, and thirteen days later, on May 23, 1873, the NWMP was hastily formed. An initial contingent of 150 men was dispatched from eastern Canada to Winnipeg, Manitoba, later that summer. Recruits enlisted for three

---

2   Paige Raibmon, *Authentic Indians: Episodes of Encounter from the Late-Nineteenth-Century Northwest Coast* (Durham and London: Duke University Press, 2005), 42.

3   Macdonald's interest in the RIC was evident in a letter he wrote to a Cabinet colleague in London, England, in February 1870, requesting "all the information he could obtain on the organization of the RIC." S.W. Horrall, "Sir John A. Macdonald and the Mounted Police Force for the Northwest Territories," *Canadian Historical Review 52*, no. 2 (June 1972): 181–82. Also see Greg Marquis, "Policing Two Imperial Frontiers: The Royal Irish Constabulary and the North-West Mounted Police," in *Laws and Societies in the Canadian Prairie West, 1670–1940*, ed. Louis Knafla and Jonathan Swainger (Vancouver: UBC Press, 2005), 185–210; R.C. Macleod, *The NWMP and Law Enforcement, 1873–1905* (Toronto: University of Toronto Press, 1976), 162.

years of service and were paid one dollar a day.[4] The mandate of the Riders of the Plains, as Mounties were sometimes called, was clearly summarized in the final stanza of "The Riders of the Plains," a poem written for the *Saskatchewan Herald*:

> Our mission is to plant the right
> Of British freedom here—
> Restrain the lawless savages,
> And protect the pioneer.
> And 'tis a proud and daring trust
> To hold these vast domains
> With but three hundred mounted men—
> The Riders of the Plains.[5]

Shortly after the police force was formed, the scarlet-clad Mountie became a widely popular figure. The print media and the force's own commanding officers played a central role in cultivating the legend of the Riders of the Plains.[6] George Arthur French, the NWMP's first commissioner (1873–1876), was the first to make strategic use of the media to cultivate positive public opinion about the force. French enlisted the help of journalist and artist Henri Julien from the *Canadian Illustrated News* to record the march west of a second contingent of Mountie recruits in 1874.[7] French was aware that Macdonald's successor, Alexander Mackenzie, was interested in disbanding the NWMP and he was hopeful that Julien's accounts would convince Canadians

---

4   Desmond Morton, "Cavalry or Police: Keeping the Peace on Two Adjacent Frontiers, 1870–1900," *Journal of Canadian Studies* 12, no. 2 (1977): 29–30.

5   Although the poet used the initials "W.S." as a pseudonym, the author is thought to be Constable T.A. Boys, who served as a member of the NWMP from 1875 to 1878. For the entire poem, see "The Riders of the Plains," quoted in Andrew R. Graybill, *Policing the Great Plains: Rangers, Mounties, and the North American Frontier, 1875–1910* (Lincoln: University of Nebraska Press, 2007), 5.

6   This material on the NWMP and the media also appears in Bonnie Reilly Schmidt, "'The Greatest Man-Catcher of All': The First Female Mounties, the Media, and the Royal Canadian Mounted Police," *Journal of the Canadian Historical Association* 22, no. 1 (2011): 202–244.

7   "Henri Julien," *Dictionary of Canadian Biography Online*, http://www.biographi.ca/en/bio/julien_henri_13E.html.

that the police force was a necessary and viable enterprise.[8]

French's tactic worked. Julien's account of the NWMP's arduous journey to the foothills of the Rocky Mountains captured the public's imagination, and the police force remained. But his strategy also proved to be a double-edged sword. It was not long before commanding officers found it necessary to create regulations prohibiting lower-ranking Mounties from speaking to the media. By the end of the nineteenth century, the force's regulations stipulated that any police officer who communicated to journalists without the approval of the commissioner was liable to face arrest, trial, and a heavy fine.[9] The police force remained intent on reinforcing its popular image, but on its own terms. It was the start of a long and often fractious relationship between the mounted police and the press.

Because Canada was a colony of imperial Britain, ideologies of race and class from the seat of the Empire occupy an important place in the history of the police force. The close link between the NWMP and the Empire was evident during Queen Victoria's Diamond Jubilee celebrations in London, England, in 1897 when a small contingent of NWMP officers made their debut on the international stage. The men caused a sensation amongst the crowds when they appeared on horseback wearing their red tunics, white gauntlets, black boots, and new felt hats, which were on display officially for the first time.[10] To observers, the dashing Mounties symbolized romance and adventure on the furthest edges of the Queen's Empire. Their appearance at the celebrations solidified the relationship between the British monarchy and the police force, and since that time, contingents of RCMP officers have appeared at every royal funeral, wedding, and coronation.

THE GENTLEMAN AND THE COWBOY

Gentlemanly values such as manners, courtesy, and respectability were often attributed to the Riders of the Plains, further enhancing

---

8   Rob C. Mawby, *Policing Images: Policing, Communication and Legitimacy* (Portland, OR: Willan Publishing, 2002), 37.

9   A.L. Haydon, *The Riders of the Plains: A Record of the Royal North-West Mounted Police of Canada, 1873–1918* (Toronto: The Copp Clark Co., Ltd., 1919), 333.

10   S.W. Horrall, *The Pictorial History of the Royal Canadian Mounted Police* (Toronto: McGraw-Hill Ryerson, 1973), 107.

their popular appeal. Social class figured just as prominently as rank in the hierarchical organizational structure of the NWMP and mirrored practices commonly found in nineteenth-century British military units. Historian A.L. Haydon claimed in 1919 that the NWMP officer was a gentleman and a man of action who possessed an inner strength that demanded respect for his authority.[11] Lower-ranking non-commissioned officers and constables were usually culled from higher levels of society than those they were policing. According to the NWMP's Colonel Samuel Steele, recruits were "smart young fellows from the old country [Britain] and eastern Canada, well-educated, but unaccustomed to manual labour, lured to the wild west by the halo of romance."[12] Criminality was assumed to be a function of the lower social orders, so it was important that members of the NWMP be socially superior to those who broke the law.[13]

All Mounties were trained to follow codes of gentlemanly conduct modelled by commanding officers who were from the upper classes of British and Canadian society. Commanders were well educated and most had received officer training at the Royal Military College in Kingston, Ontario. Many served with the British military in locations throughout the Empire. All adopted symbols that conveyed their social status and rank. Commissioned officers enjoyed the services of special constables who were hired specifically as officers' servants to perform "domestic assistance" for them in the field.[14] Gentility gave the men of the police force "distinctiveness and exclusivity in the popular view" according to another historian who observed that most of the officers were "well bred."[15] Ideas of class and race were foundational to the identity of the NWMP and were deeply embedded in the organizational structure of the police force from the outset.

The importance of maintaining upper-class codes of conduct and hierarchical social structures was emphasized by public figures such

---

11   Haydon, *Riders of the Plains*, ix.

12   Colonel S.B. Steele, *Forty Years in Canada: Reminiscences of the Great North-West with Some Account of His Service in South Africa* (New York: Dodd, Mead & Company, 1915), 96–97.

13   Macleod, *The NWMP and Law Enforcement*, 88.

14   Officers' servants disappeared from the police force in the "first decade of the twentieth century." Ibid., 80.

15   Walden, *Visions of Order*, 31.

as Robert Baden-Powell, the founder of the Boy Scout movement and British hero of the Anglo-South African war. Baden-Powell frequently singled out the men of the NWMP in his speeches and writings as the epitome of manliness, men "whose manhood was strong and rich, and whose lives were pure."[16] In contrast to such portrayals, English feminists began to critique codes of gentlemanly behaviour by arguing that the motivation behind courtesy and chivalry was a belief in the inferiority of women. While women were expected to act with deference and subordination toward men in Victorian society, men were expected to act in a gentlemanly manner toward the "weaker sex," as women were known. Chivalrous behaviour, such as the lifting of a hat or the opening of a door, was increasingly seen by feminists as condescension to an inferior rather than a demonstration of respect for an equal.[17] All the same, Mounties continued to value gentlemanly behaviour as an outward sign of true manliness well into the twentieth century.

As the nineteenth century drew to a close, the health and survival of the white race, contingent on Darwin's theories of the survival of the fittest, was cause for concern for people across the Empire.[18] There was a growing emphasis on virility and physical strength, and men on both sides of the Atlantic Ocean looked to the outdoors and wild, untamed geographical spaces to reassert their manliness. The emergence of the cowboy figure coincided with this interest. Cowboys represented a rugged masculinity, and they were often portrayed in highly romantic terms. Values such as honour, endurance, hard work, discipline, and loyalty to Empire were often ascribed to the cowboy. In his memoirs, Colonel Samuel Steele insisted that the "cowboy has no superior in the world, and in spite of his free life he takes to the order of military experience as if he were born to it."[19] The popularity and influence of the cowboy are visible in the uniforms of police and military units from

---

16   Robert Baden-Powell, "Baden-Powell's 'Boy Scouts Scheme,'" quoted in Robert H. MacDonald, *Sons of the Empire: The Frontier and the Boy Scout Movement, 1890–1918* (Toronto: University of Toronto Press, 1993), 245.

17   Cicely Hamilton, quoted in Carol Dyhouse, *Feminism and the Family in England, 1880–1939* (Oxford: Blackwell, 1989), 152.

18   MacDonald, *Sons of the Empire*, 16.

19   Steele, *Forty Years in Canada*, 213–14.

this period. Indeed, Baden-Powell's boy scouts wore neckerchiefs and a felt Stetson hat, both recognizable parts of cowboy dress.

THE ANGLO-SOUTH AFRICAN WAR

The merging of the two iconic cultural images, the cowboy and the English gentleman, was complete by the time of the Anglo-South African War. In 1900, Donald Smith (Lord Strathcona and Mount Royal), Canadian High Commissioner in London, formed and equipped an elite mounted Canadian regiment at his own expense to serve in the war. Strathcona's Horse, as it was known, was made up of "cowboys and frontiersmen of Western Canada and members of the North West Mounted Police," demonstrating a close connection between cowboy culture, the NWMP, and the pursuit of war.[20] Once in South Africa, the regiment soon gained international fame as an elite fighting force. When conventional warfare was replaced by guerrilla tactics during the conflict, "the regiment spent the next seven months scouting for the columns pursuing the elusive Boer commandos."[21] As mounted troops with light equipment and uniforms more suited to climatic conditions on the South African veldt, the men of Strathcona's Horse excelled as scouts.

Strathcona's Horse was commanded by Colonel Samuel Steele, one of the more colourful members of the NWMP. He is described in the *Dictionary of Canadian Biography* as "Physically strong and courageous ... tall, barrel-chested, and handsome, inspiring confidence in men and admiration in women."[22] In this description, Steele's physical attributes are equated with imperial masculinity, inspirational leadership, manliness, and sexual attraction. But the description of Steele's body also implied that policing and war were masculine

---

20   "Lord Strathcona's Horse: History of a Regiment," http://www.strathconas. ca/regimental-history. Researcher Sandra Gwyn places the number of NWMP members in the regiment at 537. Sandra Gwyn, *The Private Capital: Ambition and Love in the Age of Macdonald and Laurier* (Toronto: McClelland & Stewart, 1985), 336.

21   R.C. Macleod, "Steele, Sir Samuel Benfield," *Dictionary of Canadian Biography Online*, http://www.biographi.ca/en/bio/steele_samuel_benfield_14E.html. The term "Boer" referred to Afrikaners, peasant farmers who were considered to be churlish and unmannered yokels, or "boors." The term is now considered to be a pejorative. *Random House Webster's College Dictionary* (New York: Random House, 1992).

22   Macleod, "Steele, Sir Samuel Benfield." Thank you to Mark Reid of *Canada's History* for drawing this reference to my attention.

pursuits dependent on physical strength and a tall, muscular physique. Revisionists have since refuted idealized representations of Steele, who was remembered by one fellow officer as "ungentlemanly" for his frequent use of foul language, drunken behaviour, and the "negligent and callous treatment of his men" that verged on the sadistic. Steele was said to have once ordered a dozen men "suffering from piles to gallop flat out for five miles, his cure being to burst them and make them bleed."[23]

The effectiveness of the Horse's scouting techniques masked the darker side of warfare that the men were engaged in. Reports emerged in August 1900 that the regiment had conducted an impromptu court martial and hanging of six Boers suspected of killing members of the South African Light Horse. Although Steele denied these reports in his memoirs, historian Carman Miller has determined that there was little doubt that the hangings occurred and were later covered up by those involved, including Steele.[24] In this case, reality was far from the gentlemanly ideal propagated by popular discourses about the police force. Despite the controversy, members of the NWMP distinguished themselves on the battlefield, and popular appeal, thanks to the media's coverage of the war, once again prevented politicians at home from disbanding the police force. In all, seven Mounties died during the conflict and several received medals for exemplary service.[25]

The successes of Steele and his mounted regiment impressed Baden-Powell, who was by this time a British war hero for his successful defence of the town of Mafeking. Near the end of the conflict, when he was given the task of organizing the South African Constabulary (SAC), the general recruited men from every region of the Empire to man his police corps.[26] Steele was one of his more notable recruits. Steele later claimed that he helped the general organize the SAC based "on the character and methods" of the NWMP.[27] The pursuit of war

---

23   Gwyn, *The Private Capital*, 362. Ibid.

24   Miller, referenced in Macleod, "Steele, Sir Samuel Benfield." Gwyn also draws attention to this incident in *The Private Capital*, 363.

25   For a list of medals awarded to members of the NWMP for exemplary service during the war, including the Victoria Cross awarded to Sergeant Arthur Richardson, see Haydon, *The Riders of the Plains*, 256–58.

26   MacDonald, *Sons of the Empire*, 114.

27   Ibid., 113 fn.

defined the men of Strathcona's Horse as patriotic and loyal to the Empire. They emerged as exemplars of Canadian masculinity whose actions were tempered by codes of gentlemanly conduct and notions of chivalry. In recognition of the contributions made by Strathcona's Horse, and perhaps in acknowledgement of their popular appeal, King Edward VII officially granted the prefix "Royal" to the name of the NWMP in 1904.

REALITY NOT ROMANCE

Not everyone agreed with the romantic representations of the men of the NWMP, however. The police force experienced a number of problems during its early years, revealing that not all Mounties acted in a gentlemanly manner or with integrity when enforcing the law. At the end of the nineteenth century and into the twentieth, commanding officers struggled with a number of issues such as desertions, resignations, improper conduct, and breaches in discipline. Venereal disease became so rampant amongst the men of the police force in the 1880s that the police surgeon at Fort Walsh requested an assistant to help him deal with the number of men infected. By 1884, when the total complement of the NWMP was 557 men, the number of cases of venereal disease had grown to 132. Commanding officers were so concerned about the problem that they considered charging infected police officers for their medical care and confining them to their barracks as punishment.[28]

Desertions were commonplace when men could not purchase their discharge. In 1914, 10.3 percent of members of the RNWMP deserted and 18.32 percent were dismissed for bad conduct.[29] In 1912, Florence Foster of Calgary, Alberta, petitioned the federal minister of justice for a divorce. Foster complained that her Mountie husband, Fred Jenkins, had deserted her when he was sent to London in 1911 to take part in the coronation celebrations of King George V. Jenkins deserted the RNWMP shortly after landing, remarried under an assumed name, and continued to live abroad with his new wife. He later admitted to Foster that he had married her under an assumed name

---

28   James Dashuk, *Clearing the Plains: Disease, Politics of Starvation, and the Loss of Aboriginal Life* (Regina: University of Regina Press, 2013), 154.

29   Steve Hewitt, *Riding to the Rescue*, 34.

and refused to support her financially.[30] The minister of justice determined that although her husband had married her using a false name and had deserted her, the marriage remained valid.[31] While her husband failed to live up to the values embraced by the RNWMP, Foster was expected to continue to abide by the social values associated with appropriate femininity and remain married to the bigamist Foster.

The consumption of alcohol was a particularly thorny issue for commanding officers given that the police force was created, in part, to control the illegal whiskey trade that was decimating the Aboriginal population. British General Fred Middleton wrote in 1885 that the men of the NWMP were "some of the greatest scamps in the country, broken-down gentlemen who in many cases are called here inebriates."[32] For Middleton, the men were not good examples of sobriety in a region where alcohol was not permitted. Settlers also resented liquor prohibition and took exception to being regulated by the police in this way, given that senior officers of the NWMP were "notoriously heavy" drinkers. So incensed was the white population over this double standard that one NWMP constable posted outside a saloon in Prince Albert, Saskatchewan, was arrested and fined by a local magistrate for monitoring the patrons inside.[33]

Not all Mounties were brave and heroic, either. Sub-Inspector Francis J. Dickens, son of the British author Charles Dickens, was an alcoholic whose commission with the police force was purchased for him by his aunt and co-executor of his father's estate, Georgina Hogarth. She organized his nomination to the NWMP to help him escape the "temptations of London." Dickens was placed in charge of a small unit of twenty-three NWMP officers who were stationed at Fort Pitt, Saskatchewan, in 1885. He is known for his infamous desertion of the settlers at the fort during the Riel Resistance as Cree chief Big Bear

---

30   Marital desertion was not the sole preserve of men in the force's history. In 1886, one Mountie wife deserted her husband while he was stationed in Regina, Saskatchewan. She left to take up residence with a former member of the police force living in St. Paul, Minnesota. Sarah Carter, *The Importance of Being Monogamous: Marriage and Nation Building in Western Canada to 1915* (Edmonton: University of Alberta Press; Athabasca: Athabasca University Press, 2008), 95.

31   Ibid.

32   Quoted by Morton, "Cavalry or Police," 31.

33   Ibid., 33.

prepared to burn it down. Dickens allowed the civilian men, women, and children at the fort to surrender to the Cree before he escaped with his men by floating downstream on a scow toward Battleford, Saskatchewan. He left behind a number of settlers and a wounded constable at the fort, who were subsequently captured by the Cree.[34] While Dickens later called his decision a "retreat" rather than a desertion, he faced criticism in later years for his questionable actions and lack of leadership. Dickens's example demonstrates that the men of the NWMP were clearly not as well trained or equipped for military engagement as Macdonald had initially envisioned.

One of the more formidable challenges for the NWMP was policing the Aboriginal population, which sometimes placed the police force between indigenous groups and the federal government. Following the Riel Resistance, the NWMP was charged with aiding in setting up reserves to control the Aboriginal population and with implementing the federal government's pass system. The pass system prohibited Aboriginal people from leaving their reserves without permission from the local Indian agent. It was intended to limit the mobility of treaty Indians by restricting their access to the land they once used for food and to prevent their interaction with white settler communities. Although the NWMP recognized that the system had no legal basis for enforcement under treaty rights and protested the action, the police force bowed to pressure exerted by government officials to enforce it.[35] The pass system helped fulfill Prime Minister Macdonald's vision of a white settler society with an Aboriginal population that was wholly assimilated.[36] In the end, the NWMP ensured that Aboriginal people were confined to their reserves, an act that did little to enhance the trust between the police force and the indigenous communities it policed.

---

34   Eric Nicol, ed., *Dickens of the Mounted: The Astounding Long-Lost Letters of Inspector F. Dickens, NWMP, 1874–1886* (Toronto: McLelland & Stewart, 1989), 15; 242–54. Also Morton, "Cavalry or Police," 33.

35   Michael Dawson, *The Mountie from Dime Novel to Disney* (Toronto: Between the Lines, 1998), 13–14.

36   Dashuk, *Clearing the Plains*, 161–62. The forced move of treaty Indians onto reserves was part of a Conservative party policy called the "National Policy" which included the construction of a national railway to the Pacific Ocean. The plan necessitated the removal of Aboriginal people from the land to build the railway. By 1883, between fifteen and twenty thousand people were living on reserves. Ibid., 184.

As World War I approached, the Mountie served as a reminder of a fading Empire and the values that were shifting in the face of rapid modernization and the threat of a new global conflict. Commanding officers were challenged to balance the force's heroic image and idealized past with a desire to appear more modern and progressive as the century advanced. That was because they continued to embrace the Victorian values, traditions, and paramilitary organizational structures that were so foundational to the beginnings of the police force. Nowhere was this more evident than in the RCMP's persistent refusal to consider hiring women.

MATRONS, SPECIALS, AND THE UNPAID MOUNTIE

[A]s for prospective dangers in the enterprise, I didn't take them into account. When I undertake to do a thing, I just start doing it. The man or woman who is deterred from doing a thing which he or she would like to do never gets anywhere.

—Katherine "Klondike Kate" Ryan

NWMP Matron and Constable Special

1922

Throughout much of its history, the identity of the RCMP has rested on the image of the heroic Mountie as a virile and manly representation of Canada. But women have been involved in the policing activities of the RCMP since its beginnings. By the turn of the twentieth century, they occupied paid positions as matrons and gold inspectors for the NWMP, a little-known contribution that has long been omitted from the historical record. Matrons and gold inspectors were later replaced by Mountie wives, who played a significant role in the work of the RCMP until the final decades of the twentieth century. The force's reliance on the unpaid and unacknowledged work of women was a practice that not only marginalized their contributions but allowed the RCMP to maintain its iconic image. But it also reinforced the idea that policing was a solely masculine occupation, an argument that justified the delay in hiring women as police officers for decades.

EARLY CANADIAN WOMEN IN LAW ENFORCEMENT

Historical accounts of women in law enforcement in Canada are scarce. Researchers generally recognize Rose Fortune (1774–1884) as the first woman to assume a policing role in Canada. Fortune was a freed

African American slave living in the Annapolis Valley in Nova Scotia in the eighteenth and nineteenth centuries. She was a savvy entrepreneur who initially established a business transporting luggage for ship passengers from the port to local rooming houses in her wheelbarrow. Her transportation business eventually evolved into one of Annapolis Royal's first cartage companies, a business that remained in her family for over one hundred years. Fortune was also a self-appointed police officer in the port of Annapolis Royal. Her quasi-police duties included maintaining the peace, monitoring the town's youth, establishing and enforcing curfews, even "spanking local mischief-makers."[1] The community's acknowledgement and acceptance of her voluntary police service situate her as Canada's first policewoman.

Apart from Fortune's accomplishments, little is known about women in policing in Canada until the end of the nineteenth century and the appearance of the police matron. The history of police matrons is complicated by the variety of roles they were hired to perform and the titles they were given, which varied among police departments.[2] In the United States, for example, most matrons worked in jails but some also had powers of arrest, patrolled city streets, and aided male detectives in cases involving women and children. In Chicago, Illinois, Mary Owens was assigned the rank of "policeman" in 1893,[3] an unusual move for a police department in those years. Although Owens was a matron, her title and pay matched those of a policeman.[4] Others were trained social workers who had police powers and made court appearances. For example, in 1905, social worker Lola Baldwin was placed in charge of a force of social workers granted full police powers by the city of Portland, Oregon. They were charged with protecting the

---

1   "Rose Fortune," Association of Black Law Enforcers, http://www.ableorg. ca/pdf/fortunebutler.pdf. Also in Marilyn Corsianos, *Policing and Gendered Justice: Examining the Possibilities* (Toronto: University of Toronto Press, 2009), 12.

2   Women working in law enforcement held a variety of titles such as "patrol women, safety workers, women constables, and police women" in Britain, Canada, and the United States. Tamara Myers, "Women Policing Women: A Patrol Woman in Montreal in the 1910s," *Journal of the Canadian Historical Association* 4, no. 1 (1993): 230, fn. 2.

3   Dorothy Moses Schulz, "From Policewoman to Police Officer: An Unfinished Revolution," *Police Studies* 16, no. 3 (Fall 1993): 90.

4   Dorothy Moses Schulz, *From Social Worker to Crimefighter: Women in United States Municipal Policing* (Westport, CT: Praeger, 1995), 21.

women of Portland from an influx of lumbermen, miners, and labour-
ers attracted to the city following the Lewis and Clark Exposition.[5] In
Canada, matrons served in similar capacities. They worked with incarcerated women and children and sometimes served as moral regula-
tors, policing public spaces thought to be morally dangerous to women.[6]
Toronto was the first Canadian city to officially hire a woman as a
matron in 1887, followed by Vancouver in 1912.[7] Their social service
was not considered to be real police work because they dealt mainly
with women and children.

The appearance of the policewoman at the turn of the twentieth
century further complicated the history of women in law enforcement,
since the work they performed often replicated the work of matrons.
Policewomen at that time were primarily concerned with the moral
protection and sexual regulation of working-class women and children. The first policewoman in New York City, Mary E. Hamilton, in
her early book on the subject, listed her duties as social work, crime
prevention, and protective services for women and children.[8] Similarly
in Britain, women employed as policewomen during World War I were
chiefly concerned with public morality and controlling the behaviour
of working-class women, particularly in garrison towns coping with
an influx of soldiers.[9] British policewomen patrolled public spaces and
houses of prostitution, lectured teenagers smoking in the streets, separated "couples thought to be embracing too closely," and monitored a
variety of public behaviours considered to be immoral.[10]

In Canada, the goals of the moral reform movement were par-
ticularly instrumental in women's entrance into law enforcement.
Middle-class reformers, including reform groups such as the Montreal
Local Council of Women, lobbied local and federal governments and

---

5   Ibid., 22.

6   Corsianos, *Policing and Gendered Justice*, 13.

7   Ibid.; Chloe Owings, *Women Police: A Study of the Development and Status of
the Women Police Movement* (Montclair, NJ: Patterson Smith, 1925 & 1969), 62.

8   Mary E. Hamilton, *The Policewoman: Her Service and Ideals* (New York:
Frederick A. Stokes Company, 1924), 5.

9   Philippa Levine, "'Walking the Streets in a Way No Decent Woman Should':
Women Police in World War I," *Journal of Modern History* 66, no. 1 (March 1994): 44.

10   Ibid., 45.

police departments for the appointment of policewomen to help tackle issues such as temperance, eradicating prostitution, compulsory education, and "the desire to rescue delinquents."[11] Like those performed by matrons, the duties of policewomen were viewed as an extension of the private sphere of middle-class women's lives and were not considered to be real police work.

By the end of World War I, several Canadian cities had employed policewomen. Most had powers of arrest, identified themselves as police officers, and carried badges, although none had a uniform or carried a firearm.[12] The Vancouver Police Department holds the distinction of hiring the first policewomen in Canada on July 8, 1912. News reports from the period announced that Mrs. Lurancy Harris and Miss Minnie Millar were the "first of their sex to act as constables in Canada," an occasion that made for sensational headlines in newspapers across North America.[13] Harris and Millar were given full powers of arrest when they were sworn in, an indication that their work consisted of more than matron duties. They patrolled city streets, parks, and dance halls in addition to escorting women and child prisoners, investigating neglected or delinquent children, and enforcing the law regarding compulsory venereal disease treatment.[14] A few weeks after she was hired, Millar made history as the first Canadian policewoman to make an arrest. She arrested William Borden for "making himself 'objectionable' to women at a public beach" on August 5, 1912.[15] By 1925, Vancouver had three "women police and one matron," distinct functions indicating that an expansion of women's policing roles was taking place in the city.[16]

---

11 Carol Lee Bacchi, *Liberation Deferred?: The Ideas of the English-Canadian Suffragists, 1877–1918* (Toronto: University of Toronto Press, 1983), 9.

12 Corsianos, *Policing and Gendered Justice*, 15. The cities included Winnipeg, Vancouver, Halifax, Ottawa, Kingston, Toronto, St. Thomas, and London. The federal government also employed two women in the immigration department to "serve deportation warrants and make arrests of 'undesirable' female immigrants." Myers, "Women Policing Women," 234, 235 fn. 21.

13 Darah Hansen, "Equal Opportunity Policing: Vancouver Police Department Celebrates 100 Years of Women in Uniform," *Vancouver Sun*, August 18, 2012.

14 Owings, *Women Police*, 62.

15 Corsianos, *Policing and Gendered Justice*, 15.

16 Owings, *Women Police*, 62.

Similarly, in Ottawa in 1913, Florence Campbell was hired as a policewoman with full powers of arrest in response to pressure from local women's groups. Her duties included matron work, court responsibilities, and investigating child abuse and neglect.[17] The police department in Toronto followed suit, hiring two women in 1913 to serve as constables with full powers of arrest. By 1918, however, Toronto policewomen were relegated to office duties related to "marital infelicity" and were focused on mending "bad marriages" rather than patrol work.[18] It was an ominous trend. Between 1920 and 1945, the number of policewomen on patrol in Canada declined. The decline was attributed to the introduction of a crime control model of policing, a rise in the use of physical force, high unemployment rates amongst men following World War I, and resistance by male police officers to the idea of women police.

Many Canadian departments continued to employ a small number of policewomen during the 1950s and 1960s. Several also began to dress them in uniforms for the first time during this period. However, their work was increasingly limited despite attempts by the women to be recognized as law enforcement officers. In Ottawa, the city hired twenty-six meter maids who formed a separate Women's Auxiliary Division within the police department. "Their request to be called 'policewomen' was denied as they were not considered equal to their male constable counterparts," despite the same training, powers of arrest, and recruitment standards (excepting height and weight) as men. The women were not issued handcuffs or firearms and were automatically dismissed if they married or became pregnant.[19] Despite advances in some jurisdictions, the occupation of policing continued to limit the roles women played.

THE NWMP MATRON AND A "WOMAN SPECIAL"

Although women's role in policing was expanding in Canadian municipal police departments during the first decades of the twentieth century, the NWMP resisted the engagement of women in any policing

---

17   Cori Slaughter, "Women's Journey into Policing," (Ottawa, ON: Ottawa Police Service, 2003), unnumbered.

18   Myers, "Women Policing Women," 237.

19   Slaughter, "Women's Journey Into Policing," unnumbered.

capacity. In the final years of the nineteenth century, women's groups began to lobby the federal government to pressure the police force to hire women. Politically powerful groups such as the Women's Christian Temperance Union (WCTU) focused not only on temperance but on a wide range of social issues related to women and morality.[20] In 1896, the Edmonton chapter of the WCTU wrote to the minister of justice requesting that female prisoners be "placed under the charge of women gaolers instead of men gaolers" in the North-West Territories, the area policed by the NWMP.[21]

The minister was receptive to the idea and directed the NWMP comptroller to write a full report on the conditions in which women prisoners were held while under arrest. The comptroller resisted the idea of hiring matrons, citing the provision of separate cells and conveniences for women as extremely difficult in isolated outposts. He also worried that such special considerations would be expensive since it was "most difficult to secure female assistance in the Territories at what, elsewhere, would appear to be reasonable rates."[22] Despite the comptroller's objections, an order-in-council was issued by the federal government on February 1, 1897, directing the NWMP to hire women gaolers. The order was later amended on April 9, 1898, to include women escorts for female prisoners. Matrons were to be paid up to two dollars a day, plus rations, and women escorting female prisoners were to receive the same rate of pay in addition to railway fare and accommodation expenses.[23]

While official documents regarding the work of NWMP matrons are rare, popular histories are fruitful sources of information regarding their employment with the police force. In 1896, the NWMP served as a symbol of the authority of the Canadian state during a time when

---

20   Schulz, *From Social Worker to Crimefighter*, 17. Also see "The Woman's Temperance Union," *New York Times*, May 15, 1882.

21   Department of Justice, Memorandum to NWMP, December 15, 1896, LAC RG-18-A-1, vol. 150, no. 211-98.

22   NWMP, Memorandum to Deputy Minister of Justice, March 16, 1898, LAC RG-18-A-1, vol. 150, no. 211-98.

23   NWMP, Memorandum to the Commissioner, April 20, 1998, LAC RG-18-A-1, vol. 150, no. 211-98.

the boundary between the Yukon and Alaska was in dispute.[24] The NWMP was involved in more than establishing Canadian sovereignty in the region, however. The police force also enforced laws concerning sexual morality in the communities of Dawson City and Whitehorse during the Yukon gold rush. For Yukon's social elite, the potential of the morally corrupt prostitute to spread disease amongst male miners was linked to ideas about the preservation of the white race and female sexual purity. Accordingly, the NWMP surgeon was charged with examining prostitutes in Dawson City twice a month, incarcerating infected women, and treating them for venereal diseases. The NWMP also ensured that prostitutes remained confined to their own communities and were excluded from all public buildings where they might come into contact with respectable middle-class women and children.[25] It was within this context that the NWMP in Dawson City hired several women to serve as police matrons. A matron by the name of Selina Howard held the position between 1901 and 1904, and a Mrs. Warnes was hired as matron in the fall of 1915.[26] There is no evidence to indicate the numbers of matrons the NWMP employed. We do know that by 1904 the federal government had determined that matrons would not be taken on as part of the police force but were to serve in a social-service capacity.[27]

Although little is known about most NWMP matrons, the exception is Katherine "Klondike Kate" Ryan. The RCMP does not have a service record for Ryan in its archives in Ottawa, since many NWMP personnel files dating between 1904 and 1920 were destroyed by fire.[28] But information about Ryan's life and work can be gleaned from print media reports from the period and from popular histories. Kate

---

24　Pierre Burton, *The Klondike Quest: A Photographic Essay, 1897–1899* (Erin, ON: Boston Mills Press, 2005), 57.

25　T. Ann Brennan, *The Real Klondike Kate* (Fredericton, NB: Goose Lane Editions, 1990), 112.

26　Helene Dobrowolsky, *Law of the Yukon: A Pictorial History of the Mounted Police in the Yukon* (Whitehorse: Lost Moose, 1995), 116.

27　"Women employed as matrons—not to be taken on strength of the Force," LAC, file RG 18-A-1, vol. 290, 702-04.

28　RCMP Historical Section, email communication to author, March 8, 2012. Information about the fire was found on an RCMP website, http://www.rcmp-grc.gc.ca/hist/archiv-eng.htm (accessed March 8, 2012, now defunct).

Ryan was credited as the first white woman to enter the Klondike in 1898, mushing "on foot a distance of six hundred miles."[29] When she arrived in Whitehorse in 1900, Ryan established a reputable restaurant business and invested in local mines.[30] Although Ryan's adventures on the Stikine Trail were legendary during the gold rush, they were later overshadowed by her domestic abilities, such as cooking for the men of the NWMP, nursing, and performing "deeds of mercy" for injured and starving miners that earned her a reputation as the "miner's friend."[31]

In February 1900, Parliament passed a law authorizing the NWMP to hire a "Woman Special" to assist in the care of female prisoners. Five days later, Ryan was hired as Whitehorse's first matron. In 1903, Ryan was assigned the rank of constable special and her duties, in addition to those of a matron, included searching female passengers on trains and steamers who were attempting to smuggle gold dust or nuggets out of the territory to avoid paying taxes.[32] Ryan was credited with being "able to examine her own sex with a thoroughness that delicacy prevented the men of the Northwest Mounted Police from performing."[33] She was not issued a firearm or a uniform but wore an armband on her sleeve to give her a professional appearance while performing her law enforcement duties.[34] When Ryan left the Yukon in 1919, she recommended to the NWMP's commanding officers that the position of female gold inspector be abolished, making her somewhat complicit in the demise of future law enforcement roles for women in the police force.[35]

Ryan was so esteemed by the RCMP that when she died in Vancouver in 1932 the police force provided an honour guard for her funeral,

---

29   William Lewis Edmunds, "The Woman Called Klondike Kate: One of the First Few Women to Enter the Klondike in the Trying Years of '98: A Hint of the Varied Experiences in Her Eventful Life," *Maclean's* 35, no. 24 (December 15, 1922): 64.

30   Dobrowolsky, *Law of the Yukon*, 116.

31   Edmunds, "The Woman Called Klondike Kate," 64.

32   Brennan, *The Real Klondike Kate*, 138.

33   Edmunds, "The Woman Called Klondike Kate," 64.

34   Brennan, *The Real Klondike Kate*, 139.

35   Edmunds, "The Woman Called Klondike Kate," 64.

a rare privilege that few women have been accorded.[36] Ryan's example illustrates that women occasionally blurred the social boundaries between masculinity and femininity with great success during the early years of women in policing. Despite Ryan's accomplishments, the position of NWMP matron was short-lived and she quietly disappeared from historical narratives after the gold rush ended.

As early as 1897, in a memorandum informing his commanding officers of the order-in-council regarding matrons, Commissioner Lawrence Herchmer (1886–1900) stated that matrons would be "if possible, the wife of a member of the Force," an injunction that was later reiterated by an assistant commissioner in a second circular on the subject dated April 25, 1898.[37] The idea that wives of NWMP officers should perform matron and escort duties would become routine as the twentieth century wore on. The expanded role of Mountie wives not only contributed to the disappearance of the matron but negated the necessity of hiring women in any official capacity, allowing the masculine image of the police force to continue its dominance.

THE FIRST MOUNTIE WIVES

By the 1880s, the force's romantic image was so attractive that young men from across the Empire applied to join. Capitalizing on this development, the NWMP reduced the daily rate of pay for new recruits from seventy-five cents to forty cents based on the expectation that young men would continue to respond to the promise of adventure.[38] These wages are noteworthy given that matrons were being paid up to two dollars a day plus rations and expenses in 1898. New recruits were also required to sign on for five years, during which time they could not marry or ask for furlough. The prevailing theory was that unmarried men made

---

36   Two members of the RCMP, Major Z.T. Wood and Inspector C.E. Wilcox, were also pallbearers. Brennan, *The Real Klondike Kate*, 195. Also Dobrowolsky, *Law of the Yukon*, 116.

37   Circular memo no. 229, the Commissioner to Officer Commanding, February 9, 1897, LAC RG-18-A-1, vol. 150, no. 211-98; Circular memo no. 281 to the Officer Commanding (All Divisions) April 25, 1898, LAC RG-18-A-1, vol. 150, no. 211-98.

38   Colonel Sam Steele recalled that he was unable to "fathom the reason for this change, but before that I heard senior officers state that our men were too well educated, that a rough lot would have been better, and there were frequent arguments on the subject." Steele, *Forty Years in Canada*, 143–44.

better police officers since the federal government considered the cost of transporting, feeding, and housing hundreds of wives and children in primitive conditions on the western prairie to be prohibitive.[39]

In contrast to the lower ranks, commanding officers were permitted to marry, and their wives served as examples of respectable English middle-class womanhood in remote outposts. During Victoria's reign, middle-class women were expected to serve and protect "family and civilization from the very society created by men, who, in turn, expected the women to be gentle, graceful, dainty, and nurturing."[40] Many women who married the NWMP's commanding officers adhered to their womanly roles by becoming actively engaged as representatives of the Empire in colonial settlements. One notable example was Mary Drever, who married Commissioner James Macleod (1876–1880) in 1876, the "first white woman in Fort Macleod and the first married woman of a NWMP officer."[41] Mary played an important role in the history of the NWMP primarily for her correspondence with James. Between them, they wrote over 250 letters spanning twenty years (1874–1894), offering us a glimpse into settler life, the daily workings of the NWMP, Victorian marriage, and the politics behind establishing a police presence on the prairies.[42]

Mary and James were inseparable and when they were together they were often considered to be a "single unit," so much so that Mary's life was sometimes placed in danger.[43] Family legend has it that Mary was also "permitted to wear the red coat of the mounties" during her

39   Marquis, "Policing Two Imperial Frontiers," 196.

40   Sarah Watts, *Rough Rider in the White House: Theodore Roosevelt and the Politics of Desire* (Chicago: University of Chicago Press, 2003), 82.

41   Sherrill MacLaren, *Braehead: Three Founding Families in Nineteenth Century Canada* (Toronto: McClelland & Stewart, 1986), 157. Thank you to Reg Jones, a descendent of Mary Drever, for sharing this reference with me.

42   The Macleod letters are part of the collection of the Glenbow Museum and Archives in Calgary, Alberta. See http://www.glenbow.org/ to view the letters online.

43   One account records that an "Indian named Bad Boy resented the terms of Treaty #7 and 'undertook to annoy Mrs. Macleod at every opportunity' by physically intimidating her and brandishing a revolver at her. Mary clearly represented white authority." Joy Duncan, "They Also Served," *Red Serge Wives*, ed. Joy Duncan (Alberta: Co-Op Press, 1974), 25.

travels on horseback with James.[44] Once at Fort Macleod following her marriage, Mary ensured that she was seen in public. Every morning before breakfast, Mary would join her husband on horseback to inspect his men on the parade square,[45] an activity that was meant to remind the men of middle-class standards of propriety. Although her confinement to the private realm would have been considered an outward sign of her monogamy, Mary's presence during troop inspections suggests that the social boundaries between men and women were sometimes blurred for the sake of the Empire.

Though she occupied a subordinate role in society and marriage with no power or rights as a citizen, Mary's public activities were linked to the political objectives of the NWMP. In September 1877, Mary, along with the wives of two other NWMP officers, travelled with the commissioner and 108 of his men to participate in ceremonies to mark the signing of Treaty 7 with the Blackfoot Confederacy.[46] During the signing, Mary entertained the white women who were present with a formal tea party where all the "niceties of a Toronto drawing room" were observed.[47] The women's tea party was a significant feature of the gathering. Temperance was an important part of the NWMP's mandate to put an end to the illegal whiskey trade and eliminate alcohol consumption amongst Aboriginal people. The ritual of a formal tea party also communicated to the Blackfoot that a viable and civilized settler society was being established. The women acted as witnesses to the agreement, and their names and signatures appear on the copy

---

44   MacLaren, *Braehead*, 157. There is no official or biographical evidence to confirm whether the legend is true.

45   Duncan, "They Also Served," 25; also MacLaren, *Braehead*, 159.

46   Commissioner Macleod is generally credited in official histories of the NWMP as promoting "peaceful understanding" with the tribes of the Blackfoot Confederacy. Horrall, *The Pictorial History of the Royal Canadian Mounted Police*, 54. Macleod has been acknowledged in Aboriginal oral histories as "somewhat of a hero amongst the Blackfoot Confederacy" for clearing up the whiskey trade at Fort Whoop-Up and putting a stop to some of the violence taking place. See Treaty 7 Elders and Tribal Council et al., *The True Spirit and Original Intent of Treaty 7* (Montreal & Kingston: McGill-Queen's University Press, 1996), 111–13.

47   Duncan, "They Also Served," 25.

of Treaty 7 that was later distributed to the signatories.[48] Although the presence of the women at the signing is overlooked in most accounts, their roles as witnesses to this historic document indicate the status and position they held in settler society.

Another nineteenth-century Mountie wife bears mentioning for the important historical role she played in documenting NWMP history. Geraldine Moodie was the granddaughter of the famous Canadian author Susanna Moodie. She was also the wife of NWMP inspector John Douglas Moodie, a distant cousin. Following their marriage, Moodie and her Mountie husband "embarked on a thirty-two year adventure" that took them to many NWMP posts in western Canada, the Hudson Bay area, and the eastern Arctic.[49] Moodie was a talented photographer who left an extensive photographic record of early settler and NWMP life. She was the first woman to operate a photographic studio in western Canada, opening her business in Saskatchewan in July 1895. Specializing in portraiture, Moodie captured many NWMP officers and members of Aboriginal communities on film. She was also a savvy businesswoman who copyrighted her images and marketed photographs of the NWMP as Christmas cards.[50] However, like most Mountie wives, Moodie has been relegated to the margins of RCMP history and her contributions have been obscured by the dominant image of the heroic rider of the plains.

MOUNTIES AND MARRIAGE

The solitary Mountie hero may have been the masculine ideal in romanticized narratives about the police force, but the reality was that most young men who joined the police force were interested in marrying. Many purchased their release from their RCMP contract to get married. Those who could not afford to purchase their release deserted before

---

48   A missionary's wife, Elizabeth McDougall, also witnessed the treaty. Email communication from archivist Jim Bowman, Glenbow Museum, Calgary, Alberta, August 28, 2008. The original treaty is located at Library and Archives Canada in Ottawa; Glenbow holds one of the copies made for the signatories. To view the entire treaty including the names of the signatories and witnesses, see Haydon, *The Riders of the Plains*, 394.

49   Donny White, *In Search of Geraldine Moodie* (Regina: Canadian Plains Research Centre, University of Regina, 1998), 10.

50   Ibid., 7; 10-11.

their contract expired.[51] Lengthy waiting periods were interminable to a young couple in love, and secret weddings were not unusual. In December 1904, Walter Munday married without the knowledge or permission of his commanding officers. By the time his marriage was discovered, he had been promoted to corporal, a rank that was permitted to marry at the time. As punishment for violating the force's marriage regulations, however, the couple was required to accept an isolated posting at Cumberland House in the North-West Territories.[52]

Marriage regulations were occasionally relaxed throughout the twentieth century, particularly during periods of low recruitment. Jean Loates recalled that Mounties had to wait twelve years to marry when she first met her Mountie husband in 1932.[53] That year, the RCMP experienced a 74 percent increase in engagement numbers when it took over provincial policing functions in Manitoba, New Brunswick, Nova Scotia, and Prince Edward Island. By 1936, however, discharges outnumbered engagements, and marriage waiting periods were reduced to six years.[54] When RCMP officers were eligible to marry, they were required to meet a number of strict criteria known as "The Big Rule." Dorothy Standish Paull remembered that by the time she married Constable Tom Paull in December 1937, RCMP officers "had to have six years of service and a certain amount of [financial] security" before submitting an application to marry.[55] In the 1950s, constables were required to remain single for their first five years of service, be twenty-four years old, and have two thousand dollars in the bank before permission to marry was granted.[56] As late as 1973, when the

---

51   In 1913, 10 percent of the police force purchased discharges before their contract expired and 7 percent deserted, despite a period of high wages. Marquis, "Policing Two Imperial Frontiers," 197.

52   Duncan, "They Also Served," 51.

53   Jean Alexandra Loates, "Why I Joined the RCMP—Wives' Division," *The RCMP Quarterly* 39, no. 2 (April 1974): 18–19.

54   Hewitt, *Riding to the Rescue*, 33; Loates, "Why I Joined the RCMP—Wives' Division,"18–19.

55   Dorothy Standish Paull, *Scarlet Fever: A Story of Early Years in Banff and My Life as a Royal Canadian Mounted Policeman's Wife, 1914–1956*, ed. Laura Chvojka (White Rock, BC: Self-published, 1993), 38.

56   Loates, "Why I Joined the RCMP—Wives' Division," 159–60.

RCMP was considering hiring married men as well as women, recruits were "required to remain single for two years after their basic training" even though the police force hired married men as special constables or as volunteers for its auxiliary force at the time.[57]

For its part, the RCMP persisted in viewing single male police officers as more economically viable than married men. Dave Moore recalled receiving a transfer from British Columbia to northern Alberta as a single man in the 1950s. He was able to pack all of his belongings in his force-issued trunk, purchase a bus ticket, transport his trunk on the bus, and arrive at his new posting, all for $5.75. Moore speculated, "Now if I was married, it would probably [cost] around $5,000.00. You could move a [single] person like that and it didn't cost anything."[58] Bill Jones was transferred seven times in nine years as a single man in the 1960s, not an unusual circumstance for many unmarried Mounties.[59]

A violation of RCMP marriage regulations sometimes resulted in immediate dismissal. In 1945, Brad Bradley married his wife, June, in Saskatoon without permission. He was immediately dismissed and fined fifty dollars. In 1946, he reapplied to the RCMP and was granted acceptance on one condition: that he perform guard duty on Parliament Hill for the time he should have waited before marrying, and on a single man's pay. It was not until 1950 that Bradley, who by then had a daughter, received a married man's salary.[60] Bradley's punishment had more than economic ramifications for his family: it was also a shaming tactic that called into question his masculinity when his wife was forced to enter the workforce to earn extra money.

Mounties were still willing to take a chance on marrying without permission, despite threats of dismissal. Dave Moore recalled that while he was stationed in northern British Columbia in the 1950s, one member he worked with got a nurse pregnant. The couple travelled to Ketchikan, Alaska, and got married. "She was an officer in the Canadian navy officer's mess and she knew the [RCMP] inspector ... She thought

57 "Mounties May Recruit Married Men," *Globe and Mail*, January 13, 1973.

58 Dave Moore, interview with author, September 9, 2008.

59 Bill Jones, interview with author, October 3, 2011.

60 Ruth Lee-Knight, *When the Second Man Was a Woman*, ed. Heather A. Punshon (Saskatoon: Imagine Publishing, 2004), 177.

that if she could talk to him about it, maybe they could get permission," said Moore. As soon as the officer found out that they were married, her husband was fired. In another instance, a number of RCMP officers from Alberta were secretly married in Montana. When the RCMP found out about the marriages, all six men were fired. According to Moore, the best man at one of the weddings was also charged with "being a party to an illegal offense. Well, he got a warning out of it. He got sent up to the Arctic. To hide him."[61]

Moore had difficulty meeting the RCMP's regulations for his own marriage. Although he had the required five years of service, he did not have the necessary funds in the bank to demonstrate he could support a wife. But Moore had a "very friendly bank manager who lent me $1,200.00 for one day. I needed that piece of paper." The following day, after Moore's commanding officer made his enquiries, the bank manager quietly retrieved the money from Moore's account.[62] Moore's experience illustrates how many men informally resisted the marriage regulations imposed on them, sometimes with a little help from members of the community.

The RCMP could not prevent its men from marrying indefinitely and commanding officers found other ways to exercise their authority over the personal lives of members. Prospective wives and their families were subject to intense scrutiny by the police force. Jean Loates recalled the paperwork her fiancé had to submit along with his application to marry her in 1936. Jean's age, family background, and religion were all documented, and inquiries into her character, reputation, and genealogy were made. Jean's father was outraged that an organization with such an "irreproachable reputation for justice and fair play" would subject one of its members and his future wife "to such sadistic indifference" when permission to marry arrived just three days before the planned wedding date.[63] Granting permission to marry at the last possible minute appears to have been a trend in the RCMP during the Depression years. In 1937, Dorothy and Tom Paull were "plenty concerned" as their wedding day drew near and they still had not received permission

---

61   Dave Moore, interview with author, September 9, 2008.

62   Ibid.

63   Loates, "Why I Joined the RCMP—Wives' Division," 160.

to marry from headquarters in Ottawa. They, too, received permission to marry just three days before their wedding date.[64]

In 1959, Constable Mel Cheavins was denied his application to marry his fiancée, Betty, because she was a telephone operator. His commanding officer determined that members of the police force would be better off looking for a nurse or teacher as a spouse because they had a "higher standard of education."[65] The officer's assessment of Betty represented a double standard, given that men applying to the police force at that time were only required to possess a grade eleven education. Betty and Mel did eventually marry in 1960, but not before a second rejection by the RCMP when the police force discovered Betty's grandparents had emigrated from Romania, then a communist country. During the Cold War, applying to marry a woman whose relatives were potential communists was sufficient grounds for rejection.

THE UNPAID MOUNTIE

By the middle of the twentieth century, the occupation of policing professionalized and moved away from social relief and law enforcement activities to crime-fighting strategies. As a result, the number of police officers marrying increased. Technological advances, crime detection laboratories, professional training, managerial efficiency, the arrival of the police car, and changes in promotion, pay, and benefits convinced some men to view employment with the RCMP as a long-term career, one that would support a wife and family. As more and more Mounties married, women began to make numerous contributions to the work of the RCMP, work that was not officially acknowledged by the police force.

Memoirs and biographical material published by the "unpaid Mountie" or the "second man," as Mountie wives were known, have filled a significant gap in the history of women and the RCMP. The writing and publishing activities of the unpaid Mountie not only contested their absence from the historical record, but destabilized conventional representations of the Mountie hero as a solitary and self-sufficient historical figure. These largely anecdotal accounts began to be published in the first decades of the twentieth century. They reveal that Mountie wives were a source of cheap, reserve labour for the RCMP.

---

64   Paull, *Scarlet Fever*, 38.

65   Lee-Knight, *When the Second Man Was a Woman*, 159.

The first role many Mountie wives were expected to fill, with or without pay, was that of matron. Doris Hester recalled performing matron duty in the 1930s for her husband, Leo, who was in charge of transferring a number of "gypsy women, including one with a very young infant" from Fort Macleod to Lethbridge, Alberta. Doris was relieved of her charges and her duties at the Lethbridge barracks, all without pay.[66] Lee Christensen acted as matron for a female prisoner sentenced to six months in jail for attempting to murder her husband with an axe. Since the jail in Fort Smith, Northwest Territories, could not accommodate a female prisoner for a month, the woman was held at the detachment guard house until a vacancy became available. Christensen was required to supervise the prisoner on a daily basis and ensure that she was gainfully employed around the detachment.[67]

Because Mountie wives worked in spaces attached to their home, their contributions to the policing activities of their husbands were simply viewed as an extension of the domestic sphere. Their detachment duties included cleaning the cells and offices, which were usually attached to the living quarters. They also fed prisoners. Since many isolated locations did not have restaurants or hotels, wives were expected to provide visiting RCMP officers, government officials, or court personnel with accommodations and meals.[68] Some wives answered the police radio and took messages when their husbands were out on patrol. In the 1950s, Eunice Campbell remembered that the police radio was directly beside the kitchen in the detachment in Strasbourg, Saskatchewan. Since the radio was only capable of receiving messages, which were broadcast at 10:00 a.m. and 4:00 p.m., Eunice was expected to be on hand during those times to record messages when her husband was absent. She was paid one cent an item, a paltry sum she never bothered to collect.[69]

---

66   Doris Hester, "Joy to the World," *Red Serge Wives*, ed. Joy Duncan (Alberta: Co-Op Press, 1974), 151–52.

67   Christensen and her husband also performed game-warden duties, dispensed medical supplies on behalf of the Indian Department, and were raising three preschool-aged children. Lee Christensen, "Gainful Employment," *Red Serge Wives*, ed. Joy Duncan (Alberta: Co-Op Press, 1974), 103.

68   Sgt. B.F. Nowell, "Salute to the Wives," *RCMP Quarterly* 40, no. 4 (October 1975): 23.

69   Lee-Knight, *When the Second Man Was a Woman*, 149.

When she arrived at her husband's first posting in Torquay, Saskatchewan, in the 1960s, Betty Cheavins was surprised to learn that her living room also served as the courthouse and that one of the bedrooms was to serve as the judge's chambers when the circuit judge was in town. She was also expected to act as radio operator during stakeouts and roadblocks, relaying messages between her husband on the road and officers in a nearby detachment when his police car was out of their radio range.[70] In the 1970s, Florence Wilson was once pressed into service as a stenographer for an inquest into a drowning death in Stony Rapids, Saskatchewan, since she was the only person in the community who had "some experience with shorthand."[71]

Many wives recounted their difficulty coping with living in primitive conditions without privacy and basic household or sanitation conveniences. RCMP officer Claude Tidd and his wife, Mary, lived in a log cabin in the Yukon in the 1920s and carried their bathtub inside once a week to bathe.[72] In 1953, the detachment at Strasbourg, Saskatchewan, just forty-five minutes north of Regina, might as well have been located in the middle of the previous century. The living quarters were attached to the fire station, and a door in the living room opened directly into the fire hall. The second floor housed the Masonic Lodge. Eunice Campbell recalled that the house had a coal and wood stove and a wooden toilet with a ten-gallon pail they referred to as the "honey bucket," which had to be transported through the kitchen to be disposed of out the back door.[73] The living quarters of RCMP families were routinely inspected by commanding officers, who checked for cleanliness and order. Home inspections ensured that the cleanliness of living quarters and detachment offices adequately reflected the values the police force wished to convey to the communities it policed. It was an "unwritten law" that senior officers ensured that the Mountie's wife "could suitably meet social demands that his potentially higher

---

70   Ibid., 162.

71   Ibid., 106–7.

72   Claude Tidd joined the RNWMP in September 1914 and married Mary in 1925. Tidd was an avid amateur photographer and captured hundreds of images of working and domestic life in the Yukon on film. See http://www.tc.gov.yk.ca/digitization/public/fonds_tidd_en.php.

73   Lee-Knight, *When the Second Man Was a Woman*, 147–48.

rank would create."[74] Wives were expected to respond with deference toward senior officers during these inspections, suggesting that they were subject to the same hierarchical organizational structure as their husbands. Sadie Conrad recalled that, in hindsight, preparing for some commanding officer to "come in with his white gloves to check on my housekeeping" was an invasion of privacy and highly manipulative.[75] But Conrad did not speak out against the practice, knowing that the officer's written report would become part of her husband's service record. She was aware that her domestic performance was linked to her husband's career advancement.

Occasionally, being a Mountie wife had its career advantages. Gail Nelson was appointed a justice of the peace in 1968 by the provincial government of British Columbia. Her appointment meant that her husband would no longer have to travel a return distance of three hundred miles to obtain a search warrant or a summons, but could simply apply to his wife.[76] Wives in larger urban centres sometimes kept their jobs after marrying. Elizabeth Atkinson began work as a public servant for the RCMP in 1952 in a city detachment where she met and married her Mountie husband. While she continued to work for the RCMP in a paid administrative role as a secretary, she occasionally accompanied her husband on surveillance stakeouts in the evenings. She recalled being his "cover" in the car with him while he conducted his surveillance activities.[77] Elizabeth enjoyed her voluntary work as a surveillance operative, a role that would later become a full-time position for women in the RCMP in 1973.

Some Mountie wives with careers outside of the police force resisted the expectations placed upon them by the RCMP. In the 1970s, Mary Fairbanks worked as a nurse in several of her husband's postings, but with every move she lost seniority. Finally, when her husband was posted to an isolated one-man detachment without a hospital, Mary's career came to a halt. Although she had small children to look after by this time, she refused to clean cells or answer the radio and

---

74   Ibid., 40.

75   Ibid.,120.

76   Duncan, "They Also Served," 58.

77   Elizabeth Atkinson, interview with author, May 14, 2008.

telephone at the detachment unless she was paid for the work. She also insisted that the police radio be moved from their bedroom into the living area. Fairbanks engaged in a politics of refusal when she attempted to assert the value of her labour over assumptions about her role as a wife. She is certain that her refusal to meet expectations as a Mountie wife was recorded on her husband's personnel record. It was possibly a contributing factor that the force withheld promotion from her husband as a disciplinary measure since he never achieved a rank higher than corporal.

Other wives crossed the boundary between the private and the public spheres, making the reality of women's involvement in police work more fluid than official accounts and policies would suggest. Patrice Smallwood remembered "getting a talk" from the section sergeant on her arrival at her husband's new posting in the Arctic. He cautioned her "not to get involved in the running of the detachment" or to appear as though she was in charge.[78] Even though she wanted nothing to do with detachment work, Smallwood commented that she was drawn in automatically as far as the community was concerned.[79]

This became obvious one day when her husband was away on patrol with the constable. When the telephone rang with the report of a fight taking place in town in front of the Hudson's Bay store, Smallwood replied that all of the police officers were away and that there was no one to attend the scene. After the third telephone call, Smallwood realized that people in the community expected her to do something about the situation. So she walked into town, where she approached a large gathering of people in front of the store. Smallwood recalled,

> As I got nearer they all stopped and waited for me to get there ... I mean I really was shaking in my boots and I thought, "What am I going to do?" You could tell who had been scrapping because there was two guys and they were a little bloodied up. So I looked around and somebody standing near the first fellow I said, "You take him home!" Somebody standing next to the other fellow I said, "You take him home!" and they did ...

---

78   Patrice Smallwood, interview with author, September 9, 2008.

79   Ibid.

> Maybe it was coming from me rather than maybe [my
> husband] or somebody who they may have wanted to
> scrap with ... That's when I realized that the force did
> have power and reputation.[80]

As a Mountie wife, Smallwood symbolized civic authority despite a lack of police powers or training. She may not have possessed any official authority, but in the minds of the members of her community, her informal power as a Mountie wife was recognized.

Smallwood's venture from the domestic to the public sphere as the "second man" during a community emergency blurred the boundaries between ideas of masculinity and femininity in much the same way the work of Klondike Kate Ryan had decades earlier. When asked if she thought that her work as an unpaid Mountie laid the groundwork for the eventual inclusion of women in the RCMP, Smallwood replied, "I never felt that we did police work. We [wives provided] a lot of support systems for the force, there's no question. But on the whole, I don't feel I did police work as such. I never thought that we were a prerequisite for women members."[81] There is little doubt that the unpaid work of Mountie wives, and their general willingness to be subjected to RCMP policies despite the fact that they were not employees, greatly benefited the police force. As the RCMP prepared to swear in its first female constables in 1974, the work of the first matrons, female constable specials, and the unpaid Mountie was suddenly consigned to the margins of history as speculation about who would be the "first" woman in the RCMP began in earnest.

---

80   Ibid.

81   Ibid.

THE PUSH TOWARD REFORM

We're tired of being nice about trying to get an official inquiry into women's rights in Canada. If we don't get a royal commission by the end of this month, we'll use every tactic we can. And if we have to use violence, damn it, we will.

—Laura Sabia
President, Canadian Federation of University Women
January 1967

The RCMP's journey toward hiring female Mounties was long and complex. There was no one specific reason or event that convinced the force's commanding officers to suddenly change their hiring policy. Instead, it was a series of social, political, and cultural shifts that were taking place in Canada between 1960 and 1974 that challenged the RCMP to seriously consider women as police officers. These events, along with a number of internal upheavals, converged to apply pressure on commanding officers to initiate reforms. In the end, the RCMP, under the leadership of a new commissioner, finally acted to admit women for the first time in its history.

MASCULINITY AND THE RCMP IN THE TWENTIETH CENTURY

In the early decades of the twentieth century, a new ideal male body type emerged as the socially desirable standard for men. Across the Empire, an emphasis on size, power, and aggression eventually replaced the nineteenth-century ideal that favoured a lean, smaller male body type. In his annual report to Parliament in 1919, the RCMP's commissioner stated that only men with a "robust" physique were capable of policing the nation. He reiterated that the police force was "no place for weaklings."[1] The physiques of NWMP applicants were carefully measured and a thirty-five-inch chest was considered the acceptable minimum requirement for engagement.[2] Recruitment officers were also instructed to consider whether an applicant's physique complemented the Mounties' famous red serge tunic, an assessment that was duly noted on the interview form.[3] A Mountie's size, strength, and appearance were all thought to increase the public's respect for his law-enforcement capabilities as well as his social standing within the community.[4]

As the twentieth century progressed, the commissioners of the RCMP remained actively engaged in managing the masculine identity and image of the police force. While some commissioners worked to maintain the force's iconic image, others were more interested in promoting the force as progressive and modern. In 1963, Commr. George McClellan (1963–1967) claimed that he was not interested in projecting an image but the work of the RCMP.[5] By 1965, he had changed the uniform for general police duties to a more practical forage cap, blue trousers, ankle boots, and brown jacket.[6] But McClellan's successor, Commr. W.L. Higgitt (1969–1973), later overturned these changes, arguing that it was "important to restore rather than further erode our image."[7] Higgitt issued new standing orders that reinstated the

1   House of Commons Parliamentary Papers, "Report of the Royal North-West Mounted Police for the Year Ended September 30, 1919," quoted in Steven Hewitt, "The Masculine Mountie: The Royal Canadian Mounted Police as a Male Institution, 1914–1939," *Journal of the Canadian Historical Association* 7, n.s. (1996): 162.

2   Hewitt, "The Masculine Mountie," 162.

3   Ibid., 162, fn. 44.

4   Michael Dawson, "'That Nice Red Coat Goes to My Head Like Champagne': Gender, Antimodernism and the Mountie Image, 1880–1960," *Journal of Canadian Studies* 32, no. 3 (1997): 123–24.

5   George McClellan, quoted in Peter Trueman, "We're Not in a Popularity Contest," *Toronto Daily Star*, March 25, 1963.

6   Darryl Butler, email message to author, April 8, 2010.

7   The commissioner, quoted in Administrative Instruction 327, "Dress Regulations," RCMP Administrative Manual, September 30, 1970, reprinted in Jack Ramsay, "My Case Against the RCMP," *Maclean's* (July 1972): 23.

Stetson hat, long-sleeved shirt, tie, riding breeches, Strathcona boots and riding spurs for operational duties. Higgitt insisted that the traditional uniform would enhance the appearance and prestige of the RCMP.[8] But wearing dark blue wool breeches and riding boots with spurs while driving a police cruiser or chasing suspects on foot or in the summer heat, became a contentious issue amongst the rank and file. Nevertheless, Higgitt clearly viewed the appearance of his police officers as a valuable tool in communicating ideals about masculinity and authority to Canadians, even if it was at the expense of his men.

The RCMP looked for other ways to promote its men as ideal representations of Canada. The force frequently posted its most physically imposing police officers to tourist destinations. Dave Moore recalled that in the 1950s, the RCMP only sent tall members to the tourist destinations of Banff and Jasper, Alberta, "because they were always getting their picture taken." The RCMP's red serge review order uniform was also an important part of the force's representation. According to Moore, riding breeches and boots were a cavalry type of uniform that "only looked good on a tall person, not on a female that is only five foot one inch."[9] For Moore and many in the RCMP, it was only the large, masculine body that could effectively represent the country and state authority to visitors. By the late 1960s, however, it appeared to be an increasingly outmoded idea. Calls for the reform of the RCMP grew despite the best efforts of the police force to perpetuate the image it was known for around the world.

EXTERNAL PRESSURE: THE WOMEN'S MOVEMENT

Growing demands for an equal role for women in all sectors of Canadian society increased during the 1960s, as the women's movement gained momentum across the country. The agitation for women's rights, especially regarding employment equity, exerted pressure on the federal government to legislate reforms. On May 3, 1966, representatives from thirty-two women's organizations from across Canada met in Toronto and formed the Committee for the Equality of Women in Canada (CEWC). The CEWC's membership prepared a brief for Liberal

---

8   Administrative Instruction 327, "Dress Regulations," reprinted in Ramsay, "My Case Against the RCMP," 23.

9   Dave Moore, interview with author, September 9, 2008.

Prime Minister Lester B. Pearson requesting the formation of a Royal Commission to investigate the state of women's rights and to make recommendations for change. In the brief, they reminded the prime minister that the government was required to meet "the standards set by the [United Nation's] Universal Declaration of Human Rights," to which Canada was a signatory.[10] The eight-hundred-word document addressed seven areas of discrimination against women in Canada, including the discriminatory treatment of women employed by the federal government.[11] It was presented to the prime minister's designate on November 19, 1966. To the CEWC, the establishment of a Royal Commission, as opposed to a Human Rights Commission, was necessary because the group thought that a Human Rights Commission examining the status of women would be headed by a man and that all the commissioners would be male. Their fears were well founded. When the Canadian government began planning a conference to mark the UN's International Year of Human Rights in 1968, not one woman was appointed to the planning committee.

After several weeks of silence from the prime minister, the influential president of the Canadian Federation of University Women (CFUW), Laura Sabia, grew impatient. On January 5, 1967, Sabia impulsively told journalist Barry Craig of the *Globe and Mail* that the CEWC planned to march three million women to Ottawa in protest if the government refused to grant an investigation into women's rights. Craig published Sabia's threat the next day. Judy LaMarsh, the only female cabinet minister in the Liberal government at the time and a CEWC ally, later reported that Pearson was sufficiently "frightened" by the report and that he wanted to re-open talks regarding a Royal Commission on women's status.[12]

Prior to this time, women's issues were seldom addressed in the House of Commons and most Canadian politicians did not generally view women as a political constituency. That began to change following the

---

10   Cerise Morris, "'Determination and Thoroughness': The Movement for a Royal Commission on the Status of Women in Canada," *Atlantis* 5, no. 2 (Spring 1980): 13.

11   Ibid.

12   Ibid., 15. The fight for equal rights for women exacted a toll on LaMarsh, who did not seek a third term as a Member of Parliament. Judy LaMarsh, *Memoirs of a Bird in a Gilded Cage* (Toronto: McClelland & Stewart, 1969), 302.

publication of the Craig article, and male politicians began to press the government on the issue. On January 10, Member of Parliament T.C. Douglas (Burnaby-Coquitlam, British Columbia) rose in the House of Commons to question the prime minister as to whether or not it would be advisable for the government to appoint a Royal Commission so that Canada "might bring the status of women into line with that which is prevalent in some other western countries."[13] Other politicians were openly hostile to the idea of an investigation into women's rights. Conservative Member of Parliament Terry Nugent (Edmonton-Strathcona, Alberta) bluntly called the idea of an inquiry "utter balderdash," remarking that the best approach to handling women was to simply agree with them when they were right and agree with them when they were wrong.[14]

On February 3, 1967, the prime minister announced in the House of Commons that the government had decided to establish a Royal Commission on the Status of Women in Canada (RCSW).[15] The RCSW held a series of public hearings between April and October of 1968 in numerous locations across the country. They received a total of 468 briefs and some 1,000 letters of opinion from individuals and organizations in addition to submissions from 890 witnesses.[16] In their final report released in December 1970, the commissioners made 167 recommendations that clearly documented women's concerns over inequality between genders in Canadian society. The commissioners used the UN's Universal Declaration of Human Rights (1948) as a guideline to formulate their conclusions, adopting the general principle that everyone was entitled to the rights and freedoms that were outlined in that document.[17] It was the RCSW's recommendations concerning

---

13   T.C. Douglas, "Request for Study of Status by Royal Commission," *House of Commons Debates*, January 10, 1967, 11587.

14   Christina Newman, "What's So Funny about the Royal Commission on the Status of Women?" *Saturday Night* 84, no. 1 (January 1969): 23.

15   L.B. Pearson, "Announcement of Establishment of Royal Commission to Study Status," *House of Commons Debates*, February 3, 1967, 12613. Order-in-Council PC 1967-312 was approved by the Governor General on February 16, 1967.

16   *Report of the Royal Commission on the Status of Women in Canada* (Ottawa: Information Canada, 1970), x. Hereinafter referred to as *Report of RCSW*.

17   *Report of RCSW*, xi.

the RCMP, however, that shook the masculine foundations of the police force. The RCSW's commissioners noted that, although policewomen were common in municipal forces across Canada, the RCMP had "remained strictly a male preserve." They recommended that "enlistment in the Royal Canadian Mounted Police be open to women."[18]

The police force later insisted that it was not influenced by the findings of the RCSW and there is no direct evidence that it was.[19] Some of the senior RCMP officers who were involved in the decision to hire women do not recall the decision being made in reaction to outside political or social pressure—only that it was inevitable, a decision whose time had come.[20] Superintendent William MacRae, the training officer at the RCMP's training academy, insisted during several interviews with journalists that "I am gratified no one pressured the RCMP into recruiting women. It was a timely thing and the RCMP simply realized there is a definite place for women within the force."[21] One high-ranking commanding officer stationed in Ottawa at the time recalled that the RCSW "must have had some influence, but it had no direct influence. It wasn't something that pushed us. But it certainly had some influence, just hearing them talk about it." He also commented that the issue of women in the RCMP was discussed with Solicitor General Warren Allmand, who "didn't have anything against it that I remembered, but he reserved judgment on the final decision, so I don't recall him arguing against it." In the opinion of this senior officer, Allmand appeared "ambivalent" about the issue and was leaving the decision up to the RCMP.[22]

Lower-ranking officers who were working for the RCMP at the time disagreed. Insp. J.J. Poirier of the RCMP's Information Division

---

18   *Report of RCSW*, 133–34. The release of the final report made international headlines. For example, see Jay Walz, "Ottawa Panel Urges Women's Equality," *New York Times*, December 8, 1970.

19   See "Policewomen, Why Not?" *Royal Canadian Mounted Police Gazette* 37, no. 7–8 (1975): 3.

20   Dave Moore, interview with author, September 9, 2008; Henri LeBlanc, interview with author, October 14, 2008.

21   Marsha Erb, "Women RCMP Officers Inevitable: MacRae," *Saskatoon Star Phoenix*, November 8, 1974. Also in Liz Primeau, "They Always Get Their Person," *Vancouver Sun Weekend Magazine* 25, no. 11, March 15, 1975.

22   Henri LeBlanc, interview with author, October 14, 2008.

commented to journalists that the change was in response to "a series of pressures, including the evolution of women's roles" and the findings of the RCSW.[23] And Insp. G.R. Crosse commented to one journalist that increasing pressure from women's groups was a factor.[24] One corporal, interviewed decades later, was convinced that the RCMP was told by the Solicitor General to make a decision regarding the hiring of women; they had waited long enough.[25] In his opinion, it was a very political decision that emanated from the Solicitor General's office.

Female police officers agreed that the pressure exerted by the RCSW's findings was instrumental. Joyce Bennett maintained that "left on its own, I don't believe the RCMP would have acted" to hire women, and that the RCSW was the impetus.[26] Carolyn Harper thought that the fact that other police departments were opening up to women influenced the decision, as did the UN's declaration proclaiming 1975 as International Women's Year. Harper speculated, "It had to have been a political decision somewhere in Ottawa."[27] Marianne Robson agreed, stating that the RCMP was under pressure as International Women's Year approached: "The [RCMP] were mandated by the government that they were going to take women because of pressure from the United Nations."[28] While there are conflicting interpretations of the level of influence the findings of the RCSW had on the RCMP, it is clear that by the time the RCSW's findings were released, the RCMP recognized that it would have to reconsider its hiring policies.

In September 1970, three months prior to the release of the RCSW's final report, the RCMP had distributed questionnaires to police agencies

---

23   "Ms to Join the Crimebusters," *Province* (Vancouver), May 25, 1974.

24   Ruth Warick, "Women Join Ranks," *Leader-Post* (Regina, Saskatchewan), September 20, 1974.

25   Bill Jones, interview with author, October 3, 2011.

26   Joyce Bennett, interview with author, October 10, 2008.

27   Carolyn Harper, interview with author, June 28, 2010. In 1972, the twenty-ninth session of the General Assembly of the United Nations adopted Resolution No. 3275 proclaiming 1975 as International Women's Year. By ratifying the agreement, Canada was obligated to promote equality of opportunity and treatment for all employees with a view to eliminating employment discrimination in Canada. United Nations General Assembly Resolution #3275 (XXIX), "International Women's Year," December 10, 1974, http://www.un-documents.net/a29r3275.htm.

28   Marianne Robson, interview with author, July 29, 2008.

across North America and Europe to determine where women could best be utilized. Further, Commr. W.L. Higgitt had established a committee to examine the possibility of hiring women, suggesting that the RCMP had advance notice of the commission's final recommendations. The committee consisted of four senior officers who studied the issue "for a couple of weeks" before reporting back to the commissioner's planning board on their findings. In their report, they recommended that women be hired as police officers. They found that other police forces had successfully utilized women as detectives investigating major crimes, cases of rape, and crimes involving juvenile girls. They also included a few recommendations for developing a uniform and kit for women.[29]

It would take the police force another four years to arrive at a decision, however. The commissioner informed the Solicitor General that "while we have recognized the principle that there is room for female police officers, we have yet to define the specific role to be played."[30] In 1973, John Munro, the minister responsible for the Status of Women, commented in his annual report to Parliament that "a study is being conducted into Force requirements to determine where females, if engaged as regular police officers, could be used to best advantage."[31] Where to utilize women and in what capacity was still an issue, and the commissioner remained undecided.

Canadian politicians were cognizant that women were being hired as police officers in other jurisdictions and questioned the RCMP's hesitancy.[32] New York City had assigned women to patrol work for the first

29   The commissioner's planning board at the time consisted of the commissioner and his deputy commissioners. They discussed problems in the police force, made policy changes, and issued new directives to the appropriate directorates and divisions. Dave Moore, interview with author, September 9, 2008. The members of the planning board also went on regular retreats with the Solicitor General to discuss "the different problems of the force." Henri LeBlanc, interview with author, October 14, 2008.

30   Commr. W.L. Higgitt, quoted in Dawson, *The Mountie*, 149.

31   John C. Munro, *Status of Women in Canada: 1973* (Ottawa: Information Canada, 1973), 22.

32   The question of when women were going to be hired as police officers by the RCMP was raised several times in the House of Commons in 1973. See *House of Commons Debates: Official Report*, vol. III (1973), 2813; vol. V (1973), 4611.

time in 1972.[33] Washington, DC, became the first American city to hire women to work in patrol in 1971, and by 1972 the department had hired a total of 125 women specifically for patrol duties.[34] In Wales, the South Wales Constabulary had employed policewomen in uniformed work, as well as in its criminal investigation, traffic, and drug sections, since 1969.[35] In March 1973, the Attorney General of British Columbia, Alex Macdonald, suggested that the RCMP hire women for traffic patrol, freeing male officers to deal with more "serious crime such as the illicit drug trade." The RCMP responded that, although the police force utilized women in laboratory and research work, the "idea of expanding women's roles" was not under consideration, contradicting earlier assertions that they were already looking into the possibility.[36] Despite the gains being made by women in policing in several western societies, the RCMP appeared to be conflicted over the issue.

Women were making employment gains in other sectors that had previously been closed to them. In their final report, the RCSW's commissioners also recommended that the Canadian armed forces enlist married women and admit women to the military college.[37] By 1971, women were working "on the same basis as men in all classifications and trades except combat arms, sea-going duties and isolated positions" in the military.[38] The decision to open up trades to women was the direct result of the RCSW's recommendation that Canadian women should have the same opportunity to benefit from the scientific and

---

33   Kathy Burke and Neal Hirschfeld, *Detective: The Inspirational Story of the Trailblazing Woman Cop Who Wouldn't Quit* (New York: Scribner, 2006), 47.

34   Susan E. Martin, "Sexual Politics in the Workplace: The Interactional World of Policewomen," *Symbolic Interaction* 1, no. 2 (Spring 1978): 45.

35   Sarah Davies, "Police Force Recalls Days When Female Officers Were 'Of No Advantage'," March 8, 2013, http://www.walesonline.co.uk/news/wales-news/2013/03/08.html (accessed March 20, 2013, now defunct).

36   "RCMP Won't Be Hiring More Women," *Province* (Vancouver, BC), March 7, 1973.

37   *Report of RCSW*, 136.

38   The armed forces had determined that "approximately 10,000 positions could be filled by women without affecting the operational/combat role of the Forces," suggesting that the military sought to ameliorate recruitment shortages by hiring women, thus freeing up men for combat duty. By September 1974, there were "2,695 service women, including 597 officers" in the armed forces. Marc Lalonde, *Status of Women in Canada: 1975* (Ottawa: Information Canada, 1975), 33.

technological education that the military provided to men. The commissioners stopped short, however, of recommending women's full participation in combat duty. The military's decision to exclude women from combat duties was based on the belief that a lack of physical strength posed a threat to the cohesion and safety of combat units on the battlefield, a highly gendered space considered the heart of masculine identity and military service.[39]

Despite the advances being made by women in other jurisdictions, the RCMP continued to struggle with the types of duties women should perform. Given that the RCMP had not employed policewomen in the preceding decades, commanding officers lacked a frame of reference to help them make their decision. In 1969, the police force employed hundreds of women in a variety of positions as public servants who chiefly performed administrative work. The police force had also employed one hundred women as civilian members by that time. Some female civilian members worked as food services supervisors or as translators, but the majority worked as scientists or fingerprint technicians in crime detection laboratories. The issue over what duties women would perform was further complicated by the responses the RCMP was receiving to its questionnaire. Responses were inconclusive, according to the police force, for two reasons. The first was that other police agencies had only recently integrated women into the rank and file. Secondly, the RCMP maintained that the diverse and extreme working conditions their members experienced had "few if any parallels" within the police community, making it difficult to make comparisons.[40]

The RCMP's concern about extreme working conditions stemmed from an overemphasis on the importance of physical strength and size as necessary prerequisites for policing remote areas. Dave Moore remembered that before 1974, the RCMP made a practice of sending

---

39   Donna Winslow and Jason Dunn, "Women in the Canadian Forces: Between Legal and Social Integration," *Current Sociology* 50 (2002): 651. It was not until 1988, following a discrimination complaint, that a Canadian Human Rights Tribunal ordered the military to fully integrate women into regular and reserve forces, including combat roles. The following year, Private Heather Erxleben became Canada's first regular forces infantry soldier. Ibid., 663.

40   S/Sgt. S.E. (Fred) Stark, *The Role of Female Constables in "E" Division*, RCMP "E" Division Staffing and Personnel Branch (April 1986), 1.

their largest and strongest male officers to the north or to mining or logging communities to control drunk and brawling men. Moore characterized these areas as places where you could get into a fight "every night if you wanted to" and where "you could get into a fight every Saturday night whether you wanted to or not."[41] An imposing stature and physical strength were viewed as assets at these postings. But the commissioners of the RCSW saw it another way. They were "convinced that enlisted women could make a special contribution, particularly in the North, in other aspects of police work."[42] "Other aspects" may have been a reference to the RCMP's dealings with female prisoners. The RCSW's commissioners received several briefs during their hearings objecting to the fact that "women who have been apprehended are sometimes searched by male police officers" at isolated detachments.[43] Many reported abusive treatment by members of the RCMP during their arrest and incarceration.

Women were already proving to be effective in other areas of police work. In the 1960s, several police departments in North America were experimenting with using women in plainclothes capacities. In 1967, Theresa Melchionne, a deputy commissioner in the New York City police department, wrote about the effectiveness of women working undercover. She argued that the "public at large does not perceive women as police officers. Nor does the criminal," giving female officers a distinct advantage over their male counterparts. Melchionne advocated using women "as decoys" during undercover operations, including gambling, criminal surveillance, drug enforcement, and robberies.[44] In general, suspects looked for men who were physically imposing, as all police officers were at the time. They also assumed that police forces did not hire women. It was an assumption that made women especially effective at performing undercover or surveillance work.

Interestingly, the RCMP began to hire women as civilian members to work in a specialized plainclothes surveillance section in 1966.

---

41   Dave Moore, interview with author, September 9, 2008.

42   *Report of RCSW*, 134.

43   Ibid.

44   Theresa M. Melchionne, "Current Status and Problems of Women Police," *The Journal of Criminal Law, Criminology, and Police Science* 58, no. 2 (June 1967): 259. Also Burke and Hirschfeld, *Detective*, 65–69.

Jean Adams was the second woman hired to work in the Security Service (SS) section's new surveillance unit that had been established one year earlier in Ottawa. SS surveillants were responsible for gathering intelligence on foreign diplomats and spies operating in Canada, as well as Canadian citizens suspected of subversive political activity at home. Adams recalled tracking Russian spies as well as conducting surveillance on Canadians whom the RCMP suspected of being involved in the murder of Québec's Minister of Labour Pierre Laporte and the kidnapping of British diplomat James Cross during the October Crisis of 1970.[45] Women proved to be especially effective at this type of work because they escaped detection. Uniformed duties were another thing, however, and whether women could perform them was still an unknown to the men in charge of the RCMP.

NEGATIVE PUBLICITY AND THE RCMP'S IMAGE

While the commanding officers of the RCMP grappled with the question of women working in uniform, the pressure to reform appeared from an unexpected source. The romantic image of the police force as an honest, incorruptible, and efficient law enforcement service was called into question by authors Lorne Brown and Caroline Brown, who published an unauthorized history of the police force in 1973. The Browns discussed the origins and early history of the NWMP, the relationship between the RCMP and the labour unrest of the interwar years, and the force's relationship with minority groups and youth involved in the protest movements of the 1960s.

The Browns positioned the 1960s as a time when the image of the RCMP experienced "a marked decline, as did that of other police forces" as young people critically questioned and protested many aspects of society, including the activities of the police—and with good reason, according to the Browns. They highlighted the case of Robert Eadie,

---

45   Jean Adams, email communication to author, April 6, 2011. Contrary to Adams's account, the RCMP's website lists 1971 as the year that women first began to serve as special constables and civilian members. See "First Female Milestones," http://www.rcmp-grc.gc.ca/recruiting-recrutement/fem/hist-eng.htm (accessed March 21, 2012, now defunct). According to journalist John Sawatsky, the formation of informal surveillance units within the RCMP began during the Cold War period in the early 1950s, but a formal surveillance section within Security Service did not emerge until 1955. John Sawatsky, *Men in the Shadows: The RCMP Security Service* (Toronto: Doubleday Canada, 1980), 34.

who, in 1971, revealed in an interview with the Canadian Broadcasting Corporation (CBC) that he had been coerced by the RCMP into providing them with information on the illicit drug trade in Cornwall, Ontario. Eadie, who was just eighteen years old at the time, claimed that the RCMP had threatened him with a return to prison if he did not inform on drug dealers. Eadie complied and became a paid informant for the RCMP until he was beaten up by six men after the RCMP refused to provide him with protection.[46] Eadie's claims did little to reinforce the romanticized image of the men of the RCMP.

The RCMP also received unfavourable press for its response to a growing number of movements across Canada demanding social change. Organized labour, women's rights groups, gay and lesbian groups, and student movements in Canadian universities were all the subjects of RCMP surveillance. The women's movement was also the focus of the RCMP's SS, which compiled biographical sketches of leaders, read the movement's literature, cultivated informants, and monitored marches and rallies.[47] For example, members of the RCMP attended the meetings of the Vancouver Women's Caucus, fearing that the movement had been infiltrated by communists. They also followed the caucus's Abortion Caravan as it travelled across the country in May 1970 to protest Canada's abortion law.[48]

The media's coverage of police abuses of power during the 1960s was clearly problematic for commanding officers who were concerned with the eroding image of the police force. In 1961, RCMP Commissioner C.W. Harvison (1960–1963), in an address to the Canadian Association of Chiefs of Police, lobbied for the formation of a committee

---

46   L. Brown and C. Brown, *An Unauthorized History*, 138–39; 143–45. The Browns' work received national coverage when CBC Radio broadcasted a debate between Lorne Brown and retired D/Commr. William H. Kelly in a program titled "RCMP's Reputation Debated." Brown and Kelly argued "vigorously" about the RCMP's image versus the reality of the activities of the police force. "RCMP's Reputation Debated," CBC Radio, originally aired June 10, 1973, http://www.cbc.ca/archives/entry/rcmps-reputation-debated.

47   "RCMP Spied on Rita MacNeil, Feminists in 1970s," Canadian Press, August 4, 2008, http://www.ctvnews.ca/rcmp-spied-on-rita-macneil-feminists-in-1970s-1.313362.

48   Christabelle Sethna and Steve Hewitt, "Clandestine Operations: The Vancouver Women's Caucus, the Abortion Caravan, and the RCMP," *Canadian Historical Review* 90, no. 3 (September 2009): 486. Five hundred activists travelled across the country and protested on Parliament Hill for two days.

to study the reasons for the "unwarranted" criticism of police officers and to study the "fairly widespread idea that policemen are less interested in human rights, fairness, and justice than other groups."[49] And in 1968, RCMP Superintendent E.A.F. Holm urged the development of a campaign to inform the public about what the police stand for and the importance of the image of the police in maintaining public cooperation and ensuring citizen responsibility. Holm acknowledged that without the respect and assistance of the general public, the police would become ineffective in enforcing the law.[50]

The media continued to inform Canadians about illicit RCMP activities. In particular, there was a great deal of criticism of the RCMP's misuse of power after the federal government invoked the War Measures Act during the October Crisis in Québec in 1970.[51] The Front de libération du Québec (FLQ), a group of Québec nationalists, kidnapped British diplomat James Cross on October 5. Five days later, they kidnapped the provincial minister of labour, Pierre LaPorte, after the provincial government refused to meet their demands. In response, Prime Minister Pierre Elliot Trudeau's federal Cabinet passed emergency legislation on October 16, invoking the *War Measures Act*. The act granted the police and the military special powers of arrest across Canada, including the suspension of habeas corpus for detainees suspected of political insurrection.[52]

But it was the RCMP's illegal activities following the end of the October Crisis in December 1970 that had the most serious ramifications for the police force. Over the next ten years, also known as the RCMP's "dirty tricks" era, the SS conducted a series of unlawful activities against the independence movement in Québec, including illegal wiretaps, opening mail, stealing documents, conducting break-ins, bombings, and acting without search warrants.[53] On December 7, 1976,

---

49   C.W. Harvison quoted in "Canadian Chiefs of Police Conference," *RCMP Quarterly* 26, no. 3 (January 1961): 200.

50   Supt. E.A.F. Holm, "Police Image: A Paper Given at the Annual Dinner of the B.C. Provincial Police Held in Victoria on October 19, 1968," *Scarlet and Gold*, 50th Anniversary ed., (1968): 44–45.

51   See http://www.rcmp-grc.gc.ca/hist/comms-eng.htm.

52   Clément, "The October Crisis of 1970," 167–68.

53   Ibid., 176.

investigative journalist John Sawatsky wrote an article for the *Vancouver Sun* detailing a series of more than four hundred illegal break-ins in Québec by the RCMP.[54] Sawatsky alleged that a cover-up of these activities extended to the upper echelons of the police force. The revelations resulted in the formation of both a federal and a provincial commission to investigate; both reported their findings in 1981. Québec's provincial commission, known as the Keable Commission, found that the RCMP had conducted an unjustified attack on the civil liberties of Québec citizens. The federal commission, known as the McDonald Commission, recommended that the RCMP's SS be replaced with a civilian agency, leading to the formation of the Canadian Security and Intelligence Service (CSIS) in 1984.

It was against this backdrop that the RCMP faced its most serious public relations challenge to date: the criticism of the RCMP by a former Mountie. In July 1972, Jack Ramsay broke ranks and publicly criticized RCMP policies and operational procedures in a damning article he wrote for *Maclean's* magazine.[55] Titled "My Case Against the RCMP," the article was an unprecedented public airing of a number of grievances by an insider that further tarnished the image of the police force. Ramsay described what he perceived to be abusive training methods at the RCMP's academy, racism amongst RCMP officers, and the police force's antiquated marriage policies, low pay, militaristic rank structure, and poor morale amongst the rank and file.[56]

Ramsay's own illegal activities, however, would not be exposed until 1999. That year he was charged and later convicted of the attempted rape of a fourteen-year-old Cree girl he had incarcerated at the RCMP barracks in Pelican Narrows, Saskatchewan, in 1969. At the time of the attempted rape, Ramsay was a corporal at the

---

54   John Sawatsky, "Trail of Break-Ins Leads to RCMP Cover-Up," *Vancouver Sun*, December 7, 1976. Sawatsky won the Governor General's Michener Award for Meritorious Public Service Journalism for this article.

55   The RCMP's policy of forbidding its members to speak to the media continued in various forms throughout the twentieth century. For example, see Standing Orders 1970 (Section 4, no. 1156) quoted in L. Brown and C. Brown, *An Unauthorized History*, 127–28.

56   Ramsay, "My Case Against the RCMP," 58–74.

detachment.[57] As the commissioners of the RCSW discovered, Ramsay was not alone in his abuse of female prisoners. In January 1973, Cst. Allan Howard was charged with indecent sexual assault against a Métis woman in Saskatchewan, whom he forced to commit a sexual act with him while she was incarcerated. Howard pleaded guilty to the charge; he was dismissed from the RCMP and fined one thousand dollars. That same year, the president of the Saskatchewan Indian and Métis Society complained to the federal government that incarcerated Aboriginal women were being sexually harassed by members of the RCMP.[58] The abuse of power that some Mounties adopted was made possible by the powerful image of the RCMP as well as geographical isolation, which allowed abuse to occur without fear of discovery.

INTERNAL PRESSURE: UNIONIZATION

There were a number of internal pressures facing the commanding officers of the RCMP in the 1970s that had a direct bearing on the decision to hire women. In the spring of 1974, thousands of RCMP officers met in major centres across the country to discuss the possibility of forming a union, even though they were governed by order-in-council PC 2213 (October 7, 1918) prohibiting them from forming one.[59] Mounties aired a number of grievances against the RCMP including unreasonable transfer policies, low wages, and a "military system of operation."[60] Overtime pay was also an issue. Mounties were expected to provide free labour after regular working hours, an indication of the strength of military codes of conduct still in operation in the police force at the time. The airing of grievances and talk of unionization were unprecedented and came as a shock to an older generation of

---

57   On appeal in 2001, the verdict was overturned and a new trial was ordered. Ramsay then pleaded guilty to the lesser charge of indecent assault and was sentenced to one year of probation and 120 hours of community service. Christie Blatchford, "Peeling Back an MP's Past Lives," *National Post*, November 22, 1999; Jill Mahoney, "Former Reform MP Sues RCMP, Crown," *Globe and Mail*, May 27, 2002.

58   L. Brown and C. Brown, *An Unauthorized History*, 149. Also "RCMP Harassing Indians, Committing Sexual Offences Against Women, Head of Group Charges," *Globe and Mail*, January 13, 1973.

59   "RCMP Union Membership Illegal Under 1918 Rule," *Vancouver Sun*, May 1, 1974.

60   Peter Moon, "RCMP Morale Problems Traced to Rapid Growth," *Globe and Mail*, May 27, 1974.

commanding officers who still believed in the unquestioned obedience of the lower ranks.

The labour unrest erupted in British Columbia on May 1, 1974, when 250 RCMP officers met in Burnaby to vent their frustrations.[61] The next day, more than "600 Toronto-area Mounties—nearly two-thirds the division" gathered to hear the president of the Metro Toronto Police Association urge them to form a union. When a vote was taken, 605 out of the 620 votes cast were in favour of pursuing the prospect of organizing.[62] Eight days later, an estimated 2,500 Mounties from Ottawa and Toronto met at the Ottawa Civic Centre to agitate for change.[63] In response, newly appointed Commr. Maurice Jean Nadon (1974–1977) and D/Commr. Peter Bazowski met with representatives (some elected by rank-and-file police officers and others appointed by commanding officers) from every division across the country. They developed a fourteen-point plan for a formal employee-relations system of representation, which they called Division Staff Relations Representatives (DSRR). The proposed system stipulated that an elected representative from each division across Canada would meet with the commissioner and his deputies once a year to address grievances and discuss personnel issues. On May 30, 1974, a referendum was held across Canada asking Mounties to accept the DSRR model as an alternative to seeking unionization.[64] Mounties voted in favour of the proposal and the RCMP immediately gave its men a general pay increase and instituted a policy for overtime pay.

Surprisingly, it was during discussions about the formation of the DSRR system that the decision to hire women as members of the

61   The men heard a speech by an "official of the Vancouver city police union," who reported on current wage negotiations with the city of Vancouver. "Mounties Want Voice With Brass," *Vancouver Sun*, May 2, 1974.

62   Sawatsky, *Men in the Shadows*, 229. Also see "Metro Mounties Discuss Union at Noisy Rally," *Toronto Star*, May 3, 1974.

63   Commr. Maurice Nadon, "The Tenth Anniversary Dinner: Division Staff Relations Representatives," May 1984. Hereinafter referred to as Nadon speech, 1984. At a similar meeting in Montreal almost two weeks later, five hundred RCMP officers were in attendance. Sawatsky, *Men in the Shadows*, 230.

64   As a show of good faith, the commissioner sought the immediate repeal of order-in-council PC 2213 from the Solicitor General. The order was repealed shortly after the acceptance of the DSRR model as proposed in the referendum. Nadon speech, 1984; also Sawatsky, *Men in the Shadows*, 237.

RCMP was made. As Henri LeBlanc remembered it, the "subject of women in the RCMP was one of many items on the agenda" at the early DSRR meetings. The topic was discussed informally and arguments for and against the hiring of women were made. LeBlanc recalled that "we had all kinds of soothsayers who said it will never work, we'll have to babysit them, all this kind of talk, you know. Mostly from senior non-commissioned officers."[65] During the final meeting prior to the Canada-wide vote, the commissioner urged the men in attendance, "Either we do it, or we don't do it." Nadon argued that there was pressure from the media and he also noted that other police forces had hired women and they were doing well. He assured those present that "if it doesn't work, we'll just fold it up,"[66] a comment that suggests that the engagement of women was initially viewed as experimental. In fact, the day the commissioner announced that the RCMP would be accepting applications from women, he told a journalist that "married men will be eligible for regular duty and women for most regular duty."[67] His use of the word "most" may have been a slip of the tongue, but it reveals that the tenuous nature of the decision still resonated in the commissioner's mind.

Ultimately, the commissioner, his deputies, and the division representatives made the decision to employ women in the RCMP. According to LeBlanc, it "wasn't a one-man decision" but one that occurred within broader discussions taking place during the labour unrest of the spring of 1974.[68] Publicly, the RCMP continued to insist to the media that "the initiation of women into the force is no bow to the age we live in and no fulfillment of any stereotype ... It is simply an evolutionary process, one that was to be expected and one that will in all likelihood

---

65   Henri LeBlanc, interview with author, October 14, 2008.

66   Ibid.

67   "Ms to Join the Crimebusters," *Province*, May 25, 1974. Discussions regarding hiring married men were taking place as early as January 1973. "Mounties May Recruit Married Men," *Globe and Mail*, January 13, 1973.

68   Henri LeBlanc, interview with author, October 14, 2008.

be carried off without a hitch."[69] Despite the force's stance, there is little doubt that the RCMP felt the pressure to reform from a number of constituents and institutions. Whether their plans to initiate women into the RCMP could be achieved "without a hitch," however, remained to be seen.

---

69   Primeau, "They Always Get Their Person."

THE ARRIVAL OF WOMEN IN THE RCMP

The fact that we have recruited women in the RCMP without any
outside pressure reflects an enlightened attitude within the force.
—Supt. William F. MacRae
The *Vancouver Sun*, 1975

No matter how the RCMP chose to portray its policy changes, the
hiring of women and married men for the first time in the force's
history gave the appearance that the police force was intent on mod-
ernizing. On May 24, 1974, Commissioner Nadon announced to journalists that the RCMP would begin hiring women as regular members
of the police force. Nadon was the RCMP's sixteenth and first bilingual
commissioner when he took the helm of the organization on January 1,
1974. He was known for his people skills and for repairing the reputation and image of the RCMP. One of Nadon's senior officers commented
decades later that Nadon was the first commissioner who chose not to
ignore demands for women's right to join the RCMP, speculating that
Nadon's wife probably influenced him regarding the hiring of women.
He characterized the commissioner as very receptive to the idea of
female Mounties, perhaps the reason why some officers may have felt
that an "enlightened attitude" now existed within the police force.[1]

From Nadon's perspective, the RCMP was entering a time of re-
newal. He remarked that the "force is now embarked on a program of
change unprecedented in our history. It is a program that I endorse,
support and will press."[2] True to his word, in a media release a few

---

1   Cameron Montgomery, interview with author, May 24, 2007.

2   Nadon speech, 1984.

months later, the RCMP informed Canadians that thirty-two women had been selected as the first female members of the police force. They represented every province in Canada except Prince Edward Island.[3] The new recruits were scheduled to be sworn in simultaneously across the country on September 16, 1974, before being posted to the RCMP's training academy in Regina to begin twenty-two weeks of training.[4]

The simultaneous swearing-in ceremonies and the assignment of random regimental numbers to the first female recruits were designed to prevent any one woman from claiming that she was the first female Mountie to be hired by the RCMP. These actions did not, however, shield the first female Mounties from the pressure of being the first in the way the RCMP's commanding officers had hoped. Instead, they drew attention to the women as different from male police officers and fed assumptions that they needed preferential, rather than equal, treatment to succeed.

THE FORMATION OF TROOP 17 (1974/75)

The hiring of the first female Mounties was a public relations boon for the RCMP. So novel was the idea of female Mounties that the commissioner's announcement made national headlines. News about the RCMP's decision was communicated to Canadian women through the media.[5] One member of Troop 17 remembered that after hearing the announcement on the radio, she "went down to the RCMP, made some inquiries, came home, filled out the form, and threw it in the mail."[6] Trish O'Brien read an article in the local newspaper that reported the RCMP was considering hiring women as regular members. When she heard the commissioner's announcement on the radio, she "called down to the local detachment that night," but they did not have any

---

3   The woman selected from Prince Edward Island was not old enough to be hired in September 1974. She was sworn in after her nineteenth birthday and joined the second all-female troop in March 1975. Marianne Robson, interview with author, July 29, 2008.

4   Royal Canadian Mounted Police, press release, Ottawa, Ontario, September 12, 1974. RCMP Historical Collections Unit Archives.

5   For example, see "RCMP to Accept Women," *Vancouver Sun*, May 24, 1974.

6   Allison Palmer, interview with author, June 11, 2008.

information and asked her to call back on Monday, which she did.[7] Beverley MacDonald heard the announcement on her car radio while on her way to work that morning. She immediately pulled into the nearest detachment, where the young constable at the desk had to ask his sergeant if it was true that the RCMP was hiring women. When the sergeant confirmed that he had just heard it on the radio too, the constable asked him, "What do I do?" The sergeant replied, "Give her an application."[8]

What motivated these women to apply? Several women had brothers, uncles, and fathers in the RCMP or in other police forces, a factor that had a bearing on their decision. Bev Hoskar and her father and brother were the first "sister, brother and father team in the RCMP." Indeed, five of the first female Mounties had fathers who were police officers.[9] Janet Porter had two older brothers who were in the RCMP. They were at odds over her decision to apply. One brother was very protective of her. He thought that the work was too dangerous and that she "wouldn't fit in with the environment." The other brother thought that she should "get in at the beginning" and give it a try.[10]

Apart from influential family members, many of the first female Mounties were looking for a challenge, job security, better pay, and a career. Tina Kivissoo, according to one media report, "exchanged the glamorous life of a model for handcuffs and a revolver." Kivissoo was not interested in working at a "nine-to-five job."[11] Others were discouraged by the lack of advancement opportunities and low wages in pink-collar occupations. Carol Franklin cited her job as a bank teller as a factor in her decision to apply to the RCMP. When the branch she worked at brought in men as management trainees, even though they had never worked in a bank before, her frustration reached the breaking point. The men were being promoted over the female employees with experience in the industry. Franklin decided, "I need to do some-

---

7   Trish O'Brien, interview with author, November 13, 2008.

8   Beverley MacDonald Busson, interview with author, November 9, 2006.

9   "But No Nelson Eddy," *Regina Leader-Post*, March 4, 1975.

10   Janet Porter, interview with author, October 20, 2008.

11   "First Women Constables Recruited for RCMP," Canadian Press, September 16, 1974.

thing that is gonna get me out of here."[12] She was not alone. Many of the letters received by the RCSW expressed anger at poor wages for women and employers' insistence on promoting men over women for management positions.[13]

While the promise of a challenging career and job security appealed to some of the first female recruits, others were altruistically motivated. Several women stated that they wanted to make a difference in people's lives. Allison Palmer, for example, wanted "to be doing something where I felt I could make a difference in the community."[14] Some had more practical reasons. Marianne Robson, who had taken criminology and social work courses as part of her bachelor of arts degree, was already on a waiting list for a large urban police force at the time of the RCMP's announcement. This particular police force, however, had established a quota of just eight women police officers at any one time. Since all of the female positions were filled, Robson grew tired of waiting for a woman to resign or get pregnant. She applied to the RCMP as soon as her father, who heard the news on the radio, told her they were accepting applications from women.

The first female Mounties held a variety of occupations prior to being hired as constables. Several had been employed as public servants for the federal government and others worked as secretaries for the RCMP. Three were employed as schoolteachers and some worked as nurses or bank tellers. Many of the women who were hired had post-secondary education. One held a master's degree in archaeology. Robson recalled, "Everybody was single, but we had one girl ... [who] had been married but divorced, and one single mom."[15] The women were also older than most of the male recruits who were being hired at the time.

None of the women from Troop 17 saw themselves as feminists who were breaking down employment barriers for women in Canadian society. Given the RCMP's surveillance of the women's rights movement during this period, it is possible that an effort was made

---

12   Carol Franklin, interview with author, April 20, 2010.

13   Joan Sangster, *Transforming Labour: Women and Work in Postwar Canada* (Toronto: University of Toronto Press, 2010), 258–60.

14   Allison Palmer, interview with author, June 11, 2008.

15   Marianne Robson, interview with author, July 29, 2008.

by RCMP recruiters to hire women who held more politically conser-vative views. Allison Palmer remembered that none of them felt they were there to make a point about women's rights. Instead, they were there "because we wanted to be there." They were interested in po-lice work and enjoyed being surrounded by other like-minded women who were going through the same experiences. It was a positive atmo-sphere that resulted in the formation of lifelong friendships.[16]

The women were somewhat naive about what they were getting into, though. Robson recalled, "You know, you're going to go into a men's organization, and you're going to be successful, and you're gon-na survive, and the world will be good, and treatment will be equal … I never even thought of those things. I mean, I was twenty-two years old."[17] In hindsight for Robson, it was youthful naïveté rather than the movement for women's rights that may have had the biggest impact on the decisions made by the first women to join the RCMP.

THE SWEARING IN OF FEMALE MOUNTIES

On September 16, 1974, all thirty-two women were sworn in.[18] A Canadian Police Information Centre (CPIC) communication from the commissioner transmitted to every division seventeen days earlier revealed that the RCMP planned to tightly control the ceremonies, which were going to receive live coverage from the media.[19] On the day of the ceremonies, the commanding officer of the RCMP's train-ing academy in Regina, also known as "Depot" to members of the RCMP, sensed the historical significance of the occasion. C/Supt. Henry P. Tadeson closely monitored the women's engagement as he received CPIC messages from each division advising him of their dates of arrival at Depot. "D" Division (Winnipeg, Manitoba) was the first to report that they had engaged three women as constables at

---

16   Allison Palmer, interview with author, June 11, 2008. Also Maj. D.E. Toole, "A View From the Sidelines," *Royal Canadian Mounted Police Gazette* 37, no. 7–8 (1975): 8.

17   Marianne Robson, interview with author, July 29, 2008.

18   Royal Canadian Mounted Police press release, Ottawa, September 11, 1974.

19   The commissioner, RCMP Canadian Police Information Centre (CPIC) commu-nication, August 30, 1974, RCMP file DPT-575 (17-74/75). Access to Information file GA-3951-3-03134/08. CPIC was a networked computer database operated by the National Po-lice Service that linked all justice and law enforcement agencies across Canada at the time.

$10,794.00 per annum. The words "First One" were written on the hard copy of this message sent to Tadeson, who noted on the bottom, "Copy to museum for posterity purposes."[20] Tadeson was correct in appreciating that history was being made. The simultaneous engagement of an entire troop across six time zones was a precedent that has never been duplicated by the RCMP.

The participation of the media was another indicator of the significance of the event. The CBC carried the swearing in of four women in Ontario live from the RCMP's Toronto headquarters. The Canadian Press (CP) captured a photograph of them signing their oath of office as A/Commr. E.R. Lysyk looked on. Male recruits did not usually merit this type of attention from the media, let alone the presence of such a high-ranking officer during a swearing-in ceremony.[21]

The decision to conduct simultaneous ceremonies was meant to both control the media message and protect the women. Publicly, the RCMP emphasized that their intention was to transfer the pressure of being the "first" onto a group of women rather than an individual.[22] Linda Rutherford, a member of Troop 17, thought that it was a good idea: simultaneous engagements meant that no individual woman was more important than the other women in the troop, a factor that later contributed to troop unity when they were under pressure.[23] However, it was also a paternalistic approach that catered to male perceptions of female vulnerability. Commanding officers were not sure how the women would react to the intense media scrutiny, and they worked to ensure that the ceremonies went smoothly while under the watchful eye of journalists.

To further discourage anyone from claiming to be the first, all of the women were issued regimental numbers randomly within a limited

---

20   The RCMP's museum was located on the property of the training academy at that time. CPIC number SB2629, D Division, September 16, 1974. RCMP Heritage Collection Unit Archives, Regina, Saskatchewan.

21   *The World at Six*, "RCMP Welcomes First Female Officers," CBC Radio, September 16, 1974, http://www.cbc.ca/archives/entry/1974-rcmp-welcomes-first-female-officers. See *Chronicle-Herald* (Halifax), September 17, 1974; also "RCMP," *Daily Colonist* (Victoria), September 17, 1974.

22   "Women RCMP Officers Inevitable: MacRae," *Saskatoon Star-Phoenix*, November 8, 1974.

23   Linda Rutherford, interview with author, April 20, 2010.

sequence. Their random assignment was a significant departure from the RCMP practice of issuing the numbers sequentially.[24] As a paramilitary institution, hierarchy and rank contributed significantly to the culture of the RCMP, making regimental numbers extremely important. A lower regimental number signified longer service and greater seniority; police officers with seniority were generally considered for promotion before candidates with shorter service. Although it is true that one woman technically received the lowest regimental number of the thirty-two issued on September 16, no one woman was able to claim with certainty her seniority over the other recruits sworn in on that day.

Rather than shielding the women from attention, these special arrangements stimulated journalists' interest in them. In fact, the presence of the media at the ceremonies was problematic for one of the women. Carol Franklin was shocked to learn she was enlisting for five years, a detail no one had bothered to mention to her until the ceremony, but by then it was too late to question the policy in front of the media.[25] Franklin was taken by surprise but felt she could not question the RCMP officer in charge about this requirement in front of the media. Rather than protecting Franklin, the presence of the media proved to be a hindrance to more fully understanding the extent of the commitment she was making.

The women of Troop 17 were re-enacting a ceremony that had been observed by their male predecessors for one hundred years. The repetitive act of the swearing in was a benchmark of RCMP culture that symbolized loyalty and deference to the Queen, the Canadian state, and commanding officers. The women were not merely reproducing or mimicking a swearing-in ritual, however, but were modifying its function as a singularly male rite. It was a precedent that journalists were intent on capturing for Canadians.

---

24   Regimental numbers have been issued sequentially since 1875. Dale Sheehan and Redd Oosten, *Behind the Badge: History of the Royal Canadian Mounted Police "Depot" Division* (Regina: Centax Books, 2006), 242–43; 272. Allison Palmer, email communication to author, March 30, 2010.

25   Carol Franklin, interview with author, April 20, 2010. The Canadian Armed Forces also engaged their recruits for a five-year period at the time, a characteristic the RCMP shared with the military. Lalonde, *Status of Women in Canada*, 34.

TROOP 17'S ADVISOR

The women were scheduled to begin their basic training one week later at Depot, where another precedent awaited their arrival. The RCMP had seconded a female officer from the Canadian military to assist the women as they transitioned from civilian life to members of the RCMP. While every male troop had a troop counsellor, none had an additional advisor from an outside institution.[26] Maj. Doris Toole was an armed forces personnel officer with sixteen years of service, including work as the officer in charge of female recruit training at Canadian Forces Base (CFB) Cornwallis.[27] She had also served as the training officer and regimental commander during an exchange program with the United States navy, overseeing six hundred women who were undergoing recruit training.

In July 1974, Toole accompanied her director of women personnel to a luncheon at the RCMP's officers' mess in Ottawa, where they met with an assistant commissioner and two officers from the RCMP's personnel branch. According to Toole, "I must have passed muster because the next thing I knew I was told I was being seconded to the RCMP for approximately ten months."[28] Under the terms of her secondment, the RCMP reimbursed the Department of National Defence (DND) for Toole's salary and the police force was responsible for her travel costs and payment for any "temporary duty" she performed. The RCMP also provided accommodation for her in the officer's mess at the training academy.

Toole spent the month of August 1974 at RCMP headquarters in Ottawa reviewing their regulations to determine what changes needed to be made to accommodate women. For example, she discussed health issues with senior staff, particularly the need for a maternity leave policy that stipulated when a female officer should leave operational duties

---

26 Every troop at the academy in the 1970s had a troop counsellor assigned to it. The counsellors were instructors at the academy who listened to any problems that the recruits were experiencing. Some counsellors were more actively engaged with their assigned troop than others.

27 "Forces Woman to Aid RCMP Training," *Halifax Chronicle-Herald*, September 21, 1974; "Saint John Woman to Assist RCMP," *Evening Times-Globe* (Saint John, New Brunswick), September 26, 1974.

28 Doris Toole, email message to author, July 6, 2008.

for reassignment during pregnancy.[29] Although she was not involved in the selection of the first thirty-two women and did not see their personnel files, she did discuss the RCMP's choices with senior staff and was given an overview of the backgrounds of the new recruits.

In September, Toole moved to Regina to begin her work as advisor to Troop 17. Her primary task was to act as liaison between the women and the police force and to monitor training classes, provide advice to the recruits regarding the upkeep of their uniform and kit, and advise the troop counsellor, Cpl. Ken Wilkens, of any problems that arose. Toole referred any queries from the media to RCMP staff. In preparation for the women's eventual posting to the field, Toole made three visits to RCMP detachments in Saskatchewan, where she participated in regular patrols as well as one drug raid. She also talked to male members about female Mounties and tried to address their concerns "as well as those of some of their spouses." She later debriefed Troop 17 about these visits.[30]

The recruits responded to the presence of Maj. Toole in a variety of ways. One remembered that some of the women resented the fact that Toole was from the armed forces and was not a member of the RCMP. They assumed that she "didn't know what was expected" because she was a military officer.[31] It was one more way female Mounties were seen by the men at the academy as needing special treatment. Louise Ferguson recalled that Toole did not want the women to take physical education or self-defence classes with male recruits, a decision that Ferguson thought was "a little different than the objective we were trying to achieve" while training to be police officers. Ferguson also recalled that Toole's military rank was a source of tension for some men at the academy, who would "walk around the block not to have to salute her" due to her higher rank.[32] Others such as Linda Rutherford had great respect for Toole and put the major "on a pedestal." Rutherford confessed that she was "in awe" of Toole's military rank and she

---

29 Ibid.

30 Doris Toole, email message to author, July 8, 2008.

31 Allison Palmer, interview with author, June 11, 2008.

32 Louise Ferguson, interview with author, November 9, 2006.

felt more secure knowing that Toole was advocating for the troop.[33]

There were also generational differences. Three of the women interviewed for this study recognized, in hindsight, that the younger recruits had more difficulty coming to terms with the presence of Maj. Toole than the older women in the troop. They considered Toole "old" even though she was just thirty-eight years of age at the time. As one woman explained, "We were young!" and some of the women failed to appreciate Toole's "sacrifice."[34] Trish O'Brien remembered that some of the younger women thought Toole was always checking up on them, behaving more like a drill sergeant than an advisor. "We really didn't understand her role totally," commented O'Brien.[35]

From an overall perspective, however, the secondment of Maj. Toole remains an important part of RCMP history. Toole represented the first and only time the RCMP seconded an advisor from outside the police force to assist in the training of one of its troops. Her presence was an indication of the unease with which the force approached the training of the first female Mounties. As one officer at the academy at the time later explained, the force was unsure of how women would respond to the tough physical training and regimented lifestyle. For the most part, commanding officers were relieved that Toole was there.[36]

TROOP 17 AT DEPOT

In the 1970s, recruit training at Depot was strenuous and discipline was strict, much as it had been for one hundred years. It served a dual purpose: to prepare a new police officer for work in the RCMP and to afford the RCMP the opportunity to assess the new recruit.[37] Journalist Tony Leighton, in a feature article on the academy for *Equinox* magazine, summarized training at Depot as "one of the most demanding police-training programmes in the world, a grueling hybrid of military boot camp and

---

33   Linda Rutherford, interview with author, April 20, 2010. In 1969, the Canadian Armed Forces had just twenty-nine women with the rank of major out of a total of three thousand personnel with that rank, making Toole a trailblazer in breaking down gender barriers in her own right. *Report of RCSW*, 137.

34   Trish O'Brien, interview with author, November 13, 2008.

35   Ibid.

36   Cameron Montgomery, interview with author, May 24, 2007.

37   "A Guide to Success: Basic Recruit Training," RCMP recruiting guide, 1975.

modern police college."[38] The idea for a training academy for the RCMP dates back to 1869 and Prime Minister John A. Macdonald's vision of a mounted constabulary. In 1880, Macdonald dispatched Commr. A.G. Irvine (1880–1886) to Dublin to study the RIC's "Depot of Instruction."[39] Irvine was impressed with the idea of a permanent training facility where all recruits would be posted for a six-month period for training in courses taught by officers from the British military.[40]

Despite Irvine's enthusiasm, the Canadian government did not immediately act on his recommendations. It was not until the Riel Resistance of 1885 that the federal government was convinced that it was time to expand its policing operations on the prairies. A formal training academy was established in Regina later that year. It featured a riding facility, stables, and forty prefabricated buildings organized around a parade square that is still in use today. Sixty horses and one hundred men could be quartered on the site, where foot drill, mounted infantry drill, veterinary science, revolver training, shoeing and saddling horses, musketry, police regulations, and the country's laws were taught.[41] Full-time staff members were appointed from the Royal Military College at Kingston, Ontario, or were non-commissioned officers who had served with the British military in colonial postings such as India.[42]

Little had changed in the RCMP's training program by the 1970s, and instructors engaged in a rigid program that instilled discipline and loyalty. Individual identities were subsumed during the training

---

38   Tony Leighton, "Red Serge and High Spirits: Blood, Sweat and Fears—Life in the RCMP Training Depot" *Equinox* no. 22 (1985): 40. Also see Bonnie Reilly Schmidt, "Contesting a Canadian Icon: Female Police Bodies and the Challenge to the Masculine Foundations of the Royal Canadian Mounted Police in the 1970s," *Contesting Bodies and Nation in Canadian History,* eds. Patrizia Gentile and Jane Nicholas (Toronto: University of Toronto Press, 2013), 368-385.

39   The RCMP's use of the name "Depot" for the training academy may also refer to the fact that in the 1880s the NWMP initially established an "outpost and supply station along the banks of Wascana Creek" at the current site. See James McKenzie, *Troop 17: The Making of Mounties* (Calgary: Detselig Enterprises Ltd., 1992), 9.

40   Sheehan and Oosten, *Behind the Badge*, 13.

41   Ibid., 12; also Marquis, "Policing Two Imperial Frontiers," 191.

42   Sheehan and Oosten, *Behind the Badge*, 14. Greg Marquis has shown that instructors at Depot were British non-commissioned officers from the royal marines and cavalry. Marquis, "Policing Two Imperial Frontiers,"190–91.

period as a new police identity emerged. For example, on first arrival at the academy, all recruits were supplied with fatigues and told that they had to run double-time together between all classes with their heads bowed "because they lacked the knowledge to pay proper 'compliments' to their superiors."[43] Esprit de corps and troop unity were important components of the training. The welfare and survival of a troop during the training period were dependent on notions of group conformity. Those who refused or failed to pull their weight were held to account by their troopmates. Bill Jones, who went through recruit training in the 1960s, was the recipient of a hazing on one occasion when he arrived late to help his troop clean their dormitory. Jones recalled his troopmates dumping him in a tub of cold water and holding him under for thirty seconds to teach him a lesson. He also heard stories about recruits being "horse troughed," a punishment that required a trough full of horse manure and urine in which to throw a recruit who was not pulling his weight.[44] Hazing rituals in homosocial institutions such as the RCMP were often fuelled by aggression and competition, seen at the time as important elements for male bonding and male friendships.[45]

Training staff were known to lean on new arrivals, overdosing them with discipline and attention to detail, particularly in the drill hall.[46] Marching has historically played an important role in the maintenance of the image of the RCMP. Mounties have marched during royal visits, state funerals, rodeos, coronations, and police funerals for more than a century. Foot drill at Depot was a conditioning process meant to transform a troop of thirty-two civilians into a cohesive paramilitary unit that could "change direction without losing a beat" the instant a command was given.[47] Drill also served as a form of mental training

---

43   Leighton, "Red Serge and High Spirits," 42.

44   Bill Jones, interview with author, October 3, 2011. Horse troughing "was one method that a squad had of punishing one of its members who was not giving one hundred percent to the squad's training activities." Supt. J. Religa, quoted in Sheehan and Oosten, *Behind the Badge*, 351.

45   Kathy Peiss, quoted in Mike O'Brien, "Manhood and the Militia Myth: Masculinity, Class and Militarism in Ontario, 1902–1914," *Labour/Le Travail* 42 (Fall 1998): 133.

46   Leighton, "Red Serge and High Spirits," 42.

47   Ibid., 42; 46.

designed to reprogram civilians into police officers. New recruits were taught how to manage their feelings and emotions during drill exercises, one of the purposes of the yelling that drill instructors regularly engaged in. Yelling was a tool used to instill aggression and mental toughness in a recruit, qualities seen as vital to the performance of police duties in the field.[48] By the end of their training, a troop could perform a twenty-minute drill routine that included all of the basic marching movements that had been part of European military training for some two centuries.[49]

In addition to drill, running, self-defence tactics, and swimming were part of the RCMP's physical training curriculum in the 1970s.[50] As a benchmark of physical fitness, recruits were required to run the Cooper test, which measured cardiovascular fitness based on running a mile and a half in twelve minutes.[51] Recruits were also required to complete the Physical Abilities Requirement Evaluation (PARE), which simulated common physical demands of police work such as chasing a suspect up a staircase. Participants had four minutes to complete two obstacle courses.[52]

The pressure to meet these standards was intense at Depot in the 1970s and not all recruits responded positively to the rigorous training. Instructors used a strategy known as "making the troop pay" with extra physical activities when a weaker member lagged behind. Instructors believed that the weakest link would "shape up, so that

---

48   Susan Ehrlich Martin, "Police Force or Police Service? Gender and Emotional Labor," *Annals of the American Academy of Political and Social Science* 561 (January 1999): 121.

49   McKenzie, *Troop 17*, 31.

50   Recruits and instructors could participate in several extracurricular activities to challenge themselves physically. They included running in the 200 Mile Club, the 500 Mile Club, the 1,000 Mile Club, the English Channel Swim (1,290 lengths of the pool at Depot), the Diefenbaker Swim (100 miles, the length of Diefenbaker Lake), and Bench Press (150 percent body weight for males, 100 percent for females). Record holders in these activities were posted on display boards in the gymnasium hallway. Sheehan and Oosten, *Behind the Badge*, 299–301.

51   The test was developed by Dr. Kenneth Cooper, author of the bestselling book *Aerobics*, first published in 1968. Cooper's test was part of a conditioning program for astronauts, the military, and law enforcement agencies. "Dr. Kenneth Cooper," Cooper 40 Aerobics, http://www.cooperaerobics.com.

52   Sheehan and Oosten, *Behind the Badge*, 299; 301.

the rest of the troop wouldn't have to keep 'paying' for his or her in-adequacies."[53] If a recruit was continually dragging the entire troop down, troopmates would sometimes "pack a recruit's bags and set them out in the middle of the parade square" as an indication that they had decided it was time for him or her to leave the academy.[54] Most troops, whether male or female, had one or two members who resigned during training at Depot.

It is not surprising, then, that the academy's commanders were uncertain how female recruits would respond to the demands about to be placed on them. How to house and train the first female Mounties featured prominently in discussions being held. With just four months to prepare for their arrival, and given the media coverage, there was a concerted effort to ensure that all thirty-two women graduated.[55] Conventional understandings about gender and women's role in society framed their discussions. As one commanding officer admitted years later, the men who were present had an image of women that started "with their mothers" and transferred onto women in general.[56] Consequently, they viewed the female recruits in paternalistic terms, as being in need of protection from the healthy young men at the academy. Initially, there was a suggestion that a fence be erected around "C" Block, the barracks where the women would be housed, to protect them from male recruits. Although it was never under serious consideration, the idea of a fence reveals the RCMP's unease over the potential for sexual activity between male and female recruits.[57]

It was not the healthy young male recruits that women recruits needed protection from, however. Several people recalled concerns about extramarital affairs taking place between female recruits and the married instructional staff. "We had raging paranoia that a male instructor was going to get involved in an inappropriate relationship with a female recruit, which to my knowledge happened on numerous

---

53   McKenzie, *Troop 17*, 37.

54   Ibid., 40.

55   Cameron Montgomery, interview with author, May 24, 2007.

56   Ibid.

57   Ibid. By December 1974 there was "at least one serious romance between a male and female recruit." Martin O'Malley, "Women Mounties Fitting In," *The Woman's Globe and Mail*, December 5, 1974.

occasions," according to Bill Jones, an instructor at the academy in the 1970s. Jones recalled the lengths to which some of the instructional staff went to be sexually appealing to female recruits:

> We had a drill instructor who ... used to wear a girdle when he taught the women's troops. We used to see him. He'd lace this thing up so his waist would look all [slim], because he had a bit of a paunch. Only wore it when he taught the women. One of the guys I worked with in self-defence, before he taught a women's class, would spend a half an hour in the weight room pumping weights so that his arms would look bigger ... Men behave stupidly around women and that was a new thing for the Mounted Police. They'd never had to deal with it.[58]

These instructors' concern about the physical shape and condition of their bodies when in front of female Mounties represented a reversal of the more conventionally held assumption that women were the only sex preoccupied with their appearance.

Accounts about the reactions of staff members to the presence of women at Depot depart significantly from images of heroic Mounties from previous decades. They typically portrayed Mounties as sexually "safe" men who were more often than not depicted in the company of their horses or dogs rather than women. Portrayals of white, unmarried men bonded together through tough military discipline and male camaraderie dominated Mountie literature and movies for decades. However, the men at Depot who viewed female Mounties as objects of male sexual desire rather than police colleagues called into question the veracity of the traditional depictions that had shaped the RCMP's popular image.

Commanders also failed to consider that other staff members might attempt to take advantage of the presence of women at Depot. Not long after Troop 17's arrival, Bill Jones inadvertently discovered that someone had created a peephole into the women's change rooms:

---

58   Bill Jones, interview with author, October 3, 2011; also Darryl Butler, interview with author, September 11, 2008.

[S]omebody had gone into the swimming instructors' office, locked the doors, and then dug a hole in the wall or in the actual doorway so they could peek through at the women changing. It was just my good luck that I went to go into the swimming office to get something from one of the staff and found the doors locked and thought, "Boy, that's really odd," because the doors were never locked during the daytime. So I reported that to my staff sergeant ... [and] we went back afterwards and found this hole in the wall. So that prompted a big investigation.[59]

The investigation concluded that a male member of Depot's support staff had created the hole in the wall.

Commanding officers and instructors at Depot were not the only ones who were unsure of what to expect. The newly sworn-in female Mounties were also unsure of what lay ahead. One woman brought her sewing machine with her to the academy. It was an extra piece of luggage that she probably did not have time to use since every waking moment of a recruit's life was scheduled. The sight of the sewing machine likely caused some apprehension for instructors already anxious about training female Mounties.[60] One female recruit, struggling up the steps of "C" Block, the women's barracks, with two large suitcases, asked her future drill sergeant, who happened to be passing by, to help her with her luggage. An instructor who was present recalled the sergeant replying, "You're in a man's outfit now, lady, carry your own bag!"[61] The *Royal Canadian Mounted Police Gazette* recounted the same incident in the following way: "She was quickly and quietly advised that recruits were not given such luxuries, after all, was she not earning the same wages as male recruits and thus subject to equal privilege?"[62] It was a quick and early lesson for the female recruit who continued to respond in a gendered way to the men around her.

---

59   Bill Jones, interview with author, October 3, 2011.

60   Carol Franklin, interview with author, April 20, 2010.

61   Darryl Butler, interview with author, September 11, 2008.

62   "The First Troop," *Royal Canadian Mounted Police Gazette*, 37, no. 7–8 (1975): 10.

The suitcase incident reflected the general unease on the part of both men and women over the blurring of gender roles that was taking place at Depot. More importantly, the assumption that this female recruit was expected to act like a man and carry her own bags if she wanted to receive equal treatment conveyed the message that masculinity was the normative standard that the women would have to measure up to. It was a portent of things to come for the women of the RCMP.

TRAINING FEMALE MOUNTIES

Adjusting to the semi-military ways of the Force was not easy and
the Drill Staff took pains to teach us to march without a wiggle!
—Constable Barbara J. Woods
RCMP Quarterly, 1975

The RCMP attempted to regulate the women of Troop 17 during
their time at the training academy much as it had male recruits
for more than one hundred years. But decisions concerning female
Mounties were based on understandings of women's difference rather
than their equality. The approach to gender roles at Depot was a complex and fluid situation, as both the men of the RCMP and the female
recruits soon discovered. This fluidity enabled female Mounties to
challenge, in subtle and varied ways, prevailing notions of masculinity as integral to the occupation. More importantly, it offered a space
for the women to assert both their equality and their difference from
male police officers even before they left the academy. Their challenges demonstrated not only their agency, but that female police officers
were more than equal to the policing challenges that awaited them in
the field.

THE TRAINING PROGRAM

The academy's instructional staff was not informed of the exact date
the women were arriving until a couple of weeks beforehand. Until
then, instructors speculated about which corporals would be selected
to train Troop 17. Commanding officers had already decided, however,
that the senior NCO from each discipline, rather than corporals, would

instruct the female troop, another departure from RCMP tradition.[1] Speculation about changes to the training program, and whether the women would be able to handle it, was also rife. The *Royal Canadian Mounted Police Gazette* later recorded that some instructors initially expected that the first item of kit to be issued to the women would be "32 large white handkerchiefs to wipe the tears away."[2] Instructors from individual units met to discuss what alterations, if any, would be required to their programs. Some felt that many facets of training such as swimming and the use of firearms could be delivered in exactly the same way to women and men. But others were unsure of the physical capabilities of women. In the physical training unit, for example, instructors initially set objectives for weightlifting that were unrealistic for women given their stature and body strength. One commanding officer encouraged the corporals to think in terms of "equivalency" rather than "equal" when setting standards for Troop 17.[3]

Drill staff wondered whether the female body could be disciplined in the same way the male body could. So important was foot drill to the RCMP that it occupied a significant portion of the training a new recruit received.[4] Instructors were concerned about a number of aspects of teaching drill to female Mounties, including how to train them not to march with a wiggle. But there were also some pleasant surprises. Drill instructor Darryl Butler recalled that because the women did not possess the same upper body muscle mass as men, they were able to swing their arms "shoulder high and straight" with greater precision than male recruits when marching in formation.[5]

In the self-defence unit, instructors were concerned that women might not even accept the idea that self-defence training was important. Bill Jones remembered a hastily convened staff meeting in which instructors debated whether the program should be modified. In the 1970s, Depot's self-defence program was "quite violent" according to Jones.

---

1 Darryl Butler, interview with author, September 11, 2008.

2 "The First Troop," 10–11.

3 Cameron Montgomery, interview with author, May 24, 2007.

4 In 1985, for example, recruits received fifty hours of drill instruction during six months of training. Leighton, "Red Serge and High Spirits," 46.

5 Darryl Butler, email communication to author, December 16, 2009.

There was a great deal of choking, hair pulling, gouging of eyes, tearing of noses and ears, and twisting of flesh during practice sessions. Jones recalled, "We basically went on the premise that you hurt the other person until they gave up. That was the way it was taught. You applied pain, and when the pain was too much for the other person, they'd quit. That was the only restriction."[6] Instructors were unsure whether the women would want to learn the techniques as they were being taught.

During these discussions, generational differences quickly emerged. "We had two distinct schools of thought in the self-defence unit. We had what I call the old school, who thought women were frail and would be easily damaged and we should not treat them the same, and then we had the younger group, which ... were recruited in the mid-sixties, and our opinion was, 'Let's just put it forward the way it is and see how they cope with it,'" according to Jones. The younger instructors wanted to work from the assumption that the women could do the training in the same way male recruits did. They wanted to wait and see what the women were capable of before making changes to some of the techniques being taught.[7]

Following the arrival of Troop 17, some self-defence instructors quickly recognized that the women's performance could not be measured by the same standards as those applied to the men. At the time, self-defence instructors not only assessed a recruit's strength and fighting technique but qualities such as aggression and the willingness to become involved in physical confrontation.[8] During his years at the academy Jones realized that "the majority" of the women were not convinced that they wanted to use the techniques being taught. "So the marking level [for women] definitely dropped. We had a number of women held back for remedial training. I had a couple particularly myself, because of their lack of willingness to get involved in the day-to-day self-defence training," recalled Jones. "We had a number of techniques that worked quite [effectively] if you weren't big and strong. And those were the ones I tried to emphasize" when training women.[9] As Jones

---

6   Bill Jones, interview with author, October 3, 2011.

7   Ibid.

8   Ibid.

9   Ibid.

explained, "[A] proper technique should be workable by anyone. You don't have to be big and strong to make a good technique work." He maintained that the self-defence program needed adjustment to reflect bodies that were built differently—not because those bodies were inferior and could not perform the work, but because the standard by which they were being measured was not an inclusive standard.[10]

The assumption that police officers had to be big and strong to be effective was an indication that male bodies were also thought of by the RCMP in gendered ways. Recruiters continued to rely on the understanding that a muscular and imposing stature and the ability to meet violence with appropriate levels of aggression made for an ideal police candidate. Many Canadian men were unable to meet the RCMP's standards. Some men dropped out of recruit training while at the academy when they were unable, or unwilling, to adapt to the rigid physical demands. Not all male recruits conformed to the RCMP's gendered understandings of masculinity, suggesting that negotiating gendered assumptions could be just as complex for the men the RCMP hired as it was for the women.

Most of the women who trained at the academy understood that their smaller size meant that they would have to be creative once they began work in the field. Shannon Brandt, a special constable hired for surveillance duties in 1975, recognized that the techniques the instructors were attempting to teach her were not viable for the work she was hired to do. Brandt was just five feet two and a half inches and weighed 105 pounds when she arrived at Depot. She recalled being pressured by instructors to be stronger, more vocal, and more aggressive in self-defence classes where they would "fling" her around during ground fighting exercises. Brandt remembered thinking, "Isn't a surveillant neither seen nor heard?" in response to their pressure.[11] She resisted their injunctions simply because it would not be valuable in the type of work she would be doing. Brandt was creating a space for alternative constructions of policing, one that questioned concepts of physical strength and aggression as preconditions for effectiveness as a police officer. It was one way that women approached the work differently than their male counterparts. But it was also an indication

10   Ibid.

11   Shannon Brandt, interview with author, June 29, 2010.

that female Mounties were confident in their abilities and understood that alternatives would have to be developed.

Instructors were not the only staff members who doubted the ability of women to meet the training program's physical requirements. Carol Hill was a twenty-four-year-old clerk typist working as support staff at the academy when Troop 17 arrived. Hill was not sure "females belonged in the force as regular members" because of their size. Hailing from a small farming community in Saskatchewan, Hill recalled male RCMP officers having to break up fights in the local bar. This experience reinforced the importance of physical size for Hill, who was unconvinced that women possessed the strength necessary to police dangerous situations effectively.[12]

While most instructors kept their opinions about women in the RCMP to themselves, one communications instructor let the women of Troop 17 know his position from the outset. Marianne Robson remembered that the "first class we had with him, we were all sitting in class, and he walked into our class, and he looked at us and he said, 'What the fuck do you think you're doing?'" Robson interpreted his comment to mean that the women had no right to be at the academy, much less sitting in his classroom. As their training progressed, however, this instructor softened his stance toward female Mounties and Robson remembered him fondly as one of her favourite instructors.[13]

Many of the men at the academy, instructors and recruits alike, decided to take a "wait and see" approach to Troop 17. It is important to remember that male RCMP officers, like many Canadian men, struggled with the shifts in gender relations that were taking place in Canada in the 1970s. The concept of biological difference that had long been used to underpin the unequal power relations between men and women in society was suddenly cast into doubt at Depot. Men had been socialized to treat women as the weaker, passive sex, and women were expected to respond with appreciation and deference toward men in return. But the sudden blurring of conventional gender roles created a great deal of uncertainty. Men at the academy did not know whether it was appropriate to use gentlemanly deportment toward women now that they were receiving the same pay and training. "Senior male recruits

---

12   Carol Hill, interview with author, April 28, 2008.

13   Marianne Robson, interview with author, July 29, 2008.

could not quite make up their minds whether or not to hold doors open for the new female arrivals and for a while, it was [humorous] to observe the reaction on both sides," according to one observer.[14] And the women sometimes expected traditional treatment from the men, adding to the confusion.

THE MEDIA AND FEMALE MOUNTIES

The RCMP correctly anticipated that a high level of national interest and positive public opinion could be generated by the media's coverage of the arrival of female Mounties at Depot. The relationship between the RCMP and journalists was often fractious in the 1970s, prompting Commr. William Higgitt to fine-tune the *RCMP Act* with an addendum prohibiting Mounties from speaking with journalists without a commanding officer's knowledge or approval. The RCMP recognized, however, that it needed the media to promote the police force as a reform-minded institution interested in gender equity and diversity. Accordingly, journalists were granted access to the preparations being made at the academy for the arrival of the first female Mounties.[15] Journalists toured "C" Block, the women's barracks, to view the renovations that were being made. Several later reported on the removal of the urinals and group showers and the installation of cubicles and bathtubs to accommodate the women. Reporters also noted that new amenities included a hand dryer for drying hair and laundry facilities. The reportage suggested that although women were joining a male institution, they still required female spaces where they could continue to engage in conventional feminine activities, calming civilian anxieties about women's changing role in society.[16]

The RCMP was also anxious to produce a record of Troop 17's activities. Commanding officers enlisted the help of a female civilian member to create an official photographic record of the first female Mounties.

---

14   "The First Troop," 10.

15   For a detailed study on the media and Troop 17, see Bonnie Reilly Schmidt, "'The Greatest Man-Catcher of All': The First Female Mounties, the Media, and the Royal Canadian Mounted Police," *Journal of the Canadian Historical Association* 22, no. 1 (2011): 202–44.

16   See "The RCMP Rookies: Mounties Get Their First Women," *Toronto Star*, December 28, 1974; Ruth Warick, "Basic Training Program Same for Fairer Sex," *Leader-Post* (Regina), September 20, 1974; O'Malley, "Women Mounties Fitting In."

Unlike the media, this photographer was given full access to the women in their barracks. In 1975, the *Royal Canadian Mounted Police Gazette* published her photographs along with an article on Troop 17. The women were photographed doing laundry, ironing, curling their hair, and polishing their shoes. The caption underneath read, "Changes in training facilities were inevitable—laundry rooms—ironing rooms—hairdressing-rooms and a little less spit and a little more polish."[17] While male recruits undertook the same housekeeping activities, they were seldom if ever photographed performing them, at least not until *Equinox* magazine published a feature article on the RCMP's training program in 1985. One photograph of a male Mountie ironing his uniform appears in that article.[18] Until then, popular representations of Mounties did not depict male recruits engaged in what was considered to be feminine work. In the *Gazette's* photographs, female Mounties were confined to their gendered roles, reassuring the largely male police readership that the women continued to be governed by their feminine nature.

After their arrival at Depot, the media was granted unprecedented access to Troop 17. Several of the women recalled a strong media presence throughout their entire six months of training. One woman remembered just wanting to fit in with the male recruits, noting that it was "hard to feel like everybody else when you're getting all this special attention."[19] It was another way the troop was set apart. Louise Ferguson recalled the troop being photographed by media from across Canada and around the world, "from places we hadn't heard of."[20] Allison Palmer remembered the media following the troop to their classes and even to the mess hall, where the women were photographed "trying to shovel food in" within the twenty minutes allotted for their meals.[21] According to Marianne Robson, the media "was around us all

---

17 "Women, Why Not?," *Royal Canadian Mounted Police Gazette*, 37, no. 7–8 (1975): 4.

18 Leighton, "Red Serge and High Spirits," 47.

19 Louise Ferguson, interview with author, November 9, 2006.

20 Ibid.

21 Allison Palmer, interview with author, June 11, 2008.

the time" and they were followed "relentlessly."[22] The only place the media was not allowed was the dormitory, but that restriction was eventually circumvented too. Carol Franklin received calls on the dormitory pay telephone from two radio stations in her hometown asking for interviews.[23]

Despite the RCMP's initial assurances that they wanted to diffuse the pressure of being the first over the entire troop, the force failed to recognize the adverse effects the media was having. Support staff member Carol Hill recalled that the arrival of the women was very high profile for the RCMP, and that it must have been difficult for Troop 17. She remembered that everything they did was scrutinized.[24] Several members of the troop cited the media's interest as the thing they liked the least about their time in training. Trish O'Brien, who described the media attention as "horrible," commented,

> I guess it was all such a big event, bigger than what we even thought. We were just there to do our thing and excited about joining and we didn't even want the media there. But they were everywhere, watching us eating, and doing our weights, and running and whatever. Sometimes your tongue would be down to your ankles and you'd have this camera in your face. And we'd want them to go away. And even in class you're listening to the lecture and they'd have the camera going … After a while I really got annoyed … That was one of the big things we found disturbing and distracting.[25]

Eventually, all of the press coverage began to take its toll on the troop.[26] The women grew tired of all the publicity, a fact that was also

---

22 Marianne Robson, interview with author, July 29, 2008.

23 Carol Franklin, interview with author, April 20, 2010.

24 Carol Hill, interview with author, April 28, 2008.

25 Trish O'Brien, interview with author, November 13, 2008.

26 One RCMP source described the media presence this way: "All branches of the press showed an extensive interest in their progress and the girls found themselves under additional pressure from the media." See "The First Troop," 11.

recorded by the press.[27] They resisted the RCMP's public relations strategy, complaining to commanders that they no longer wanted to be interviewed or photographed by journalists. The RCMP eventually relented, limiting the media's access to two of the women who were selected to act as spokespersons, easing some of the pressure on the troop.[28]

THE "SPECIAL" FEMALE MOUNTIE

As the media's intense focus on Troop 17 continued, a second all-female troop quietly arrived at Depot in January 1975. These female recruits were hired as special constables, or "specials" as they were known, to work at Canadian airports as part of a national airport security program initiated in conjunction with the Ministry of Transport on March 12, 1973.[29] Thirty-two women from across Canada formed Troop J (1975), an event that went unnoticed by the media.[30] The RCMP considered the rank of special constable as one area where the police force could best utilize women. Indeed, women had been highly successful conducting surveillance work for the RCMP since the 1960s, first as civilian members and then as specials.[31] It was a factor that influenced the force to hire women for uniformed special constable duties at Canadian airports in December 1973, five months before the decision to hire women as regular uniformed members was made.[32]

The rank of special constable was not new to the RCMP and

---

27   Primeau, "They Always Get Their Person." Also Marianne Robson, interview with author, July 29, 2008.

28   Trish O'Brien, interview with author, November 13, 2008.

29   In the 1970s, aircraft hijackings were becoming frequent, and a police presence at airports was viewed as a security measure. By 1975, the RCMP had trained 657 special constables specifically for duty at nine international and twenty domestic airports across Canada. Solicitor General Warren Allmand, *Annual Report: 1974–1975* (Ottawa: Solicitor General of Canada, 1975), 18; 24.

30   Special constable troops were assigned a letter rather than a number, a practice that differentiated them from regular troops and reinforced the hierarchy that existed amongst ranks in the RCMP.

31   Surveillance operatives working for the RCMP's Security Service were eventually promoted from the rank of civilian member to special constable in 1973. All special constables within the RCMP converted to regular member status in 1990. "Historical Evidence of A.M. Bulletin About Conversion of S/Csts. to Cst.," RCMP file G524-17 (92-11-24). Access to Information file GA-3951-3-03134/08.

32   "Policewomen, Why Not?," 3.

it vanished and reappeared at various points throughout the force's history. In the nineteenth century, gold inspectors, officers' servants, scouts, and interpreters all held the rank of special constable. The rank was widely reintroduced in the 1970s, and specials were hired to perform a number of specialized tasks.[33] Pilots for RCMP aircraft, commanding officers' drivers, and some members of the RCMP band held the rank. In 1974, the RCMP began to hire specials specifically for criminal surveillance work in major Canadian cities. Many regular members viewed the hiring of specials as a weakening of RCMP standards. In a hierarchical paramilitary institution in which rank was highly prized, specials were generally viewed with condescension because of their shortened training time, static postings, specialized duties, and lower pay. One special constable, commenting on the attitudes of regulars at Depot in 1975, noted that unless you had completed six months of training you were not considered part of "the group."[34]

Retired Mountie Jane Hall observed in her memoirs that the special rank was considered to be a "dead end." Hall erroneously believed that specials were academically less competitive than regulars and did "not need to meet the standard recruitment requirements" regular members had to meet.[35] Her comments are representative of the opinion held by many regular members that specials were inferior as police officers. However, uniformed specials met the same recruitment standards as regular members, testified in court, and had full police powers. They received the same training in academics, firearms, drill, swimming, self-defence, and physical training but all within a truncated training period of three, rather than six, months.[36]

---

33   According to journalist Paul Palango, the rank was reinstated following World War II when the RCMP began to hire surveillance specialists to track Russian spies in Canada during the Cold War. Paul Palango, *The Last Guardians: The Crisis in the RCMP ... and in Canada* (Toronto: McClelland & Stewart, 1998), 25. In 1975, the first Aboriginal special constables were hired specifically for work in Indigenous communities. They completed their training on March 14 and conformed "as closely as possible to the qualifications required for a regular member." Sheehan and Oosten, *Behind the Badge*, 295.

34   Shannon Brandt, interview with author, June 29, 2010.

35   Hall, *The Red Wall: A Woman in the RCMP* (Renfrew, ON: General Store Publishing, 2007), 45.

36   Caroline Harper, interview with author, June 28, 2010.

Physical differences were often used by regular members to justify the exclusion of specials from police culture, where they were "treated terribly" according to one retired officer.[37] The body of the male special constable, in particular, was contentious. Male specials hired for plainclothes duties such as surveillance had long hair, grew beards or moustaches, and were shorter in stature.[38] In an organization where size and strength were equated with authority and effective policing, the special was an anomaly that threatened the iconic image of the RCMP. The idea that specials were somehow lesser police officers explains why, in part, Troop J's arrival went unnoticed by the media in January 1975. Although the special troop also performed drill exercises and wore uniforms,[39] they were never introduced to the media and did not endure the constant media attention experienced by Troop 17. Questions remain about the role that commanding officers played in diverting the media away from the lower-ranking special constables. Given the weariness of Troop 17 in dealing with journalists, it is difficult to understand why the RCMP did not make members of Troop J available for interviews to help defray some of the pressure being felt by the female regulars. Clearly, commanding officers held the view that the special constable did not measure up to the iconic image that the regular member symbolized.

The attention being paid to Troop 17, who were at the halfway point in their training by that time, distracted them from helping Troop J, who wanted, but did not receive, input about their training from a "big sister." It was a tradition at Depot that a "big brother" or a "big sister" from a senior troop was assigned to a junior troop to help them adjust

---

37   Bill Jones, interview with author, October 3, 2011.

38   The minimum height requirement for regular members in 1974 was five feet eight inches for men and five feet four inches for women. See O'Malley, "Women Mounties Fitting In." For a discussion on how the minimum physical qualifications for regular members fluctuated over one hundred years, see Sheehan and Oosten, *Behind the Badge*, 17–20.

39   Special constables assigned to airport duties in 1975 were issued brown tunics rather than red serge tunics. The difference in uniforms did not matter significantly to the public. Carolyn Harper recalled being photographed constantly by passengers arriving at the airport where she was stationed. "[W]e were the first RCMP policewomen that a lot of people from around the world saw in uniform. They would get off a plane, and you'd be standing there and they'd go, 'A Mountie, a female Mountie!' and they'd take your picture." Caroline Harper, interview with author, June 28, 2010.

to life at the academy. Carolyn Harper, a member of Troop J, described the lack of interaction between the two female troops in this way:

> We were supposed to have a big sister [from Troop 17] but they didn't come near us … I don't know if it was 'cause we were specials, whether they … didn't think we weren't important enough, I don't know. And we actually complained to our corporal and said, "You know what, we haven't seen our big sister. Any help that we're getting, for uniform things and polishing our boots, and all that stuff, any information we're getting is from male troops. They're helping us out. We haven't seen one of the women come in and help us out at all." … And after we complained about that, two of them came over and talked to us for a while, and that was about it.[40]

Marianne Robson, a member of Troop 17, remembered Troop J. When asked why her cohort kept its distance from the specials, Robson reflected:

> There was some jealousy between the two troops and we were not encouraged to assist them or mentor them in any way. Of course, by the time we were halfway, Troop 17 was looking pretty tattered—hair cut off, no makeup, pretty muscular. We were a little jealous of how feminine the special troop of girls still looked, and of course up to that time we were the Queen Bees of Depot and these new gals were on our turf … But again, the strangest thing was that [we] were [not] encouraged to fraternize with this group of young women.[41]

---

40   Ibid. This problem was remedied prior to the arrival of the second female regular troop in March. Maj. Doris Toole recommended that Cst. Cheryl Joyce, a member of Troop 17, be retained at Depot for an additional three weeks to "assist the members of Troop 36 (1975) in their initial phases of training." Joyce's terms of reference included advising the women on personal problems, providing training on kit upkeep and clothing standards, the general supervision of the women's quarters, and monitoring training classes. Maj. D.E. Toole, memorandum to the C.O., Depot Division, "Female Uniformed Member of the Force as Advisor," February 25, 1975. Author copy.

41   Marianne Robson, email message to author, July 4, 2012.

This disconnect between the two troops was an indication that female Mounties also struggled with the shifts in gender that were taking place in society where the fight for women's rights was often equated with a loss of femininity. It is possible that the members of Troop 17 may have felt this more keenly than the regular female members who followed them.

It is worth noting that many of the women in Troop J initially thought they were being hired as regular members. According to Harper, none of them understood the differences between a special and regular constable when they were recruited. Harper recalled that almost all of the women in her troop were told that there was one female troop already in training in Regina and that the RCMP did not know if they were going to hire more women. They were assured that they would have a uniform and all of the same police powers; the only difference would be their static posting at an airport.[42] All of the members of Troop J erroneously believed that they might be the last female troop to be trained by the RCMP. Yet just one week after Troop 17 graduated on March 3, 1975, a second troop of female regular members arrived at Depot on March 10 to begin their training. The members of Troop J were "pretty irate" at this turn of events, and many suspected that they had been misled so that the RCMP could fill its quota for female special constables at airports.[43]

The assertion that Troop J might be the last female troop spoke to the tenuous position of women in the RCMP. It echoed the commissioner's earlier promise to the DSRRs that "if it doesn't work, we'll just fold it up." The hierarchical structure of the RCMP made it possible for recruiters to mislead the women. After all, recruits, male and female, were considered resources to be shaped and moulded by the RCMP's managers, who were accustomed to directing the lives of the lower ranks. For the women of Troop J, their rights as employees were superseded by the power and authority of senior ranking officers who needed to fill staffing quotas. By the time the women discovered that they were not

---

42   Carolyn Harper, interview with author, June 28, 2010.

43   Ibid. In 1975, Marc Lalonde, minister responsible for the Status of Women, reported that another ninety-six women were scheduled to complete their training by mid-1975, and that fifty-seven women had been hired as special constables to perform specialized duties such as airport patrols. Lalonde, *Status of Women in Canada*, 35.

regular members, they had invested a significant amount of time and resources in joining the RCMP, including quitting their jobs and relocating to Regina to go through training. Protesting this turn of events seemed to be a futile exercise for the female specials by the time they realized that they had been duped.

TROOP 17 GRADUATES

As the women of Troop 17 prepared to graduate from Depot, the police force handpicked their postings.[44] A willingness to relocate anywhere in Canada was a well-known requirement of Canada's federal police force, one that was established with applicants early on in the recruitment process.[45] Until 1975, regulations stipulated that members of the RCMP would not be posted to their home province for the first five years of their service. According to former staffing and personnel officers, it was based on the belief "that members would be compromised by their old [classmates] or buddies. By keeping the member isolated from their family and friends, we ensured their loyalty to the Force and ensured their objectivity when conducting investigations."[46] This policy contributed significantly to the masculine and paramilitary culture of the RCMP, where unquestioned obedience, unclouded by attachments and emotions, was still perceived as a valuable character trait in police officers.

The policy shifted over the years in much the same way the RCMP's marriage regulations and rates of pay fluctuated. The RCMP often changed its regulations during periods of low popularity, sluggish recruitment, or public criticism. A staffing shortage was one possible reason the RCMP changed its regulations in the early 1970s to allow recruits to be posted to their home province.[47] By 1977, however, the

---

44   All recruits were interviewed by staffing officers at the academy prior to their graduation. During the interview, recruits were given the opportunity to state their top three posting preferences. Not all requests for the first preferred posting were met, and some recruits were sent to postings they considered to be less than desirable. The RCMP had the final word on where it sent its personnel.

45   Sheehan and Oosten, *Behind the Badge*, 19.

46   Quoted in Sheldon Boles, ed., "Old Surrey Boys," *Veterans' Update*, 2nd ed. (Vancouver: RCMP Veterans' Association, 2012): unnumbered.

47   Recruitment numbers increased dramatically during the 1974–1975 fiscal year. That year, the RCMP hired 1,140 constables; 432 were married men and 113 were women. Solicitor General of Canada, *Annual Report, 1974–1975*, 24.

policy had changed again and graduates were prohibited from being posted to their home communities.[48] As they prepared to graduate in 1975, most of the women of Troop 17, but not all, were assigned to postings in their home provinces, a reflection of the RCMP's ongoing paternalistic concern for the first female Mounties.

The graduation ceremonies for Troop 17 were held at the academy on March 3, 1975. Thirty of the original thirty-two recruits graduated.[49] A number of dignitaries, including Commr. Maurice Nadon, Canada's Solicitor General Warren Allmand, Saskatchewan's social services minister Alex Taylor, and Helen Hunley, the Solicitor General for Alberta, were in attendance and made speeches.[50] Warren Allmand later confessed in an interview to being "choked up" while watching the "various demonstrations of swimming, self-defence and drill given by Canada's first female RCMP." Allmand commented that he was "moved and enthused. I felt I was observing an historical event in a force that has so much history."[51] He was not alone. Many of the two hundred people present had tears in their eyes watching military marches and listening to strains of "Amazing Grace" being played during the ceremonies. Five fathers, members of the RCMP and other police forces, presented their daughters with their identification badges. In a departure from RCMP tradition, their mothers were also invited to participate in the

---

48   Marianne Robson, interview with author, July 29, 2008. By 1987, the regulation was once again being rigidly enforced. See Anne Kyle, "RCMP Policy Can Separate Family Members at Times," *Leader-Post* (Regina), March 23, 1987.

49   One recruit purchased her discharge and returned to secretarial duties in the RCMP. Another converted to the rank of special constable to work at Winnipeg International Airport. "The First Troop," 11.

50   Hunley was also present when three of the women were sworn in six months earlier in Alberta. Hunley was a veteran of World War II, a popular businesswoman, and a future Lieutenant-Governor of Alberta. She was invited by Troop 17 to address their class at their graduation ceremony and during the evening banquet. "Allmand's Message to New Mounties Is Look Forward," *Leader-Post* (Regina), March 4, 1975. Thank you to Rhonda Semple for drawing my attention to the likelihood that Hunley's achievements positioned her as an inspirational figure for Troop 17.

51   "Allmand's Message to New Mounties Is Look Forward," *Leader-Post* (Regina), March 4, 1975.

presentation in "recognition of the silent role played by wives of RCMP officers."[52] Reports of the graduation made national headlines and the ceremony was televised live by the CBC.

Cst. Janet Graham delivered the troop's valedictory address, speculating on what lay ahead for her and her fellow troopmates:

> Many eyes will be upon us—some critical, some encouraging—watching to see if we will pass the test. It will be up to us to prove our worth ... Here at Depot we have been shown that we are capable of going beyond what we thought was our limit. With this in mind, I'd like to close with this little proverb: "Our greatest glory lies not in never falling but in rising each time we fall."[53]

Graham likely had her male colleagues in mind when she stated that female Mounties would be watched, tested, and required to prove their worth. Few could imagine just how prescient her words were.

---

52   Ibid.

53   J.L. Graham, "Valedictory Address Troop 17 (1974/75)," March 3, 1975. RCMP Heritage Collection Unit Archives, Regina, Saskatchewan.

WOMEN IN RED SERGE

We were absolutely devastated that we didn't have high browns
like the guys.

—Louise Ferguson
Troop 17 (1974/75)

By 1974, the RCMP uniform had conveyed ideas about manliness,
power, state authority, and the nation for more than a century. It
was a readily identifiable symbol of Canada, a bridge from the past
to the present and a reminder of Canada's imperial ties with Britain.
The women of Troop 17 shared these beliefs about the symbolism and
authority that the RCMP uniform represented and they were eager to
don the famous red serge.[1] Unbeknownst to them, however, dressing
female Mounties in the red serge tunic, Stetson hat, and Strathcona
boots worn by male officers was never a consideration for the RCMP
in 1974. Instead, the police force decided to negotiate the tensions
surrounding the hiring of women by developing a feminized version
of the male uniform. It was seen as one way to manage the women's
smooth transition into the rank and file, many of whom were resistant
to the idea of female Mounties.

But the creation of an alternative uniform for women proved to
be a complex balancing act for the RCMP. The women's version had
to convey both authority and femininity, a fusion difficult to achieve
in a society that viewed these concepts in dichotomous terms. Early
in their training, the first female Mounties challenged the distinction

---

1   Serge is a durable worsted woollen fabric with diagonal lines or ridges that
is typically used for military uniforms. Members of the RCMP commonly refer to their
review order dress tunics as their "red serge."

that the women's uniform represented. But the RCMP remained intransigent, preserving the iconic review order uniform as a representation of Canada that was exclusively male. The history of the women's uniform contextualizes the implications the arrival of women had for the image of the RCMP. It also illustrates how gendered assumptions about the women's difference, rather than their equality, were reinforced through their uniform.

The history of the RCMP uniform and the rules and regulations governing the wearing of one are long and complex.[2] To eliminate the potential for confusion, the information that follows focuses on the two types of RCMP uniforms most recognizable to the Canadian public: the service order or daily operational uniform, and the review order or ceremonial red serge dress uniform.[3]

THE ROMANCE OF THE NWMP UNIFORM

Historically, the RCMP's review order uniform communicated a number of ideas about civic authority, citizenship, and power within Canadian society. In 1873, the uniform played a significant role in establishing the authority and power of the Canadian state and the Queen's Empire on the western prairie. The NWMP's approach to dressing its police officers in red serge woollen tunics mirrored a long British military tradition dating back to the formation of the New Model Army during the English Civil War. At that time, red (or scarlet) was a colour widely associated with royalty since it was more costly to produce as a dye than earth tones, such as brown or blue. When a brighter, synthetic version of the dye began to be produced on a mass scale during the industrial revolution, red serge woollen tunics soon became standard apparel for many of the Empire's armies and colonial police forces.

---

2   I am especially indebted to James J. Boulton for his detailed research on the history of the RCMP uniform. See James J. Boulton, *Uniforms of the Canadian Mounted Police* (North Battleford: Turner-Warwick Publications, Inc., 1990). Also James J. Boulton, *Head-Dress of the Canadian Mounted Police, 1873–2000* (Calgary: Bunker to Bunker Publishing, 2000). Research done by Jacques Brunelle, *The Royal Canadian Mounted Police in the 1990s: A Review of the Uniform, Dress and Kit of the RCMP* (Calgary: Bunker to Bunker Books, 1994) was also extremely helpful.

3   Other orders of dress included walking out order, formal attire that included a formal full-length blue skirt, white gloves, and a clutch purse for women and high-waisted overalls, congress boots, and box spurs for men. At the training academy, members of the drill instruction staff regularly wore service order no. 2, which was composed of a blue jacket, Stathcona boots, spurs and riding breeches. Brunelle, *The Royal Canadian Mounted Police in the 1990s*, 55.

The decision on the type of uniform adopted by the NWMP evolved over a two-year period and cannot be attributed to any one person. Colonel Robertson-Ross, the adjutant general of the Canadian militia sent by Macdonald to survey conditions in the western territories prior to 1873, and a "noted devotee of military finery," was viewed by one historian as instrumental in the decision.[4] The extent of Robertson-Ross's influence is not clear, however, and it appears that commanding officers of the NWMP also submitted suggestions.[5] By January 1874, the colour of the tunic had been selected. That month, Commissioner George Arthur French wrote, "A scarlet tunic has I believe been decided upon and from what I can learn here there are very good reasons for the decision. I should therefore advise the adoption of a plain scarlet tunic similar to those worn by some of the Imperial Cavalry regiments."[6] In 1876, a hussar-style design was officially adopted as the uniform of the NWMP.[7]

Concerns about the costs of dressing the new police force were discussed in Parliament. Macdonald reassured members of the House that the NWMP would be a civil force, not a military force, "with as little gold lace, fuss and fine feathers as possible,"[8] likely a reference to the elaborate uniforms worn by the British Hussars. Parliamentarians' fears were justified because by May 1875, the NWMP's commissioner was suggesting that chevrons and gold lace for non-commissioned and commissioned ranks should adorn the tunic "to lighten it."[9] Despite Macdonald's reassurances about fuss and fine feathers, "the Mounted Police in full dress soon resembled British

---

4   Desmond Morton, "Cavalry or Police: Keeping the Peace on Two Adjacent Frontiers, 1870–1900," *Journal of Canadian Studies* 12, no. 2 (Spring 1977): 30.

5   Boulton, *Uniforms of the Canadian Mounted Police*, 20–21.

6   George Arthur French quoted in Boulton, *Uniforms of the Canadian Mounted Police*, 19.

7   Boulton, *Uniforms of the Canadian Mounted Police*, 19. Hussars were a light cavalry regiment more commonly found in European armies. They were known for their distinctive style of dress, which was modelled after that of the Hungarian Hussars of the fifteenth century.

8   Macdonald, quoted in Morton, "Cavalry or Police," 30.

9   Boulton, *Uniforms of the Canadian Mounted Police*, 21.

dragoon guards."[10] But the elaborate uniform was expensive and un-suited to rugged prairie life where the NWMP uniforms wore out "at an alarming rate."[11]

Once the men of the NWMP began their policing duties, the uni-form underwent numerous changes to accommodate the primitive living and working conditions they experienced. Official dress regu-lations were relaxed and practicality soon determined how the men dressed. The men adopted more flamboyant pieces of clothing for their uniform such as fringed buckskin tunics, slouch hats, neckerchiefs, chaps, velveteen breeches, and flannel shirts, all articles of clothing that made policing on horseback more comfortable.[12] By 1895, other elements of the uniform had been replaced. The British-style pillbox hat and white pith helmet were replaced by the Stetson hat.[13] Created in 1865 by J.B. Stetson of St. Louis, Missouri, the Stetson, popularly known as the "cowboy hat," was a wide-brimmed hat made out of felt that featured a high crown and straps that prevented it from flying off the head during windy days. Toward the end of the nineteenth cen-tury, the more practical dress had finally distanced the NWMP from its "old association with the British army."[14] In fact, images of NWMP officers from the period depict men who resembled cowboys more than members of a paramilitary police force inspired by regiments of the British military.

At the turn of the twentieth century, the NWMP uniform garnered international attention during the Anglo-South African War. Strathco-na's Horse was not only famous for being exceptional scouts but for

---

10   Morton, "Cavalry or Police," 30.

11   Brunelle, *The Royal Canadian Mounted Police in the 1990s*, 5.

12   At one point moccasins were also adopted as an official item of kit. They were discontinued in 1900. Boulton, *Uniforms of the Canadian Mounted Police*, 1; 95–96; 138.

13   MacDonald, *Sons of the Empire*, 47. There is some discrepancy over the spe-cific year the Stetson was first introduced as an official part of the uniform but most accounts date it as between 1895 and 1899. The Stetson was formally authorized as part of the official NWMP uniform by an order-in-council from the federal Cabinet on June 22, 1904. Boulton, *Uniforms of the Canadian Mounted Police*, 144; 146.

14   MacDonald, *Sons of the Empire*, 47.

their distinctive style of dress.[15] It was no coincidence that the riding breeches, neckerchiefs, cowboy hat, and riding boots they wore
were more suited to climatic conditions on the South African veldt,
which resembled those of the Canadian prairie. In particular, a special
riding boot was designed and manufactured for Strathcona's Horse
by the Slater Shoe Company of Montreal. The Strathcona boot, as it
was called, featured a laced instep with a large gusset which afforded greater flexibility for the foot. A second gusset on the upper calf
that could be loosened or tightened by an adjustable strap was also
added, making the boot beneficial for both riding and marching. In
keeping with the elite status of the regiment, the boots were issued
to all members of Strathcona's Horse, not just its officers, a significant
departure from British military tradition.[16] When the NWMP adopted
these elements as part of the official dress uniform at home, a close
connection between military prowess and the romantic figure of the
western cowboy was firmly established.[17]

The NWMP's review order uniform underwent very few changes after the police force was granted "Royal" status by King Edward
VII in 1904. In recognition of this new status, blue shoulder epaulets
replaced gold-trimmed scarlet straps on the red tunics. By this time,
the RNWMP uniform was associated with an image of Canada that
was heroic and manly, an image that the federal government now
fully endorsed and was reluctant to change.[18] The Mounties' dress
uniform reached its final form in 1914. By 1920, strict compliance
with dress regulations was expected from all members of the RCMP
as the newly amalgamated police force expanded its mandate across
the country.[19]

The unusual dress of the men of the RNWMP also served as a
symbol of eroticism, a dimension of the uniform that may explain
its ongoing appeal in popular culture. Indeed, the sexual attraction

---

15   Brunelle, *The Royal Canadian Mounted Police in the 1990s*, 56.

16   See the Canada War Museum website: "Uniforms and Equipment: The Strathcona Boot," http://www.warmuseum.ca/cwm/exhibitions/boer/strathconaboot_e.shtml.

17   The Strathcona boot was adopted as an official part of the Mountie uniform
in 1900. Boulton, *Uniforms of the Canadian Mounted Police*, 138.

18   Brunelle, *The Royal Canadian Mounted Police in the 1990s*, 55.

19   Boulton, *Uniforms of the Canadian Mounted Police*, 1.

of women to the RCMP officer was colloquially known in Canada as "scarlet fever," a characterization that suggested women were unable to resist the attraction of the handsome Mountie dressed in his red serge tunic. Dorothy Standish Paull, in her 1993 memoirs, recalled dating her future husband, Tom, who was stationed in Banff, Alberta. "We began to see each other as long as the working days would allow. I found I had not only caught his eye but Scarlet Fever as well. I was engaged to Constable Tom Paull during the summer of 1937."[20] Paull titled her memoirs *Scarlet Fever*. There is little doubt that the review order uniform was firmly established as the centrepiece of the RCMP's image by the time Dorothy succumbed to Tom's attractions.

Throughout the twentieth century, the RCMP remained committed to portraying its male police officers as gentlemen. One way this was achieved was through the creation of regulations regarding a Mountie's dress and deportment. Numerous handbooks written for new recruits provide evidence that the RCMP associated gentlemanly behaviour and self-discipline with a neat and clean appearance. For example, in one 1947 pamphlet titled *Prelude to Duty*, recruits were told to "Keep your uniform clean. There is no excuse for dirty shoes or dusty clothes ... Before going on Parade have the other fellow check you and do the same for him. There are mirrors on each floor. Use them to inspect your personal appearance before leaving the room." And in 1951, recruits were advised, "Always walk smartly about the ground of your training establishment. Be properly dressed whenever you leave your barrack room or the building in which you live. Do not wear part civilian clothes and part uniform. Always see that you are properly clad."[21] Order and manliness were defined through the strict maintenance of a clean appearance, an immaculate uniform, and military deportment, all of which were thought to contribute to a Mountie's authority over other Canadian men.

FEMINIZING THE MOUNTIE UNIFORM

Given the specific values and ideals that the Mountie uniform represented, the design of a distinct uniform for female Mounties was

---

20   Dorothy Standish Paull, *Scarlet Fever: A Story of Early Years in Banff and my Life as a Royal Canadian Mounted Policeman's Wife, 1914–1956* (White Rock, BC: Self-Published, 1993), 37. Thank you to Irwin MacEwan for this reference.

21   Sheehan and Oosten, *Behind the Badge*, 230–31.

viewed as necessary to appease a number of constituents within the RCMP who were concerned with the erosion of the image and authority of the police force following the arrival of women. The first priority for commanding officers, however, was to encourage Canadian women to apply to the RCMP. With this objective in mind, they determined that a stylish and feminine uniform would help to attract female recruits. After all, it had been a successful strategy employed by the Canadian armed forces during World War II.[22] A number of institutions had similar strategies. The occupation of nursing, for example, redesigned its uniforms in the 1940s "to publicize the makeover their occupation was undergoing." Toronto General Hospital had consulted with an "internationally known" fashion designer to create an all-white uniform for its nurses that conveyed cleanliness and respectability.[23]

When the RCMP's commissioner convened a planning committee to design a women's review order uniform on June 14, 1974, the all-male committee "felt that the adoption of a distinctive uniform should coincide with recruitment, to produce an immediate and favourable impact" on Canadian women.[24] Not all of the officers present were comfortable with this idea. They argued that one of the underlying principles in recruiting women was that they be given equal treatment wherever possible. The creation of a uniform separate from the male version was a "major departure" from those principles, one that potentially weakened "the strength of the original intent" in hiring women.[25] It proved to be a prescient concern.

Despite the reservations of some, in April 1974 the RCMP hired the executive director of Fashion Canada, "one of the best known Canadian designers,"[26] to help the RCMP's tailors meet the force's

---

22   Ruth Roach Pierson, *"They're Still Women After All": The Second World War and Canadian Womanhood* (Toronto: McClelland & Stewart, 1986), 139.

23   Kathryn McPherson, "The Case of the Kissing Nurse: Femininity, Sexuality, and Canadian Nursing, 1900–1970," *Gendered Pasts: Historical Essays in Femininity and Masculinity in Canada*, eds. Kathryn McPherson, Cecilia Morgan, and Nancy M. Forestell (Toronto: University of Toronto Press, 2003), 191.

24   Boulton, *Uniforms of the Canadian Mounted Police*, 505.

25   Boulton, *Uniforms of the Canadian Mounted Police*, 506.

26   Marsha Erb, "New Uniform Neat, Plain and Functional," *Saskatoon Star Phoenix*, November 8, 1974.

requirement for a stylish review order uniform.[27] The hiring of a fashion designer dispels the misconception that Maj. Doris Toole, Troop 17's advisor, designed or had input into the design of the women's uniform.[28] The RCMP's tailors were instructed to take the designer's recommendations into consideration when creating a final product.[29] The men on the planning committee agreed that "female members should be immediately recognizable as members of the RCMP and not confused by the public with other uniformed groups." However, the initial prototype did not bear much resemblance to the male tunic and left little room for the application of rank and service badges.[30] The RCMP's tailors worked to resolve these issues.

Designing a uniform that identified women as police officers but was appropriately feminine was a universal problem for most police departments during the 1960s and 1970s. In 1960, the Toronto Police Service had issued its policewomen with "derby style hats to prevent them from being mistaken for airline stewardesses or TTC [Toronto Transit Commission] guides."[31] Canada's first female police chief, Lenna Bradburn, who began her policing career in Toronto, recalled having been mistaken for a post office employee while wearing the hat on patrol. Bradburn became a strong advocate for wearing the forage cap issued to male police officers, a regulation that did not change in Toronto until 1991. Differences in headgear for male and female officers were, for Bradburn, evidence of the systemic discrimination against women in policing.[32]

By the fall of 1974, the RCMP's design difficulties had been overcome and senior tailor Albert Reiter and his staff were presenting

---

27   Boulton, *Uniforms of the Canadian Mounted Police*, 504. The RCMP's tailor shop is located in Ottawa, Ontario. See "RCMP Tailors Create Force's Famed Uniforms," *Gazette* (Montreal), July 9, 1986.

28   Doris Toole, email communications with author, July 8, 2008, and September 30, 2011. Some of those interviewed for this study erroneously believed that Toole was responsible for the design. Rod Olsen, interview with author, January 10, 2010; Darryl Butler, interview with author, September 11, 2008.

29   Boulton, *Uniforms of the Canadian Mounted Police*, 504.

30   Ibid., 505.

31   "Herstory: Milestones in the History of the Toronto Police Service," http://www.torontopolice.on.ca/museum/herstory-milestones_in_the_history_of_tps_women.pdf.

32   Corsianos, *Policing and Gendered Justice*, 40.

prototypes of the women's review order to the commissioner and senior officers for their approval.[33] Henri LeBlanc recalled, "I remember on a couple of occasions where we had any new piece of the uniform, they'd have someone come in and show us the uniform. We would look it over and then decide whether it was practical or not."[34] Female support staff modelled the pieces for the officers in the commissioner's boardroom. The uniform consisted of a navy blue knee-length skirt, black pumps, a white dickie, a red wool serge blazer made from the same fabric as the male tunic, a shoulder bag, and a navy blue pillbox hat.

Maj. Doris Toole, in Ottawa in mid-August 1974 to consult with the RCMP about Troop 17, was asked to attend one of the sessions in the commissioner's boardroom. She recalled that several RCMP secretaries were present and made suggestions that would, in her opinion, have made the uniform even more feminine. Toole had been an advocate for changes to the women's military uniform, which had become feminized following the unification of the Canadian armed forces in 1964. For Toole, the feminization of the military uniform "played into men's ideas of femininity" and did not reflect policies about women's equality with men within the armed forces.[35] Toole voiced her concerns over the suggestions being made by the secretaries, which were never acted upon, likely because what the participants in the commissioner's boardroom were viewing that day was the final design. Toole remembered that "at that meeting it was agreed that feedback from the Troop and Depot staff would be sought" before any further changes were made.[36] However, Troop 17 was never given the opportunity to provide their input and the design stood.

Decisions regarding the women's service order uniform were also in the final stages. Earlier in the year, the RCMP's Clothing and

---

33 "RCMP Tailors Create Force's Famed Uniforms."

34 Henri LeBlanc, interview with author, October 14, 2008.

35 Post-unification, female military officers wore miniature braids on their uniform jackets, along with a small pin worn on the blouse, to denote their rank. When a woman removed her tunic, it was difficult to see her rank unless "you looked closely at the pin" according to Toole. It was not until the 1970s that the military returned to using braid on the women's tunic to denote rank. Doris Toole, interview with author, October 10, 2008; email communication with author, October 18, 2011.

36 Doris Toole, email communications with author, July 8, 2008, and October 18, 2011.

Equipment Design Committee (CEDC) had already laid the ground-work for the development of a service order uniform after reviewing "various women's uniforms of the Canadian Armed Forces."[37] The design included a brown tunic similar to the male jacket but without breast pockets; blue "ladies-style slacks" with a yellow stripe; a blue knee-length skirt; a square leather purse with a shoulder strap; a beige long-sleeved blouse without pockets; and a black oxford-type walking shoe.[38] While the women's operational uniform bore a close resem-blance to the male uniform, there was one significant departure.[39] The female uniform also included a triangular necktie, which was made of dark blue heavy cotton and included a white elastic strip with a metal hook that went around the neck and hooked onto a metal loop on the left-hand side of the tie.

It was not unusual in the 1970s for police departments to cre-ate an alternative to the male tie in an effort to maintain a woman's feminine appearance when wearing a uniform. For example, the first women to be hired as police officers by the police department in Se-attle in 1976 wore "crossover ties that snapped in the front."[40] Sim-ilarly, the Canadian military issued a "neck tab" to female personnel instead of a tie.[41] In western societies, a tie traditionally symbolized professionalism and neatness. But the size, width, colour, and pattern also conveyed specific meanings about the wearer.[42] For the RCMP, a stylized tie conveyed that its female officers were feminine, but it also suggested that female Mounties possessed a different set of attributes from their male counterparts.

Dressing female Mounties in slacks for operational duties was another concern since pants, although practical, emphasized a wom-an's form. In the 1970s, wearing pants while working in a professional

---

37   Boulton, *Uniforms of the Canadian Mounted Police*, 506.

38   Ibid.

39   Erb, "New Uniform Neat, Plain and Functional"; "Mounties Get Their Wom-an," *Victorian* (Victoria, BC), March 5, 1975.

40   Adam Eisenberg, *A Different Shade of Blue: How Women Changed the Face of Police Work* (Lake Forest, CA: Behler Press, 2009), 73.

41   Doris Toole, email communication with author, October 18, 2011.

42   Jennifer Craik, "The Cultural Politics of the Uniform," *Fashion Theory* 7, no. 2 (2003): 129.

office was not considered appropriate for women in private industry or the public service.[43] The police force's clothing policies for its female civilian staff reflected these values. Carol Hill recalled that there was a dress code in place for female support staff working at Depot in 1974. Women were required to wear dresses or skirts; slacks were not permitted during office hours until several years later. When pants were finally allowed, female staff members were instructed to wear "dressy" pantsuits only.[44]

Female police officers wearing pants was a problem for many police departments struggling to come to terms with choosing practicality over social convention. In Seattle, one of the first female constables characterized her uniform in 1975 as a "cross between a meter maid and a flight attendant." She explained that in those days, women's pants had zippers on the side rather than the front. The women's uniform followed this fashion trend and every time female police officers had to use the bathroom, they had to remove their gun and utility belt to undo their pants.[45] A stylish side zipper rather than a front closure made the slacks feminine but impractical, given all of the equipment that police officers carried around their waist.

Some female municipal police officers in Canada were required to wear a skirt during operational duties. It proved to be highly problematic for Liz Davies, the first woman hired as a constable by a small municipal police department in British Columbia in 1973. Davies was hired before the department had a uniform for her to wear. She recalled piecing together a uniform for herself from a number of sources. Davies took a skirt worn by an earlier policewoman who had resigned from the department to a tailor to have it altered to fit her. She paired the skirt with a force-issued long-sleeved shirt and a pair of black boots that she purchased. Davies's own trench coat completed her uniform. After the department hired a second woman six months later, Davies

---

43   Valerie Steele, "Dressing for Work," *Men and Women: Dressing the Part,* eds. Claudia Brush Kidwell and Valerie Steele (Washington, DC: Smithsonian Institution Press, 1989), 71.

44   Carol Hill, interview with author, April 28, 2008. As late as 1986, when female RCMP officers wore their service order uniforms they were required to change "the trousers for a skirt when they [were] doing desk work." See "RCMP Tailors Create Force's Famed Uniforms."

45   Eisenberg, *A Different Shade of Blue,* 73.

remembered that the department "tried to get us into culottes. They didn't work at all. It was ludicrous. They seemed to be fighting putting us in pants ... We were expected to climb fences, we were expected to run after people and do all kinds of things in a uniform that wasn't really workable. So they finally had to give in and give us pants."[46] One year later, in 1974, this particular police department issued its female constables with the same uniform as male officers, resolving the functional difficulties the women were having.

Perhaps the RCMP took the experiences of these municipal police departments into account when they designed the women's service order uniform, which allowed for pants. When it came to the review order uniform, however, the RCMP's designers viewed slacks as unprofessional and unfeminine. The RCMP had strict regulations regarding the appearance of its police officers, both male and female, during public events and in public spaces. As one Dress and Deportment regulation stipulated in 1988, "Appearance in both dress and behaviour has become synonymous with the position as a member of the Force, and primarily, the basis on which he/she is judged and accepted by the public."[47] Allison Palmer, who was stationed at a tourist destination in the Rocky Mountains in the late 1970s, discovered that few people connected the women's review order uniform with the RCMP. She recalled that tourists questioned her as to whether female Mounties were really just summer students dressed in "rented" uniforms to promote Canada. She also remembered two American tourists thinking that she was wearing "the new Salvation Army uniform."[48] For Palmer, these perceptions undermined her authority as a law enforcement officer. The women of the RCMP quickly recognized that the male review order uniform conveyed specific messages to the public about authority that a feminized version of the uniform was unable to express.

---

46   Liz Davies, interview with author, July 17, 2008. By the 1950s, policewomen from some municipal departments were being issued uniforms. When the Ottawa police department hired its third policewoman, Edna Harry, in 1950, she was the first woman on that police force to be issued a uniform. It consisted of a blouse, a skirt, and a cape. Cory Slaughter, "Women's Journey Into Policing," unpublished paper, Ottawa Police Service (2003): 1–5.

47   Quoted in Sheehan and Oosten, *Behind the Badge*, 231.

48   Allison Palmer, interview with author, June 11, 2008.

The RCMP was also keen to ensure that female Mounties were appropriately heterosexual in appearance. Some members of the public speculated that because the women worked in a male-dominated institution, they were lesbians. Lesbian Mounties would have been a public relations disaster for the police force during a time when gay men and women in Canada were still not out in the workplace. The women's review order uniform was intentionally designed to communicate notions of normative femininity to the civilian population and to defray any characterizations of female Mounties as lesbians or as manly. One senior officer recalled, "As time developed, we changed our attitudes. Before, you know, we insisted [female members] wear skirts and then we went into the slacks so it's a progression over the years."[49] Displaying the femininity of female Mounties moved them outside the masculine workplace and into a more conventional realm where skirts, rather than masculine attire, were broadly accepted in Canadian society as normative dress for women.

The RCMP's interest in promoting the femininity of its female police officers to Canadians was still evident at the training academy in 1978. Every day at noon, troops practised their drill manoeuvres in front of the public in the academy's parade square. Cherise Marchand recollected that her troop was the only female troop in training at Depot between the end of May and October of that year. She commented that her drill instructor was anxious to have her troop marching on the parade square during noon parade as often as possible. "So we were wearing skirts with nylons and all of that. So we did at least four of the five parades a week."[50] The sight of female Mounties parading in skirts and heels for tourists was a stark contrast to the display of the men parading in Stetsons, breeches, and Strathcona boots. The image conveyed to the public that female Mounties were still feminine despite the fact that they were engaged in masculine activities such as drill manoeuvres.

On October 8, 1974, the RCMP announced to the media that the first women's review order uniform would be modelled for journalists at Government House, the residence of the Governor General in Ottawa. Later that day, a photograph of model Christine Shaikin wearing

---

49   Henri LeBlanc, interview with author, October 14, 2008.

50   Cherise Marchand, interview with author, October 15, 2008.

the uniform appeared in the *Ottawa Citizen* with the caption "À la RC-MP."[51] The use of French was likely a reference to the fact that the RCMP worked with a fashion consultant on the design. The women's uniform reassured Canadians that there was little change in the status quo for the RCMP despite the hiring of women. The masculine identity of the police force remained intact and men remained firmly in control.

The adoption of the women's review order dress uniform had one final hurdle to clear before becoming official. Commr. Maurice Nadon reminded the Solicitor General that any change to the RCMP's uniform regulations required an order-in-council from the federal cabinet. His request was an urgent one, since the women had already started their training in Regina. On October 3, 1974, section 194 of the *RCMP Act* was revised by cabinet to include a section on the female uniform. The revision read:

> The significant uniform of the Force, the design of which is to be approved by the Minister, shall (a) in respect of male members, consist of felt hat, scarlet tunic, blue breeches with yellow cavalry strip, brown Strathcona boots and jack spurs and (b) in respect of female members, consist of cloth cap, scarlet tunic, blue skirt and black shoes, together with such other items of uniform as the Minister approves.[52]

The distinctions were clear: women would wear a feminine version of the male review order uniform, a decision endorsed by the highest levels of the federal government.

DESEXUALIZING THE WOMEN'S UNIFORM

Many police departments, including the RCMP, were engaged in a tough balancing act when designing a uniform for women. Adding to the problem was a desire to desexualize the appearance of their female police officers. When the Ontario Provincial Police (OPP) hired its first female constables on May 24, 1974, the recruits were issued an over-the-knee,

---

51   Barry Gravelle, "À la RCMP," *Ottawa Citizen*, October 8, 1974.

52   The order-in-council was dated February 25, 1975. Boulton, *Uniforms of the Canadian Mounted Police*, 506.

straight-cut skirt, a tunic without breast pockets, and a Sam Browne holster. Jill Ryan recalled that she was later issued pants (with a side zipper) the first winter "because we were freezing in miniskirts and black nylons" while out on patrol. Ryan also received a blue blouse without pockets because the police force "didn't want our 'fullness' to be even more apparent."[53] Pockets were an operational necessity for police officers, but the OPP's desire to conceal a female police officer's "fullness" was an indication that some police departments were overly concerned with desexualizing the women's bodies.

The RCMP, despite their best intentions, was similarly inclined. In the interests of drawing attention away from the women's breasts, the original service order uniform did not have pockets on the tunic or shirt. The RCMP unwittingly issued the first female Mounties polyester blouses that emphasized their breasts. Several of the women recalled that the blouses were transparent and, because they were made out of polyester, clingy. They recounted how on cold days there were "all kinds of rude comments" from male co-workers when their nipples became obvious through the fabric.[54] The choice of fabric and the elimination of pockets on the blouses only served to enhance the female body rather than de-emphasize it. Attempts to both feminize and desexualize the uniform were not always successful.

Breasts were also problematic when it came to organizing items for the kit that was to be issued to female Mounties in Depot.[55] Undergarments had been a part of the standard kit issued to all new recruits since the nineteenth century, and the all-male committee was initially undaunted by the prospect of choosing underwear for the first female recruits. Cameron Montgomery, who was involved in meetings concerning the development of the women's kit, remembered discussions about undergarments and bathing suits for the women. He recalled one of the men had done some research and discovered that the RCMP

---

53   Jill Ryan, email communication with author, May 27, 2010.

54   Louise Ferguson, interview with author, November 9, 2006.

55   In the 1970s, recruits received their kit three times during twenty-two weeks of training at Depot: during their first week, between the ninth and twelfth week, and between the fifteenth and seventeenth week. They received approximately fifty items of kit during training, including their uniforms, badges, Sam Browne, handcuffs, bedding, bathing suits, and Stetsons. In 2006, the cost of outfitting a male officer was $3,142.97 and a female officer $3,056.27. Sheehan and Oosten, Behind the Badge, 371.

could order bathing suits with modesty panels across the front that would conceal the women's crotch. Another discovered that sports brassieres were available. The men unanimously agreed that these articles would be useful items for the women's kit. It "soon became clear we had to get somebody else involved, maybe a female" recalled Montgomery. "We didn't know what we were doing, that this isn't working, and we knew it wasn't. Like the modesty panel. That tells you a lot, doesn't it?"[56] The fact that the men did not consider it necessary to seek advice from a woman about female undergarments speaks to the tight control commanding officers were accustomed to exerting over all aspects of a recruit's training.

Montgomery's concerns were justified. Decisions about the type of bathing suits issued to the women and discussions about modesty panels became moot after the bathing suits became transparent following three months of daily wear in chlorinated water.[57] Journalist Colleen Slater-Smith reported on another problem the women were having with the bathing suits. She noted that Troop 17 were nervous about the "fall-out" of their breasts during rigorous swimming manoeuvres since the suits were cut low under the armpits.[58] Slater-Smith's reportage illustrates just how little privacy the women of Troop 17 had at the academy. It further shows that female journalists were not above writing about the women from a gendered perspective, despite the fact that they were also working in a male-dominated profession and breaking down barriers.

Apart from the inadequacy of the bathing suits, the force-issued bras fell short of the women's needs as well. The sports bras were of poor quality and lacked proper support for physical training according to Marianne Robson.[59] It would take another two years for the RCMP to do away with issuing bras to female Mounties. The CEDC finally determined that decisions regarding the type of undergarment the women wore were best left up to the women themselves and that "no

---

56   Cameron Montgomery, interview with author, May 24, 2007.

57   Bill Jones, interview with author, October 3, 2011.

58   Colleen Slater-Smith, "Troop 17 Graduates," *Leader-Post* (Regina), March 3, 1975.

59   Marianne Robson, email communication to author, October 7, 2011.

further issues would be made when the present stock was depleted."[60] It signalled the partial demise of the century-long tradition of RCMP control over every piece of the uniform and kit issued to recruits.

While the selection of undergarments for recruits may seem strange by today's employment standards, it is important to remember that the paramilitary structure of the RCMP demanded conformity. Sameness, right down to undergarments, was part of a strategy to dissolve individualism during a recruit's time at Depot. The elimination of individualism prepared a recruit to unquestioningly obey the power and authority of senior officers, not only at the academy but in the field. It explains why the officers charged with finding suitable items for the women's kit were initially unfazed by the task, and why they failed to consult any woman, even their wives, about the merits of the items they were selecting.

Despite the paternalistic concerns of commanding officers about the modesty of female recruits, aspects of the women's kit were openly sexualized by male recruits at the academy. Soon after Troop 17's arrival in 1974, male recruits learned that the RCMP was issuing them with brassieres. One instructor at Depot remembered that rumours developed that "RCMP" was stamped on the inside of the bras and an "open competition to see who could first get their hands on an issue brassiere" developed amongst the men.[61] The bras were considered a novel piece of kit that would lend credence to stories of sexual conquest. The gossip about an RCMP stamp on the brassieres was erroneous, however, as examples housed at the RCMP's Historical Collections Unit demonstrate. Nevertheless, the competition over acquiring a force-issued bra served as a reminder to both the men and women of the RCMP that underneath the women's uniform was a sexual female body that disrupted, rather than conformed to, the normative standards of policing that were so highly valued by the RCMP.

Although the RCMP wanted an attractive uniform for its female police officers, they also worked to minimize the female police body as

---

60   Boulton, *Uniforms of the Canadian Mounted Police*, 514.

61   Darryl Butler, interview with author, September 11, 2008.

a site of sexual desire. These seemingly contradictory impulses, between feminizing and de-feminizing the women's uniform, speaks to the delicate balancing act the RCMP was engaged in as it sought to maintain the feminine appearance of the women while ensuring they were recognized as members of the RCMP. The RCMP's insistence on continuing the tradition of designing and controlling every aspect of a recruit's uniform and kit meant that the gendered lines between male and female uniforms would not be crossed any time soon.

RUNNING IN DAMN HEELS

Historically, the force was always concerned with femininity ...
They also wanted to ensure that you were separate, especially
in dress uniform. That dress uniform had been men-only for one
hundred and one years. A woman was gonna come in and wear
that? Give your heads a friggin' shake! There was no way we were
gonna win that battle, although we tried. We tried.

—Marianne Robson
Troop 17 (1974/75)

The decision to dress female Mounties in a feminized version of
the male uniform served to maintain the dominance of the masculine image of the RCMP. Many of the first women who were hired
by the RCMP resisted the women's version of the uniform and struggled with the unworkability of its design. The women of Troop 17 did
not passively wait for the RCMP to make changes to their operational
uniform and kit, however. Nor did they wait for the RCMP to invite
their opinions on the design. Instead, the first female recruits contested decisions regarding their uniform by registering complaints with
their troop advisor and by writing memoranda to Depot's commanding officers.[1] Once in the field, they continued to lodge formal complaints with senior officers both at the detachment level and at RCMP
headquarters in Ottawa. Many female Mounties actively lobbied for
changes, including the right to wear the same uniform as their male
colleagues.

Three pieces of the women's uniform in particular were singled out
by female Mounties as requiring immediate change: the purse, the hat,
and the shoes. But the RCMP insisted on conforming to conventional

---

1   Marianne Robson, interview with author, July 29, 2008.

ideas of femininity when it came to dressing its female police officers and denied most requests for changes. The hierarchical control exercised by commanding officers silenced their protests and delayed changes to the original women's service and review order uniforms for years to come. Nevertheless, the women persisted in challenging the outward appearances that made them different, rather than equal, as police officers.

CARRYING A STUPID PURSE

On September 16, 1974, the CBC dispatched reporter Bob Johnstone to the RCMP's divisional headquarters in Toronto to cover one of the swearing-in ceremonies of some of the first women hired by the RCMP. Later that evening, Canadians across the country listened as Johnstone described for his audience what female Mounties would look like:

> The Royal Canadian Mounted Police today took a big step, one that will certainly change the image of the force. The force that always gets its man now has women—thirty-two of them. In simultaneous swearing-in ceremonies all across Canada, the first women joined the Royal Canadian Mounted Police ... At least on paper, the women Mounties are the same as the men. They'll wear roughly the same uniform except they'll have their choice of slacks or skirt. They'll get the same pay and be subject to the same regulations. The principle difference is that they'll carry their revolvers in shoulder-strap handbags instead of holsters.[2]

The purse was the most contentious issue for the first female Mounties in 1974. A purse was a strong symbol of femininity in society at the time, and it was used by many police departments intent on maintaining a feminine appearance for their female police officers. The purse that was issued to the first female Mounties was worn with both the service order and review order uniforms. It was a square,

---

2   Bob Johnstone, "RCMP Welcomes First Female Officers," CBC Radio, *The World at Six*, September 16, 1974, http://www.cbc.ca/archives/entry/1974-rcmp-welcomes-first-female-officers.

leather shoulder bag with straps that included inserts inside for bullets, handcuffs, and a revolver. In contrast, male RCMP officers wore a Sam Browne, as it was known in the RCMP, with both orders of dress. Sam Browne equipment had been developed in 1852 by British general Sir Samuel Browne, who lost an arm during war service in India. Browne designed a leather strap that was worn diagonally across the chest and which hooked onto the belt front and back to take the weight of the equipment belt off the hips. The diagonal strap also enabled Browne to quickly draw his sabre from its scabbard with one hand.[3] The Sam Browne had been incorporated into the British army uniform by the time of the Anglo-South African War, when members of the NWMP were first introduced to it. By 1904, the Sam Browne had become part of the RNWMP uniform for all field and parade duties. The equipment belt male Mounties wore held a holster, revolver, bullet holder, and handcuff pouch, all of which were supported on the hips by the Sam Browne.

When it came to issuing a Sam Browne to the first female Mounties in 1974 for wear operationally, however, commanding officers were once again concerned with the women's breasts. The RCMP's planning committee sought a medical opinion from the Department of Veterans Affairs asking whether the cross strap would produce breast discomfort or more serious injuries. Veterans Affairs assured the committee that no serious injury would occur.[4] In the Canadian armed forces, women working as military police officers wore "Sam Browne equipment to render the sidearm more visible" during patrols. Despite this advice, the RCMP remained committed to the idea of a handbag for female Mounties. The planning committee felt that the Sam Browne "would not be desirable," and decided that handbags "with appropriate compartments for a handgun and handcuffs" would be issued.[5]

However, a purse proved to be an operational danger to both male and female officers during operational duties. Many North American police departments were being pressured by their rank

---

3   Rebecca Stone, "Sam Browne and Beyond: A Look at Duty Belts," *PoliceOne. com*, July 20, 2005, http://www.policeone.com/police-products/duty-gear/articles/117535-Sam-Browne-and-beyond-A-look-at-duty-belts/.

4   Boulton, *Uniforms of the Canadian Mounted Police*, 311.

5   Ibid.

and file to terminate its use. In Los Angeles in 1972, women carried their revolvers in handbags but hoped that they would "eventually be permitted to wear a holster on the theory that a visible gun is much more intimidating than a hidden one."[6] Further, a handbag was more easily accessible to a suspect during an altercation than a sidearm that was carried on a police officer's person. In Toronto, where female police officers also carried purses in 1974, Marlene Watson successfully argued with commanding officers that "it was easier to get a gun out of a holster than a purse."[7] Watson's resistance to the purse resulted in the eventual issue of holsters and duty belts to female police officers working in Toronto.

A purse could also be dangerous if left unattended. This was a serious concern for Canadian municipal police officer Liz Davies, who recalled being issued a shoulder bag in 1973 with a holster sewn into it for her snub-nosed revolver. It was her male peers who lobbied the police department to change her purse to a belt and holster because of the danger it posed. Davies remembered leaving her purse unattended at accident scenes on more than one occasion. "I'd be down in a ditch with an injured person, and I'd look back and there'd be the police cruiser door open and my purse sitting there. So they [male officers] stressed to the brass that you can't do that. It's not a workable thing."[8] This police department relented and issued Davies a holster and duty belt along with a male uniform within her first year.

But the RCMP, while acknowledging the potential hazards of a purse, proposed that it could be secured under the uniform's shoulder straps to prevent it from getting into the wrong hands or being left behind.[9] It was highly unlikely that a fabric shoulder strap on a tunic would prevent a suspect from acquiring the purse during a violent altercation. Nevertheless, the RCMP proceeded with its plans to issue a square handbag similar to the one being used by the Ontario Provincial Police. While the Ontario Provincial Police (OPP) issued purses to its first female constables in May 1974, they were discontinued after

---

6   "The Female Fuzz," *Newsweek* 80 (October 23, 1972): 117.

7   Joe Fiorito, "Retiring Cop Broke Limits for Women," January 30, 2008, http://www.thestar.com/opinion/columnists/2008/01/30/retiring_cop_broke_limits_for_women.html.

8   Liz Davies, interview with author, July 17, 2008.

9   Boulton, *Uniforms of the Canadian Mounted Police*, 511.

the first five months because they were impractical.[10] In December 1974, almost three months into Troop 17's training, the RCMP temporarily issued them duty belts. This change in policy may have been in response to the OPP's experience. Sensing that their complaints were finally being heard, Troop 17 continued to pressure the RCMP to issue them a Sam Browne. But the purse remained an official part of the female uniform and the CEDC set February 1975, one month before the women graduated, as the final date for a decision regarding whether Sam Browne equipment would be issued to female members.

While commanding officers debated over the Sam Browne, the women of Troop 17 were trained to use a two-inch .38 calibre snubnosed revolver that fit into their purses, rather than a six-inch .45 calibre revolver that was used by the men and worn with a Sam Browne. It was another difference that the women thought would limit their full integration and acceptance as police officers. Louise Ferguson recalled that the troop "made a lot of noise about carrying a stupid purse." When the RCMP finally relented, Ferguson remembered that the troop "had to retrain on the bigger guns and the whole works and graduate. We had all this extra shooting and all this extra work. It was fine. We were so happy to get real guns like everybody else. We were all worried about our credibility as it was, you know. Getting to the field and to show up with a purse—you could just see the guys would just laugh you right out of the car."[11] Troop 17 recognized that carrying a purse would not only pose a danger in the field, but would erode their authority as police officers. Their resistance to carrying a purse was successful; the Sam Browne was adopted for wear with the women's service order uniform in time for their graduation in March 1975.[12] However, purses were still required when wearing the review order uniform.

THE GRANNY SHOES

The second contentious issue concerned the footwear that the RCMP issued to the women in 1974. The black oxfords worn with their

---

10   Jill Ryan, email communication with author, May 27, 2010.

11   Louise Ferguson, interview with author, November 9, 2006.

12   Boulton, *Uniforms of the Canadian Mounted Police*, 511.

operational and dress uniforms were described as "granny shoes" or "Salvation Army" shoes by some of the women of Troop 17, an indication that they considered the shoe unflattering. Their resistance to the design of the shoe illustrates that there was a tension for the women between wanting to be taken seriously as police officers and maintaining a feminine appearance. Complaints about their shoes may have been a way of expressing their fear that civilians would associate their drab footwear with volunteer or religious service, work that was previously connected to conventional understandings of women's appropriate role in society. Female Mounties were working hard to establish their legitimacy as authority figures, and the force-issued footwear, like the purse, was seen to diminish their credibility.

The women of Troop 17 were not only concerned with the appearance of their shoes. On a practical level, they encountered so much trouble with their ankles while wearing the shoes that they did not run double time in Depot during their first two weeks of training. Louise Ferguson described the shoes as having thick Cuban heels. They were about an inch and a half high, which explains how ankle injuries could occur when running in them.[13] Major Doris Toole summarized the problem that the shoes posed for the women in an article for the *RCMP Gazette*. Toole wrote that because Troop 17 did not run double during their first weeks of training, it appeared to some "to be coddling the female. But if one were to take the time to find out the reason for this difference, one would learn that the footwear issued was found to contribute to ankle injuries when running in troop formation."[14] Toole's insight regarding the shoes helped put to rest the perception that the women were receiving preferential treatment at Depot.

The oxford shoe was important for one more reason. Drill was a significant part of the development of a troop's cohesion and discipline, and troops practised their manoeuvres in front of the public on the academy's parade square daily. The Strathcona boots worn by male recruits created a stomping sound that conveyed authority, precision, and strength during drill manoeuvres. In contrast, the heeled oxfords worn by the women could not duplicate the sound made by Strathconas no matter how hard the women stomped. One instructor

---

13 Louise Ferguson, interview with author, November 9, 2006.

14 Toole, "A View From the Sidelines," 8.

recalled that when the women marched they did not make noise "because they had those little shoes that clicked as opposed to guys with boots."[15] The difference between a clicking noise and authoritative stomping drew attention to the distinctions between male and female police officers.

The issue of proper footwear for female police officers dogged other police forces too. Jill Ryan, who joined the OPP in September 1974, recalled that the pumps she was issued were extremely uncomfortable in cold weather. Although female constables in the OPP were issued pants for operational duties, they were required to wear a skirt and pumps for dress occasions. During the Pope's visit to Ontario in 1984, female OPP officers were required to wear their skirts, nylons, and pumps while policing the event. Ryan was unsure if it was due to the Pope's status or his view of women doing a man's job that the request for appropriate attire for female police officers was made. Whatever the reason, Ryan recalled that the week was so cold that the male police officers were wearing long johns under their pants. She remembered "standing out in the middle of a field with mud oozing into the top of my little pumps while the men stayed warm and dry with their ankle boots!" Ryan took action, mobilized the other women on duty, and complained to superior officers about the conditions. "We got our superiors to agree to allowing us to wear warmer black leotards—but only if we all had the same make/brand. I remember going to the Bay and buying out all of their stock!"[16] Ryan's example illustrates just how impractical some of the decisions about women's uniforms were. But it also shows that the RCMP was not alone in taking a gendered approach to dressing female police officers.

Complaints about footwear continued once Troop 17 began work in the field in 1975. Some of the women wrote memorandums to commanding officers complaining about the unsuitability of their shoes for operational duties. Marianne Robson, who was stationed in a small prairie detachment, commented, "Even our shoes had heels on. I remember chasing [a] guy and running in damn heels. And then I got picked to test out boots. I mean that was the best thing ever,

---

15   Darryl Butler, interview with author, September 11, 2008.

16   Jill Ryan, email communication to author, May 27, 2010.

ankle boots."[17] Robson began to wear the ankle boots early in 1976 and never wore the "granny shoes" again during operational duties.[18] Allison Palmer, also a member of Troop 17, had a dim view of the "armed forces–issued shoes with heels" and spent considerable amounts of time filling out paperwork to get them changed. For her, the oxford shoes did not make sense in the middle of the prairies. She commented that because most of her troop was posted to rural areas, the shoes quickly proved to be unsuitable for operational wear. "I foot-chased through a ploughed field in high heels. Totally impractical." Palmer persisted in her memo-writing campaign to be issued ankle boots. Finally, her supervisor told her to "go buy them and I'll pay for them out of the detachment [funds]."[19] Palmer's supervisor was willing to circumvent the RCMP's uniform regulations for the sake of practicality and safety, something a number of supervisors did when the first female Mounties arrived at their detachments.

By 1979, female members were still registering complaints about their shoes, although by this time they had been issued flat oxfords for operational duties. But changes to uniform regulations required the approval of headquarters in Ottawa, and on May 7, the OIC of Internal Affairs wrote to the director of Organization and Personnel outlining the complaints he was receiving about the women's shoes:

> It has come to our attention that female members (including Special Constables) are reluctant to wear the knee length skirt when employed on office duties (Service Order #1) as they are required to wear a flat heeled black oxford with this order of dress. Female members state the oxford, when wearing a skirt and nylons is unbecoming, is completely without style and certainly does nothing to enhance the uniform. The black oxford originally designed for Service Order #1 had a Cuban type heel, however, this shoe proved unacceptable as it caused twisted ankles when performing

---

17   Marianne Robson, interview with author, July 29, 2008.

18   Marianne Robson, email communication to author, February 14, 2015.

19   Allison Palmer, interview with author, June 11, 2008.

operational duties. As a result of complaints received, the shoe was changed to the present flat heeled oxford similar to male members.[20]

The tensions between the women's desire to wear attractive footwear while performing administrative duties and their need for practicality in the field proved difficult to resolve. Appeals about the overall appearance of their uniform indicated that female Mounties understood the RCMP's sensitivity to the image that the uniform conveyed. Although the RCMP eventually allowed its female members to wear the review order dress pumps with the service order while assigned to office duties, the flat-heeled oxford remained as part of the operational uniform.

PILLBOX HATS

The third piece of the uniform that female RCMP officers resisted was the cap they wore with both their service order and review order uniforms. As early as April 1974, the RCMP's CEDC studied the headdress worn by women in the military and other police departments. The male forage cap, the navy blue peaked hat with a vinyl visor and yellow hatband normally worn by men for operational duties, was not a consideration for the women.[21] In June, the committee concluded that the women's hat would be modelled after the Montreal City Police female cap. It would be made of felt, the same colour as the male forage cap, with a peak, chinstrap, and yellow band. The regimental badge would be worn on the yellow band on the front.[22] Although the cap was officially referred to as the women's forage cap, many in the RCMP referred to it as a "pillbox" hat. The pillbox was not new to the police force. It had been the standard issue to men of all ranks in the NWMP in 1874. The term "pillbox" was used because the hat resembled the cylindrical boxes used by pharmacists for dispensing tablets

20   Memorandum, Officer in Charge Internal Affairs Branch to D.O.P., "Orders of Dress—Female Black Shoes (Pump)," RCMP file G-217-1-2 (7 May 1979). Access to Information file GA-3951-3-03134/08.

21   The term "forage cap" originated in the nineteenth century when members of the British cavalry exchanged their ornate headdress for lighter caps when foraging for food for their horses. Boulton, *Uniforms of the Canadian Mounted Police*, 9.

22   Ibid., 506.

in the nineteenth century.[23] It was discontinued as part of the NWMP uniform because it was impractical, a decision from the previous century that the planning committee should have heeded.

All of the women interviewed for this research pointed to the pillbox hat as the thing they liked the least about their uniform for three reasons: it was impractical, it was unflattering, and it established the women as different from male Mounties. Louise Ferguson remembered that the "main difference from the male uniform was the funny little hat you couldn't keep on your head."[24] The hat routinely fell off when getting in and out of the police cruiser or blew off in the wind. Although there was a chinstrap designed to keep the hat in place, the women found it cumbersome when putting the hat on and taking it off numerous times throughout a shift. For Kate Morton, the women's uniform "set me up as being different, especially the hat."[25] Morton disliked the pillbox so much that a male colleague acquired a men's forage cap for her to wear while on patrol. He warned her that she had to be sure not to let her commanding officer see her wearing it. It was one way that Morton and her co-worker circumvented the RCMP's uniform regulations in an effort to alleviate the impracticality of the hat's design.

Allison Palmer used her hat to hold her notebook and packages of chewing gum while she was in the police cruiser "because we had no shirt pocket." When she had to get out of the car she "had to dump everything out to put the hat back on. I didn't particularly like it because people did think you were a railway conductor."[26] Margaret Watson also disliked the pillbox. "I just didn't like the pillbox hat. It was very unflattering ... and it would give you a horrible headache." On one occasion, Watson, who was tall and sometimes mistaken for a male police officer, arrested three gang members while on patrol. She recalled, "I think they got confused initially because it was so dark ... I don't

---

23   James Boulton, *Head-Dress of the Canadian Mounted Police* (Calgary: Bunker to Bunker Publishing, 2000), 9.

24   Louise Ferguson, interview with author, November 9, 2006.

25   Kate Morton, interview with author, February 26, 2008.

26   Allison Palmer, interview with author, June 11, 2008. In the 1970s, RCMP regulations stipulated that members were required to put their hat on every time they exited their vehicles.

think they would have pulled over if they'd known I was a woman. But I had a pillbox hat; they should've known that I wasn't male."[27] The pillbox clearly identified her as a female police officer and, in Watson's mind, set her apart as being less than authoritative when dealing with the public.

Women working in other police departments in the 1970s also disliked the impracticality of the hats they were issued. Jill Ryan described the hat she wore for the OPP as a "soft-sided hat which made us look like meter maids." Although women in the OPP were authorized to wear the same uniform as their male colleagues by 1988, their hat remained different for some time afterward, a distinction that continued to separate them from male police officers.[28] Municipal police officer Liz Davies remembered that her department experimented with women's hat styles before female members were issued the same uniform as the men in 1974. "My first hat was sort of a weird one. I remember it was a soft hat and it had a hard brim," she recalled. "It was an impractical thing. The bowler type was always kicking around [in the cruiser]."[29] While a feminine style of cap may have appealed to the men in charge of designing women's police uniforms, the unworkability of the pillbox was something women across police agencies remembered, even decades later.

Occasionally, male members of the RCMP intervened on behalf of the women in an attempt to remedy the problems they were encountering with their uniform. Darryl Butler, an instructor at Depot in the 1970s, described the women's uniforms as "terrible" and "ugly." He remembered that by the time the third female troop went through the academy in 1975, the women were still complaining about the quality of the uniform and asking why it was different from the male uniform. Butler decided to take action and bring the issues to the attention of Depot's training officer:

> The [women complained that the] slacks were conformed for the female figure, had no pockets and were

---

27 Margaret Watson, interview with author, February 25, 2008.

28 Jill Ryan, email communication with author, May 27, 2010.

29 Liz Davies, interview with author, July 17, 2008.

too bloody tight. The blues [tunics] they were given was a polyester thing, again with no pockets. The shoes were awful, the so-called boots they were given had no support. Their red serge was significantly different and the hat! Ugh. Why can't they wear the same uniform as the men? So, being a bright resourceful fellow I took a couple of the better looking [women] ... and got them dressed in all the male uniforms, including boots, breeches and Red Serge and had the Identification Section take photos. I prepared a report voicing the concerns that were given to me and sent along the copies of photographs to the Training Officer, Supt. Bill MacRae. Well, did he rip my face off. "Do you know how much time and money was spent on designing this uniform?" I guess I didn't. That was the end of that.[30]

While recouping the costs incurred in designing the women's uniform was probably a consideration, commanding officers were unwilling to allow their female officers to transgress understandings of appropriate feminine attire. Butler's photographs of women dressed in male uniforms opened a space for commanding officers to consider alternatives which were summarily dismissed. Nevertheless, female Mounties, with occasional help from male members, continued to exert pressure on the police force to make changes.

DRESSING THE PREGNANT MOUNTIE

The RCMP may have spent considerable amounts of time and money designing the women's review and service order uniforms, but their efforts were somewhat short-sighted. Commanding officers failed to consider that many of the women would eventually become pregnant and require an additional uniform. The RCMP simply assumed that female Mounties would leave operational duties as soon as they discovered they were pregnant and revert to civilian attire. It was an assumption that eliminated the necessity and cost of designing a maternity uniform. Female RCMP officers, however, viewed the situation differently and actively resisted the restrictions placed on them by a

---

30   Darryl Butler, note to author, September 11, 2008.

lack of maternity uniform when they became pregnant.

In the 1970s and 1980s, some female Mounties hid their pregnancy, choosing to remain on active duty until their uniforms could no longer accommodate their changing bodies. Three of the women who were interviewed for this research admitted to doing this after learning they were pregnant with their first child. They understood that once they divulged they were pregnant, they would be removed from operational duties and transferred to more mundane administrative tasks until they took maternity leave. Of course, not all female members resented their removal from the road. Some enjoyed the change in duties and a return to wearing civilian clothes. But civilians conducting business at detachment offices often assumed that female Mounties were public servants because they were dressed as civilians. It was a circumstance that frustrated some female Mounties during a time when they were working hard to establish their authority as police officers in their communities.

As a result, many pregnant Mounties lobbied the RCMP to design maternity wear that could be worn for both operational and administrative duties. It was not until 1987, however, that commanding officers finally relented and a maternity uniform was designed.[31] The uniform was created by the men of the RCMP's tailor shop without input from the women. Their design conformed to the widely accepted idea in society at the time that a pregnant woman should dress modestly to hide her "condition." As a result, a maternity jumper, or dress, that had thick pleats both front and back was developed. The volume of fabric made the women feel as though they were wearing a tent that only emphasized, rather than minimized, their expanding waistline. The fit of the uniform was uncomfortable: the hem of the shirt rode up over the waistline, Velcro tabs and elastic casing on the waistband constricted movement, and the tie had a tendency to slide sideways off the belly. The uniform did not include a coat, and the force-issued shoes did not allow for the fact that a woman's feet swelled when she was pregnant.[32]

Safety was another concern since the tailors' design did not accommodate a holster and a revolver. According to one media account,

---

31   Brunelle, *The Royal Canadian Mounted Police in the 1990s*, 44.

32   Sandra Tullio-Pow, telephone interview with author, March 2, 2010.

"Pregnant officers complained that the jumper-style dress with its pleated front and lack of loops made it impractical to wear a gun belt—and therefore impossible to perform their normal duties."[33] Female Mounties wanted to continue to wear their revolvers even when conducting administrative duties at the detachment, given that they were still police officers.

Police departments in other jurisdictions also struggled with how to clothe their pregnant police officers. In 1989, the OPP gave its female officers a clothing allowance to purchase civilian attire to wear when they were assigned to administrative duties. But like the women of the RCMP, female OPP officers found that the public often refused to acknowledge them as police officers when they were dressed as civilians. Some pregnant OPP officers who did not want to leave operational duties right away "simply started wearing their police husband's trousers and gun belt" to accommodate their expanding bellies.[34] The women of the OPP finally took the initiative and designed their own maternity uniform. Irena Lawrenson and her colleague Joan Tonner, who was pregnant at the time, worked with the OPP's tailor to develop a prototype. The uniform consisted of expandable pants with an elastic waistband and a loose, tent-shaped tunic top worn over the standard-issue shirt. Lawrenson and Tonner brought their ideas to the OPP's Clothing and Equipment Committee, where Tonner modelled the prototype. To their surprise, it was approved by the committee for future production.[35]

Female Mounties, like their OPP counterparts, wanted to appear professional in a maternity uniform, and they continued to petition the RCMP for changes. It was not until 1995, however, that the RCMP turned once again to the fashion industry for help with a new design. Sandra Tullio-Pow, an award-winning designer of maternity wear from Ryerson Polytechnic's school of fashion in Toronto, was hired.

For her, the original RCMP maternity uniform impeded functionality and minimized a woman's authority as a police officer.[36]

---

33   Barbara Wickens, "Dressing the Part," *Maclean's* 109, no. 19 (May 6, 1996): 11.

34   Irena Lawrenson, email communication with author, May 27, 2010.

35   Joan Tonner, email communication with author, June 21, 2010; Irena Lawrenson, email communication with author, May 27, 2010.

36   Sandra Tullio-Pow, telephone interview with author, March 2, 2010.

Tullio-Pow set out to create a maternity uniform that resembled the women's service order uniform as closely as possible. She interviewed nine pregnant Mounties from across Canada before beginning her design. Tullio-Pow altered the waistband of the trousers for greater flexibility; created a shirt with a longer and flared hemline and elastic in the middle of the back to prevent it from riding up; added side front pockets to the shirt and a functional tie that was shorter and stayed in place over the pregnant belly; and designed an all-weather maternity coat. Four prototypes were created and tested in the field in May 1996. By the end of the year, Tullio-Pow's uniform was adopted for standard issue by the RCMP after a few modifications.[37] Tullio-Pow entered her design in a juried exhibition sponsored by the International Textile Apparel Association, winning the award for Best Design for Functional Apparel for 1996.[38]

Two issues regarding the maternity uniform remained unresolved, however: where to carry a service revolver and the development of maternity body armour. The issue of where a pregnant Mountie carried her weapon remained a contentious one for the RCMP. Tullio-Pow recalled that the force refused to issue shoulder holsters to any of its police officers, male or female, because of concerns that they were less secure in dangerous situations. She did remember that the original maternity uniform had "a little gizmo entry at the side" that supposedly held a revolver. But it was too difficult to access in an emergency situation.[39]

Maternity body armour was also contentious. Tullio-Pow recalled that there were concerns that a fetus would be harmed by the impact of a bullet hitting the body armour. It was a possibility that the men who were making the decisions did not even want to entertain. But female members did not back down from addressing the issue.

---

37   The media took great interest in the development of the Mountie maternity uniform. See *Toronto Star*, "New Uniform for Mountie Mom," September 5, 1996; Barbara Wickens, "Dressing the Part," *Maclean's* (May 6, 1996): 11; Marcus Robinson, "Fashion: Mounted Police," *Saturday Night* 111, no. 8 (October 1996): 28. The RCMP also featured the maternity uniform in one of its publications: Brenda Zanin, "New Uniform Has Great Expectations," *Pony Express* (July/August 1998): 6.

38   Nancy J. Owens, ed., "Proceedings of the Annual Meeting of the International Textile and Apparel Association, Inc." (November 1998): 18–21.

39   Sandra Tullio-Pow, telephone interview with author, March 2, 2010.

According to Tullio-Pow, one pregnant member in Nova Scotia was so concerned about her safety that she had custom-made body armour designed for herself. "She was one of the ones that was working in a three-man detachment ... She was the only woman and she felt that she needed that and she went and paid for it herself," said Tullio-Pow.[40]

Struggles over the design of the maternity uniform reveal the extent of the RCMP's commitment to removing pregnant Mounties from operational duties as soon as possible. Commanding officers were undoubtedly motivated by safety and liability concerns for female members and their fetuses. But the RCMP also felt that they alone were responsible for decisions concerning their personnel. Individual female police officers did not have the right to decide at what point in their pregnancy they left operational duties; instead, it was a decision that should be made by supervisory personnel charged with managing the lower ranks.

BLURRING THE UNIFORM DIVIDE

In the 1980s, there were three women who had the opportunity to wear an altered version of the male review order uniform, including the red serge tunic, boots, Stetson hat, Sam Browne, and breeches. In each case, the uniforms were created for public events that promoted the police force, suggesting that the RCMP was sometimes willing to blur gendered lines in the interests of generating positive public opinion. Jackie Lewis, a special constable who was a lead singer in the RCMP band, recalled that in 1984 a review order red serge tunic was created by RCMP tailors especially for her to wear during performances. And in 1988, in preparation for the band's tour to Italy, she was issued custom-made breeches and boots to wear while on parade with the band. When Lewis became pregnant with her first child in 1989, tailor Albert Reiter designed a maternity uniform for her. Lewis recalled, "I still remember the way that skirt felt and you know, if it weren't so unusual for a woman [to be] wearing a long navy blue skirt, I'd still be wearing it today. It was just so, so comfortable ... I remember doing a television show just a month before [my daughter] was born and nobody knew I was pregnant. That's how beautiful that red serge was."[41] While Lewis's

---

40   Ibid.

41   Jackie Lewis, telephone interview with author, May 17, 2010.

maternity uniform was well designed and comfortable, the fact that it hid her expanding body illustrates the police force's adherence to social conventions that dictated a woman's pregnancy should not be obvious.

In 1981, two female Mounties made their inaugural appearance as performers in the RCMP's Musical Ride, a first for women in the RCMP.[42] Christine Mackie and Joan Merk received significant attention from the public and the media as the only women amongst the thirty-two performers in the Ride, described by one journalist as the "public-relations pride and joy of the Royal Canadian Mounted Police."[43] Not everyone was happy about their presence on the Ride. One middle-aged man commented to a journalist during one performance that "There are only two [women] in there, according to the paper—and I think it's a disgrace. They shouldn't have let 'em in."[44] Many of the men on the Ride were also opposed to the women joining their ranks. Mackie and Merk endured a significant amount of ill treatment during the two months of equitation training courses they were required to complete. In an interview for *Flare* magazine in 1982, journalist Charlotte Gray wrote that Merk "seemed to trigger more resentment amongst those men who didn't like riding alongside women. Her curly blond hair and feminine figure made her conspicuous and she wasn't allowed to forget it. Muttered comments about the way she rode, wore her uniform and did her stable duties were often made behind her back."[45]

Despite the criticisms, Mackie and Merk were also breaking ground as two of the few female Mounties permitted to wear a male review order uniform. Kate Morton, who turned down a position in

---

42   The development of the RCMP's Musical Ride can be traced to 1876 and Fort Macleod in present-day Alberta. The Ride was performed publicly for the first time in 1901, becoming a "regular public entertainment" by 1904. Monique Cooper and Joel Walker, *The Spirit of the Ride: The RCMP Musical Ride* (Winnipeg, MB: Heartland, 2007), 17–18.

43   Charlotte Gray, "Musical Riders: It Wasn't Easy Being the First Women on the RCMP Musical Ride," *Flare* (July 1982): 41. Thank you to Don Klancher for bringing this reference to my attention.

44   Gray, "Musical Riders," 41. By August 2013, more than half of the Mounties performing on the Musical Ride and three of the Ride's supervisors were women. *Burnaby News Leader*, "Former Burnaby Member was Pioneer on RCMP Musical Ride," August 20, 2013, http://www.burnabynewsleader.com/entertainment/220363191.html.

45   Gray, "Musical Riders," 42.

the Musical Ride in 1980, recalled that the women's Ride uniform was specially ordered "with panels inserted into the bust area to accommodate their chests" and custom-made riding breeches to accommodate a woman's hips. Female members also wore English riding boots rather than RCMP issue, "unless their feet were large enough to wear the men's boots."[46] These changes were necessary to accommodate the female body and create a visual consistency with the male uniform during performances.

The opposition to women on the Musical Ride demonstrates just how important the image of the male review order uniform was for the RCMP's most popular public relations tool. But female Mounties were determined to offer the Canadian public an alternative representation of the RCMP, one that situated them as figures of authority in their own right and on their own terms. In 1982, when Mackie was asked whether she enjoyed being on tour with the Ride, she replied, "Being a member of the Ride is a great way to see the country and represent Canada abroad. You feel pretty proud of yourself up there in the red coat."[47] The presence of Mackie and Merk on the Musical Ride signalled to Canadians, both inside and outside the RCMP, that romanticized notions about women succumbing to scarlet fever and the charms of the handsome Mountie dressed in that nice red coat were quickly disappearing.

---

46   Kate Morton, interview with author, February 26, 2008.

47   Christine Mackie quoted in Gray, "Musical Riders," 44.

THE MYTH OF PHYSICAL PROWESS

Actually, it was kind of fun when you'd go to a bar fight and you'd get going with the cowboys and they'd come out swinging and they'd see that you were a girl ... They'd never want to admit that you were the one to pull them off somebody or took them down in a fight because that would be very destructive to their egos.

—Pam Osborne
RCMP Officer

The challenges that the RCMP faced over deciding how to train and dress the first female Mounties were soon overshadowed by other concerns following Troop 17's graduation. Larger questions surfaced about the reception the women might receive at their first detachments. How would rank-and-file Mounties react to the women at their first postings? Would members of the public respect female Mounties as figures of civic authority? Could women meet the physical demands of law enforcement? Would male police officers be placed in danger as a result of women's physical limitations? Were women capable of providing backup during violence? Would they be able to exercise their powers of arrest with sufficient physical force?

These questions were based on assumptions about gender. Police departments across North America were governed by a culture of masculinity where rigidly defined notions of gender and police authority dominated, and where authority was often understood as the ability to deliver lethal force.[1] Authority was also understood in terms of mental discipline, physical toughness, and aggression, all characterized by

---

1   Hewitt, "The Masculine Mountie," 168.

a strong and imposing body that communicated the potential for the use of force. For much of the twentieth century, these ideas undergirded the organizational structure of the RCMP where hierarchical rank structures, the chain of command, control over the rank and file, and the RCMP's connection to national identity all coalesced to reinforce police work as a masculine undertaking.

SIZE MATTERS

The myth that police officers had to be burly, tall, and strong to combat violence was often cited as the central reason for barring women from the occupation. The idea that male physical prowess was necessary to be an effective police officer was pervasive by the early decades of the twentieth century. It was no coincidence that the idea coincided with women's entrance into law enforcement. Although the Vancouver city police department was the first to hire women as police officers in Canada in 1912, just one decade later their positions were being eliminated and their powers eroded. In 1919, Vancouver employed four women with full police powers and one matron working in the jail. By 1928, however, just two female constables and three police matrons, all "without police authority," were employed by the department. Commanding officers justified the removal of police powers from female officers because "women have not proved themselves as responsive to discipline as men." Women were also deemed unable to meet the physical demands of police work. Police duty was "a matter of strong-arm methods and ... women's arms are weaker than those of their brothers," making them unlikely representatives of civic authority.[2]

The idea that physical prowess was a necessity for police work became firmly entrenched in police culture as the century wore on, evidenced by the height standards most departments adopted. By 1974, the minimum height requirement for applicants to Canadian municipal departments was set at five feet ten. It was a standard that few women, or for that matter men, could meet. The RCMP was no different and most Mounties viewed their strength and height as their most effective weapon on the street because it intimidated others and

---

2   Evelyn Le Sueur, "Can Women Do Active Police Work in Vancouver?," *Canadian Council of Churches/The Social Service Council of Canada* 10, no. 12 (1928): 277.

ensured compliance from the public.[3] They belonged to a club of elite masculinity where their youth, race, size, and strength idealized them as superior to other men who were under their authority. The image of the RCMP was built around this concept, linking the size and race of the male police body to representations of Canada. It is not surprising that when the RCMP lowered its minimum height requirements for recruits to five feet eight for men and five feet four for women in 1974, it was controversial.

Not all Canadian police departments were eager to follow the RCMP by lowering their height standards. In 1979, the Ottawa police department refused the application of a woman for the position of constable because she did not meet the minimum physical requirements of being five feet ten and 160 pounds.[4] The applicant took her case to the Ontario Human Rights Commission where a Board of Inquiry ruled the "police height and weight requirements as discriminatory in effect against women,"[5] forcing the police department to modify their physical testing standards.[6] That same year, the board also adjudicated a complaint that height and weight standards at the police department in Toronto were discriminatory against men because women were not required to meet the same criteria. The commission found that "separate height and weight requirements for women applicants to the police force were not discriminatory because they were not prejudicial to men."[7] The commission's ruling signalled that physical differences could no longer be a justification for inequality, at least not in the province of Ontario.

Police departments in other jurisdictions continued to impose height and weight restrictions on applicants. By 1982, just six of twenty-four Canadian police departments had no height or weight restrictions,

---

3   Daniel Bell, "Policewomen: Myths and Reality," *Journal of Police Science and Administration* 10, no. 1 (1982): 115. The link between physical size and intimidation in American police departments is addressed in "The Female Fuzz," *Newsweek* 80 (October 23, 1972): 117.

4   Slaughter, "Women's Journey Into Policing," unnumbered.

5   Lubomyr Chabursky, "The Employment Equity Act: An Examination of Its Development and Direction," *Ottawa Law Review* 24 (305): 313.

6   Slaughter, "Women's Journey Into Policing," unnumbered.

7   Chabursky, "The Employment Equity Act," 316.

and one, the Halifax police department, set a standard height of five feet eight for both men and women.[8] These regulations continued to be challenged in courts across the country well into the 1990s as a number of communities sought to make their police departments more representative of the general population. By 1986, some police departments developed new physical testing standards when the new federal *Employment Equity Act* (EEA) came into effect. The *Act* called for the mandatory development of an employment equity program for all "federally regulated workplaces" and required federal employers to "set up proactive initiatives to promote equality for four designated groups: women, Aboriginal peoples, persons with disabilities, and members of visible minorities."[9] As a result, four Canadian municipal departments developed new standards that included weight drag, flexibility, obstacle runs, victim recovery, hand strength, and other tests designed to measure the minimum strength and agility of an applicant.[10] By 1988, the RCMP had modified its physical testing system by adapting some aspects of the standards already being used by municipal departments.[11]

VIOLENCE AND CONFRONTATION

But testing during the application process and the realities of violence on

---

8   Rick Linden and Candice Minch, *Women in Policing: A Review* (Winnipeg: Institute for Social and Economic Research, University of Manitoba, 1982), 104.

9   The act was the result of recommendations made in the *Report of the Royal Commission on Equality in Employment* by Judge Rosalie Silberman Abella, who coined the term "employment equity" in the report. Colleen Sheppard, *Inclusive Equality: The Relational Dimensions of Systemic Discrimination in Canada* (Montreal & Kingston: McGill-Queen's University Press, 2010), 28.

10   The departments using these tests included Vancouver, Edmonton, Winnipeg, and Toronto. Stark, *The Role of Female Constables*, 199.

11   Rod Olsen, interview with author, January 4, 2010. It was not until 1999 that the Supreme Court of Canada ruled that employment testing standards could not be based on capabilities that favoured men. British Columbia forest firefighter Tawney Meiorin brought suit against her employer after being laid off from her job despite a satisfactory job performance evaluation. The court ruled that Meiorin could not be laid off for failure to meet the requirements of a new physical fitness test based on men's abilities, a test that had little to do with the ability to actually do the work. Judy Fudge and Hester Lessard, "Challenging Norms and Creating Precedents: The Tale of a Woman Firefighter in the Forests of British Columbia," *Work on Trial: Canadian Labour Law Struggles*, eds. Judy Fudge and Eric Tucker (Toronto: The Osgoode Society for Canadian Legal History, 2010): 341.

the streets were two different things in the minds of many male police officers. Contrary to assumptions about women in policing, however, female police officers were not above resorting to physical confrontation when necessary. Marlene Watson, who joined the Toronto police department in 1964, received a number of physical injuries as a result of violent conflicts with members of the public during her long career as a police officer. In an interview with the *Toronto Star* on the occasion of her retirement, Watson commented, "I've been punched. I've had whiplash from kicks to the head. When you first join, you have a false sense of security. You think they won't hit you because you're a woman." She also had her tailbone broken three times.[12] Watson's assumption that she would not be assaulted because she was a woman reveals that, at least initially, she also relied on conventional understandings of gender to enforce the law.

Female Mounties were also not afraid of using physical force. Some, like Margaret Watson, "gained a sense of satisfaction in subduing a man."[13] Several women used their prior interest in physical fitness and sport to their advantage while engaged in police work. Leslie Clark's interest in martial arts had started before she joined the RCMP and continued after she was hired. At the time she was interviewed for this study, Clark held degrees in four disciplines: a second-degree black belt in jujitsu, a first-degree black belt in karate, a brown belt in judo, and a red belt in tae kwan do. Her martial arts qualifications gave her confidence in terms of fighting while carrying out general policing duties. "Fighting for me was never an issue. I've been hit, I'd hit, you know, I'm not scared of it ... I'm not scared of fighting in the general sense or in being physical," stated Clark.[14] She was clearly at an advantage when it came to physical confrontations with members of the public.

Like Clark's, Janice Murdoch's level of physical fitness challenged perceptions about the limitations of the female police body. As a dog handler for the RCMP, Murdoch was required to maintain a certain level of physical fitness that few men or women possess. She described the importance of remaining in good physical condition as a dog handler:

---

12 Joe Fiorito, "Retiring Cop Broke Limits for Women."

13 Margaret Watson, interview with author, February 25, 2008.

14 Leslie Clark, interview with author, October 9, 2008.

Dog handlers in general have a lot of injuries relating
to their cores because our job is very unnatural in that
you have this eighty pound dog pulling you off centre
all the time. So, instead of it being just a run where your
body is straight and in control, you're actually fighting
the dog all the time. So you're pulling back always on
one side more than the other. You're going over fences,
and through trees, and losing your balance a lot. Dog
handlers have a lot of back injuries because if your
core's weak, your back is going to be injured. [They
also have a lot of] knee injuries and ankle injuries. So
I do a lot of exercises to combat that. I weight train at
least once a week, I run probably three times a week,
and then I swim and I bike. I ski a lot in the winter.[15]

Murdoch was also aware that as she aged, many of the suspects
that she would be pursuing would be younger than she was, a development she considered incentive enough to stay in top physical condition.

Despite the physical capabilities of women like Murdoch, the concept of male physical prowess as the ideal standard continued within
police culture. The RCMP's own studies on female Mounties discussed
how perceptions of feminine weakness shadowed the careers of many
of the women. According to one study conducted in 1984, male recruits
at Depot "were concerned about females' (lower) physical strength,"
an assumption that marginalized women as a "minority who have to
prove themselves" even before they left the academy.[16] The study's
conclusions suggested that male recruits held specific beliefs about
women as the weaker sex even prior to their hiring. Since police agencies recruited from the local community, the attitudes and beliefs of
male recruits were a reflection of understandings about women in operation in broader Canadian society at the time.[17]

---

15   Janice Murdoch, interview with author, April 17, 2008.

16   Robert Loo, *Interim Report: Stressors for Women in the Royal Canadian Mounted Police*, (June 1984), 9–10. Access to Information file GA-3951-3-03134/08 (July 14,
2008). Hereinafter referred to as *Interim Report*.

17   Don L. Kurtz, "Controlled Burn: The Gendering of Stress and Burnout in Modern Policing," *Feminist Criminolgy* 3, no. 3 (2008), 221.

THE MYTH OF PHYSICAL LIMITATIONS

The myth of the physical limitations of female Mounties was subsequently reproduced in the field. In 1986, an RCMP study of female constables found that a woman's inability to handle violence or physical confrontation was often presumed by male respondents. This perception emerged time and again in the comments made by male police officers who were participating in the study. Women were singled out as requiring additional physical training to compensate for what was seen as their inherent physical weakness. Women were also described as unreliable and ineffective. One male constable responded that male members were constantly having to cover for the female members and could not rely on them in emergency situations. Another maintained that female Mounties needed more backup at violence-related complaints no matter how many years of service they had.[18] It was obvious that many men in the RCMP perceived all women, not just some, as ineffective as police officers based on ideas about their physical limitations.

Gendered attitudes emerged again in the same study in response to a question regarding the reasons female Mounties were experiencing difficulties adapting to police work. An overwhelming majority of male constables and their supervisors considered that, because of "physical inferiority and [the] sensitive nature of females, adaptation is hardest [to the] violent and physical aspects of police work."[19] One male constable clarified his response in this way: "Females do not have the physical size/strength to take part in violence, and as a result are apprehensive in attending situations where they may encounter any violence." Another explained that "females face an internal conflict between their natural femininity and the masculine role of police work."[20] These comments reveal how male RCMP officers associated specific characteristics with femininity, which they described as "natural" and therefore unchangeable. In contrast, police work was viewed as a "masculine role." Most male Mounties saw women as socialized to be accommodating rather than aggressive, and as emotional rather

---

18   Stark, *The Role of Female Constables*, 63; 67; 72.

19   Ibid., 144.

20   Ibid., 147.

than rational beings. It was an attitude that left little room for alternative approaches to law enforcement.

Although male police officers advanced the idea that physical prowess was an absolute necessity in enforcing the law, researchers studying the issue took exception to this viewpoint. One 1982 study of American police departments examined "the issue of the physical capability of women police"—and refuted "the commonly expressed myth that policing is essentially male work because only men have the physical strength needed to perform patrol."[21] The study's author evaluated data acquired from eight American police departments in the 1970s to determine whether claims of the physical limitations of female police officers were valid. He concluded that "women perform the patrol function in municipal, county, and state police settings as ably as men, and that it is feasible to hire and deploy women as officers the same as men."[22] His findings indicated that perceptions about the physical inadequacies of women were unfounded.

The idea that police officers were obliged to engage in a constant stream of violence requiring the continuous use of physical force was also a misconception according to criminologist Daniel Bell, who found in 1969 that "approximately 90 percent of a police officer's time was spent in noncriminal service activities."[23] In a 1993 study, another researcher found that just 15 percent of police calls involved violent intervention, most of which could be diffused if an officer had the ability to "talk to people."[24] By 2003, researchers studying the types of calls police officers responded to uncovered what they dubbed the "80-20 secret" of police work: "This secret is that 80% of a police officer's time is spent doing social-work-type jobs, such as domestic disturbances/

---

21   Roi D. Townsey, "Female Patrol Officers: A Review of the Physical Capability Issue," *The Criminal Justice System and Women: Women Offenders, Victims, Workers*, eds. Barbara Raffel Price and Natalie J. Sokoloff (New York: Clark Boardman Company, 1982), 413. Also Kimberly A. Lonsway, "Tearing Down the Wall: Problems with Consistency, Validity, and Adverse Impact of Physical Agility Testing in Police Selection," *Police Quarterly* 6, no. 3 (September 2003): 237–77.

22   Townsey, "Female Patrol Officers," 413.

23   Bell, "Policewomen: Myths and Reality": 118.

24   Jonathan M. Lazar, "Female Police Officers: Their Past, Present and Future," unpublished undergraduate paper, March 1993. Access to Information file GA-3951-3-03134/08 (July 14, 2008).

violence, disturbances of the peace, and traffic control ... [while] 20% of the time is spent fighting crime, such as homicide, narcotics, kidnapping, and armed robbery." However, most recruits graduating from police academies believed the opposite was true, that 80 percent of their time would be spent fighting violent crime.[25] This is not surprising, given that the curriculum being taught in many police academies in the 1970s and 1980s placed a heavy emphasis on the management of violence but afforded minimal amounts of time to developing skills such as resolving interpersonal disputes.[26] The academy was also a place where instructors routinely told their war stories, reinforcing for recruits that physical force was not only a necessity but a measure of success and prestige.

NEGOTIATION NOT CONFRONTATION

Interpreting whether a situation required an aggressive physical response or conflict resolution was a skillset that women, and some men, brought to the occupation. All of the female police officers who were interviewed for this research relied on negotiation rather than physical confrontation on a regular basis. RCMP constable Kate Morton recalled that she did not like engaging in physical fights. She found that if there was a way of "talking some guy into the back of the car, it was easier."[27] Similarly, Carolyn Harper discovered that her best weapons were her gender and her ability to talk her way out of dangerous situations. "If the person was male and they still had some faculties about them when a female officer arrived, they would try not to look like a fool. They would try to pull themselves together" when negotiating with her.[28]

A woman's ability to negotiate was cited by female Mounties as the central difference between the ways male and female RCMP officers approached their work. One anonymous female survey respondent stated, "There is a place for a female in any police role, both operational

---

25   Venessa Garcia, "'Difference' in the Police Department: Women, Policing, and 'Doing Gender,'" *Journal of Contemporary Criminal Justice* 19 (2003): 340.

26   Steve Herbert, "'Hard Charger' or 'Station Queen': Policing and the Masculinist State," *Gender, Place & Culture: A Journal of Feminist Geography* 8, no. 1 (2001): 59.

27   Kate Morton, interview with author, February 26, 2008.

28   Carolyn Harper, interview with author, June 28, 2010.

and administrative. You don't have to be a fighter to be a good GD police person." She cited an ability to talk your way through difficulties as essential in police work for both men and women.[29] Allison Palmer concurred, explaining:

> I would talk my way out of situations because, I mean, I'm tall but I'm small-boned. I don't have a lot of strength. I have seen female members who have ... tried to be one of the guys [during confrontations] and things escalated. So, I mean, there are women who wanted to act just like the men and there are those of us who knew we couldn't perform that way, so we had to use much more of a psychological approach rather than physical.[30]

Palmer, who was never assaulted on the job during twenty years of patrol work, recalled that she did have to get physical a number of times. She remembered that very few men would engage with her during a physical altercation unless they were too drunk to notice that they were dealing with a female police officer. Most of the time, Palmer relied on her negotiation skills to resolve tough situations and make an arrest. "When you think about it, we want to do the same job [as male officers], but you're just going to take a little different tactic to get there."[31] The alternative approaches female Mounties like Palmer employed challenged the idea that physical prowess was an absolute necessity.

When Shelly Evans was asked about differences between male and female approaches to law enforcement, she responded, "The boys still see it as the pursuits, the fighting, breaking heads, you know. There's always the helping people in the background [of their minds], but boys are still boys, you know. I think women [join the RCMP] to help people."[32] Carol Franklin also talked her way out of a number of

---

29   Stark, *The Role of Female Constables*, 82.

30   Allison Palmer, interview with author, June 11, 2008.

31   Ibid.

32   Shelly Evans, interview with author, July 30, 2008.

difficult situations. "I would be able to talk, to use that skillset. Does it always work? Of course not ... [But] you don't need to resolve issues [with force and] you don't need to get into a confrontation to be effective," said Franklin.[33] Marianne Robson, whose first posting was to a mining community, found that dealing with the public was extremely physical. Still, she relied on negotiation as much as possible. "Because I was a woman, I knew I had to use the strongest muscle I had and that was my tongue. So that [physical] aggressiveness of police officers ... I wasn't able to do that. So I treated community people the way I wanted to be treated," recalled Robson.[34]

It was a sound approach that members of the community usually respected. When Allison Palmer served a summons to a man at his house one day, she did not realize until afterwards that he was a "police hater" and extremely violent. When he was arrested one month later for attempted murder, the suspect refused to talk to male police officers at the detachment. He wanted to talk to Palmer. Palmer got the man to make a statement, for which he thanked her at the end of their interview. Her male colleagues wanted to know how she did it. Citing her counselling background and knowledge of violent behaviour, Palmer insisted that she viewed the situation as a challenge. "I guess that's part of why I liked detachment work. That was my challenge, even though I knew people were going to get hurt and end up serving time. I was helping protect somebody else from harm."[35] Palmer's preventative approach to a potentially violent situation achieved positive results.

Female Mounties' preference for preventive rather than punitive approaches to police work was most evident in arrest statistics. In fact, in research undertaken for the RCMP's Health Services Directorate in 1996, Dr. Lynn Andrews suggested that the criteria used in the RCMP's annual performance evaluations might be inappropriate for women. While high arrest rates traditionally signalled good performance for men, women's preference for de-escalating violence often resulted in lower arrest rates, suggesting that a different measure of performance

---

33   Carol Franklin, interview with author, April 20, 2010.

34   Marianne Robson, interview with author, July 29, 2000.

35   Allison Palmer, interview with author, June 11, 2008.

might be needed.[36] In the United States, lower arrest rates in the 1970s were usually touted as proof that women were incapable of effectively enforcing the law. Although women "required arrest assistance more often than men," they also made fewer arrests because of their policing style, according to one researcher. However, in Washington, DC, women not only made fewer arrests but they also "sustained a higher conviction rate making it likely that they made fewer unnecessary arrests or higher quality ones."[37] Lower arrest rates for women did not necessarily point to their ineffectiveness as police officers.

The possibility of imminent death was another reason that ideas about the importance of physical size persisted in police culture. The potential for death during the course of a shift, as well as the mandate to kill fellow citizens if necessary, united police officers across all jurisdictions.[38] It was also a factor that distinguished policing from most other occupations.[39] While occupations such as the forest or mining industries had the potential to endanger workers' lives, the police role was unusual in that it required officers to face the threat of sudden attack from another person, not the more calculable risks of physical or environmental hazards.[40] Yet according to Statistics Canada, 133 police officers (92 percent) who were murdered in Canada between 1961 and 2009 were killed with a firearm, suggesting that physical size was not a factor in preventing death.[41] Still, physical prowess remained an essential element for effective law enforcement within

---

36   Lynn Andrews, "Stress in Women Police," *RCMP Health Services Directorate* (December 1996): unnumbered. Access to Information file GA-3951-3-03134/08 (July 14, 2008).

37   Townsey, "Female Patrol Officers," 416.

38   P.A.J. Waddington, *Policing Citizens: Authority and Rights* (Philadelphia, PA: UCL Press, 1999), 112.

39   The only other group of workers more at risk of on-the-job homicide in Canada during the same period was taxi drivers, with twice the work-related death rate of police officers according to Statistics Canada. Sara Dunn, "Police Officers Murdered in the Line of Duty, 1961 to 2009," *Statistics Canada* (Fall 2010), http://www.statcan.gc.ca/pub/85-002-x/2010003/article/11354-eng.htm.

40   Robert Reiner, *The Politics of the Police*. 3rd ed. (New York: Oxford University Press, 2000), 88.

41   Dunn, "Police Officers Murdered in the Line of Duty, 1961 to 2009."

police culture. Negotiation was a skill that was not given the same priority as physical force in the RCMP, an indication that a hierarchy of skillsets was at work within the organization.

The image of the physically imposing male crime fighter was so normalized that by the time of the arrival of the first female Mounties in 1974, few Canadians, inside or outside the RCMP, could understand how women could do the job. Ideas about the necessity of physical size and strength left little room for the alternative approaches women brought to policing. Although female Mounties could meet physical confrontation and violence with force when called upon to do so, many used negotiation instead to achieve more peaceful outcomes. Their alternative responses destabilized the idea that effective policing required physical size and strength, establishing a new standard that allowed female Mounties to define police work on their own terms. Nevertheless, masculinity remained the standard that women were expected to live up to and emulate, no matter what. Acceptance of the alternatives would be slow in coming. It was one more hurdle that the women of the RCMP would have to overcome.

WOMEN AS FIGURES
OF AUTHORITY

I don't know how many times I told people, "Look, I am totally going to publicly humiliate you here in front of all your friends. I'm going to kick your ass." And they'd look at me and think, "Holy crap, she might be able to do it!"

—Shelly Evans
RCMP Officer

When the women of Troop 17 arrived at their first postings in March 1975, they did not know exactly what lay ahead. Issues surrounding their uniform, the media, and training were becoming distant memories as they assumed their policing duties. Most of the women were excited to begin their new careers. Allison Palmer remembered that she arrived so early at the detachment on her first day that she had to sit in her car listening to the radio until someone unlocked the door so she could check in for duty.[1] Not everyone shared Palmer's enthusiasm.

It quickly became evident to the women of Troop 17 that some people were unwilling to accept them as police officers. Mountie wives were especially resistant to women in the RCMP. Wives' unpaid work for the RCMP for decades prior to 1974 afforded them a unique place within the organization, and some viewed themselves as the feminine complement to the heroic Mountie. Others struggled with the idea of their husbands spending long hours working with young, single women whom they viewed as a threat to their marriages. Often, wives adopted

---

1   Allison Palmer, interview with author, June 11, 2008.

a number of gendered attitudes about women in the force that mirrored the opinions expressed by their husbands. Mountie wives registered their opposition to women in the RCMP by using informal methods of exclusion that isolated and ostracized female members socially.

Members of the public were also struggling with changing definitions of masculinity and femininity in Canadian society. Many Canadians were unsure of how to approach a female police officer, especially in those communities policed by the RCMP that had never seen one before. Some people adopted a paternalistic approach to female Mounties, encouraging them for doing a good job or assisting them in their duties. Others relied on conventional understandings of masculinity and femininity to manipulate, harass, and intimidate the women to escape arrest or evade capture. Still others resorted to physical violence, and many female Mounties had to employ the use of force to make arrests.

By and large, however, in a society where policing was equated with masculinity, the presence of female police officers was an unknown variable that generated significant confusion over how to respond to female figures of authority. Combative males were torn between engaging a female police officer in a physical confrontation and risking being bested by her during an altercation on the one hand, and obeying the commands of a female officer on the other. When they did resist, it afforded the women of the RCMP the opportunity to challenge gender distinctions through the use of force. At the same time, it presented them with a chance to exercise their agency as police officers by introducing alternatives to violent confrontation.

MOUNTIE WIVES AND WOMEN IN THE RCMP

For much of the twentieth century, the RCMP embodied a specific form of gender relations that celebrated the nuclear family in which the wages of a male breadwinner supported dependents, who were supervised by a wife who remained within the home. The nuclear family was a measure of normality during the postwar period, and Mountie wives were elemental in upholding this standard in the RCMP. In doing so, they occupied a position as the appropriately feminine counterpart to the masculine Mountie hero in their communities.[2] However, expectations surrounding wives'

---

2   Wives were more frequently and openly acknowledged for their contributions by the men of the RCMP following the hiring of female Mounties in 1974. For example, see Nowell, "Salute to the Wives," 13.

detachment work were challenged in the 1960s and 1970s as more and more Mountie wives began to work outside the home. A growing number of women refused to perform policing-related services for the RCMP while holding down a job. But many Mountie wives remained in the home, conforming to more conventional understandings of their place within RCMP culture.

Wives had a number of reasons for resisting the presence of women in the police force. One of the most common reasons was because they feared that a female police officer would be unable to back up their husbands in a dangerous situation. This suggests that they shared their husbands' perceptions about the physical limitations of female police officers. The overriding concern, however, had more to do with the threat of competition for the time and affection of their husbands. Rumours about female Mounties engaging in sexual relations with male members were circulating between detachments across the country even before Troop 17 left the training academy. Gossip had it that there was "hanky panky between some of the women recruits and the NCO instructors" at Depot, where female recruits were also "accused of having sex with their male counterparts in the residences, in police cruisers, even in the graveyard."[3] The women of Troop 17 were cognizant of this gossip, as was the media who dutifully recorded it for Canadians.[4] The rumours seemed to confirm notions that any woman who wanted to work in a male-dominated organization was only there to engage in morally corrupt conduct with men.

It was a concern that worried the RCMP's commanding officers. Given the amount of time that male and female Mounties were to spend together during the course of a shift, it became important to the RCMP to reassure Mountie wives that female police officers were not rivals. Accordingly, Commr. Maurice Nadon, in his speech to Troop 17 at their graduation ceremonies, made a rare public acknowledgment of Mountie wives for their unofficial work for the RCMP: "Wives of members stationed on detachments were in many cases unofficial, unpaid and all-too-often unrecognized—but always appreciated—members

---

3   Robert Knuckle, *Beyond Reason: The Murder of a Mountie* (Dundas, Ontario: Kayson Publishing, 1997), 109. Depot's cemetery is located adjacent to the training academy's grounds.

4   Colleen Slater-Smith, "Troop 17 Graduates," *Leader-Post* (Regina), March 3, 1975; Knuckle, *Beyond Reason*, 67.

of the Force."[5] Nadon's reference to wives as "members" of the police force may have been inadvertent, but it is unlikely that many would have contested this characterization. In a similar vein, the RCMP *Gazette*, in its extensive coverage of the graduation of Troop 17, also included an article that paid tribute to Mountie wives: "Little did they know when they pledged their marriage vows, that they were taking on an unknown partner—namely the Force. This often left them in the position of being the third party, or odd-woman out!"[6] Despite these accolades, some RCMP wives were clearly feeling the odd woman out, now that female Mounties were about to begin partnering with their husbands at work.

It was not long before the women of Troop 17 learned that the rumoured antagonism of Mountie wives was not unfounded. When Trish O'Brien was asked about her reception at her first posting in the Maritimes, her initial recollection was of the wives at the detachment. O'Brien remembered that the wives were particularly upset at her arrival. She recalled one of her male colleagues saying, "My wife said if you work with me, our marriage is over!" The wives viewed O'Brien as a threat:

> They didn't want us working with [their husbands] in the car, and all this was going on without me even knowing. No one said anything about it. And once I got in there and I got to know the people, then you started hearing stuff ... how all the wives got up in arms when they found out the female's coming here; no one wanted you.[7]

Marianne Robson described the resistance of the wives as a big internal issue within the RCMP. She was unsure if the wives really believed that female Mounties were there to "steal their husbands away," but she remembered that there was a real sense that female Mounties were viewed as a threat. "We were there to do a job and my intent was not to break up anybody's marriage or steal somebody's

5   Nadon speech, 1975.

6   Nowell, "Salute to the Wives," 23.

7   Trish O'Brien, telephone interview with author, November 13, 2008.

husband by any means," stated Robson.[8] Linda Rutherford remembered that the wives at her first posting in rural Manitoba were asked in advance by commanding officers what they thought of a female police officer working with their husbands. Her trainer's wife had "absolutely no problem" with him training a woman.[9]

Wives employed a number of tactics, including shunning and gossip, to register their resistance to female Mounties. Allison Palmer recalled that the wives at her first posting ignored her outright. They did not want anything to do with her until her trainer's wife stepped in and defended her. Palmer remembered that she was the one who finally went to a stitch and bitch and said to the women who were present, "If anyone should be jealous it should be me. She's working with my husband." One wife later telephoned Palmer to make amends. They are still friends today.[10] Janet Porter also remembered that her trainer's wife was interviewed prior to her arrival and that "everyone had to be on board" with her husband training a female member. While Porter found that the wives were nice to her, they did not ask her to dinner, to go shopping, or to otherwise join them in socializing.[11]

This tension continued for the women who followed Troop 17. Margaret Watson, who graduated from Depot in 1977, realized early in her policing career that the wives of male members were concerned about female Mounties "coming on" to their husbands. "They were not happy," recalled Watson, who said that female members had to prove themselves to the wives too. Supervisors at her first detachment even organized "contact parties" so the wives could get to know her. But it was not until Watson began to date a single constable her own age

---

8   Marianne Robson, interview with author, July 29, 2008.

9   Linda Rutherford, interview with author, April 20, 2010.

10   Allison Palmer, interview with author, June 11, 2008. All new recruits, once posted to the field, underwent a Recruit Field Training (RFT) program for six months. Each recruit was assigned a trainer, usually a more senior officer at the detachment who trained them in operational police duties. The trainer and the recruit worked through a training manual and usually rode together as a team every shift. In general, each recruit was required to complete the manual prior to their first annual performance evaluation. The completed program resulted in a pay increase. Thank you to S/Sgt. Margaret Shorter for this information.

11   Janet Porter, interview with author, October 20, 2008.

that the wives' concerns over her presence diminished somewhat.[12] When Kate Morton was posted to a small detachment on the east coast of Canada, she found that while most of her male colleagues were respectful, their wives were less trusting. She recalled that whenever the detachment had summer ride-along programs for law students, her male peers preferred that she take the female students so they would not "get in trouble" with their wives.[13]

Although Cherise Marchand had a good relationship with her male trainer and his wife at her first posting in western Canada, they abruptly ceased all social interaction with her after she completed her Recruit Field Training (RFT) program. Marchand recalled that both had treated her very well during her training, inviting her to social functions or to their home at Christmas. But as soon as her training was over, her trainer "didn't want to have anything to do with me." Marchand, who was surprised by this turn of events, speculated that once their social responsibilities and working requirements as the trainer and the trainer's wife had been met, a continuing personal relationship with her was seen as unnecessary.[14]

Carolyn Harper was posted to a large urban detachment in the 1970s where she encountered animosity from Mountie wives. Harper and the other single women at this posting discovered that the wives would not speak to them at social functions. Harper blamed their husbands for the situation:

> I actually blame a lot of the men for that because the culture is such that they really didn't take their jobs home with them. They really didn't talk to their wives about their work. Having somebody there that they knew their husband was talking to was probably more upsetting to them. I don't think they always looked to us as sexual rivals. I think they looked at us as rivals for their husbands' time. I think that it really hurt them that they knew that their husbands were talking to us about

---

12   Margaret Watson, interview with author, February 25, 2008.

13   Kate Morton, interview with author, February 26, 2008.

14   Cherise Marchand, interview with author, October 15, 2008.

things that their husbands wouldn't talk to them about
at home. [15]

As a result, female members who were single did not attend social
functions at this particular detachment when the wives were present.

Some male Mounties handled the arrival of female members better than others by introducing their wives to them right away. Carol
Franklin found the wives at her first posting very accepting and inclusive. Franklin still "writes Christmas cards to one of the members'
wives that befriended me. I feel so fortunate to have been in that
place."[16] The wives at Louise Ferguson's first detachment were also
supportive, once they had met her. "I mean, you got invited to everybody's place for supper. First of all, the guys wanted their wives to
meet me so that tension was settled down. I got lots of dinner invitations right off the bat. We all socialized together."[17] Some male Mounties recognized that it was important to quickly defuse any tensions
that may have been created in Mountie marriages by the arrival of
female police officers.

The women who were married to RCMP officers were not alone
in their trepidation over female police officers; it was a familiar response from the wives of police officers across Canada. Carolyn Harper's application to a municipal police department in British Columbia
was initially rejected in 1974. When she contacted the recruiter to ask
for the reason, she was told the department was being careful in their
selection of its first female constable because of resistance from the
wives. According to Harper, the department was treading carefully
after receiving "so many complaints from wives."[18] Harper, who was
single and twenty-one years old at the time, remembered that the
wives were especially concerned about their husbands riding around
all night with a young woman in a police cruiser. That particular police
department eventually hired a divorced woman in her thirties with
two children. Harper successfully applied to the RCMP instead.

---

15   Carolyn Harper, interview with author, June 28, 2010.

16   Carol Franklin, interview with author, April 20, 2010.

17   Louise Ferguson, interview with author, November 9, 2006.

18   Carolyn Harper, interview with author, June 28, 2010.

In 1982, researchers Rick Linden and Candice Minch, sociologists from the University of Manitoba, conducted extensive research into women in policing in North America, including the RCMP. Their discussion of family problems amongst police officers included the reasons for high rates of divorce. They pointed to the strains placed on marriages by shift work, long hours, and social isolation within communities. As well, the "entry into the department of fairly large numbers of women who may be sharing a car eight hours a day with their husbands is seen by the wives as an additional threat to their marriage."[19] Researcher A.O. Maguire, in an undated study on the RCMP, found that Mountie wives grew concerned every time they discovered that a new female police officer was arriving at the detachment. Maguire found that "in one case, the fears of the wives are alleviated when the new constable turned out to be a 'plain Jane' and was not perceived as a threat." Similarly, the wives became more accepting of female officers after they began to go out with single males on the detachment.[20] The RCMP's own research identified several issues female Mounties had to overcome as they attempted to socialize and integrate into their communities, including negativity from wives.[21]

Of course, not all Mountie wives responded to the presence of female police officers in negative ways. But like the wives of men in many male-dominated professions that were admitting growing numbers of women in the 1970s, the unpaid Mounties relied on conventional concepts of gender when resisting the idea of women working closely with their husbands. Their response demonstrates that women were not a homogeneous, unified group but, like men, were often divided when it came to beliefs and opinions regarding the shifts in gender relations that were occurring.

FEMALE MOUNTIES AND MEMBERS OF THE PUBLIC

The residents of the first Canadian communities to receive a female Mountie in 1974 responded to their arrival in a variety of ways.

---

19   Linden and Minch, *Women in Policing*, 124.

20   A.O. Maguire, "Laughing on the Outside—Crying on the Inside: A Renewed Examination of the Female Regular Members of the Royal Canadian Mounted Police," quoted in Linden and Minch, *Women in Policing*, 105.

21   Stark, *The Role of Female Constables*, 145; 161.

Most residents in small towns and rural communities had never seen a female police officer before. People at Louise Ferguson's first posting felt gratified when their community was chosen as one of the first to have a female Mountie. "Everybody in the community was really pleasant. Very nice," recalled Ferguson, who felt supported and appreciated by the public.[22] At Allison Palmer's first posting, people viewed her as a novelty. She recalled one incident when she stopped to have a coffee with some of her male colleagues. "Somebody had never seen a female member before and paid for my coffee," said Palmer, who never discovered the identity of her benefactor. She also recalled that her colleagues were somewhat upset that they had never experienced the same from a member of the community.[23]

After a while, however, so much attention was like living in a fishbowl for the women of Troop 17. Janet Porter, posted to a small town in the prairies, remembered that the whole community knew she was coming and that heads turned whenever she drove through town in the police cruiser.[24] Linda Rutherford found the attention difficult at times: "It was hard. You'd stop the police car at an intersection, and people would be walking by and they'd be pointing. I had no privacy. You couldn't go anywhere. Everybody knew who I was and they'd be pointing ... I remember so distinctly people pointing. It was a novelty."[25] Marianne Robson remembered being stared at wherever she went, both on and off duty. She commented, "I guess it was just so unusual, so unique, that people wanted to see what it was all about."[26] It was attention that the women of Troop 17 did not anticipate or want.

The rarity of female Mounties contributed to their social isolation. Researchers in one 1982 study concluded that small and isolated communities posed particular challenges for the women of the RCMP, especially when they attempted to socialize off duty. Because the

---

22   Louise Ferguson, interview with author, November 9, 2006. According to one RCMP study conducted three years later, many communities felt privileged to receive the first female Mounties and readily accepted them as police officers, although there were a few skeptics. Sgt. D.R. Baird, *Policewomen in the R.C.M.P.*, October 14, 1977, 6–7. Access to Information file GA-3951-3-03134/08.

23   Allison Palmer, interview with author, June 11, 2008.

24   Janet Porter, interview with author, October 20, 2008.

25   Carol Franklin, interview with author, April 20, 2010.

26   Marianne Robson, interview with author, July 29, 2008.

women were so well-known in the community, it became difficult for them to escape the "pressures of the police role." Although male RCMP officers were also recognized in their communities, it was a problem that was particularly acute for women "who have no friends or working associates in remote areas." Researchers discovered that social isolation contributed to low morale and led to lower retention rates for women in the RCMP.[27]

In addition to social isolation, the lack of privacy sometimes posed safety concerns for young female Mounties in the 1970s. Donna Burns recalled that groups of young men at her first posting, who were well-known to the local police, attempted on several occasions to intimidate and frighten her. Because it was a small town, they knew where she lived. They sat outside her apartment in their vehicles late at night, put sugar in her gas tank, and followed her around while she was patrolling. Burns commented, "There were numerous times when the groups would be following me while out on patrol and just trying to set me up" in potentially harmful situations.[28] However, she stood her ground and refused to be intimidated. Burns always felt supported by the male members she worked with, many of whom she referred to as "gentlemen" who did not hesitate to back her up in dangerous situations. Their support afforded her a level of personal security that contributed to her growing confidence as a rookie police officer.

It took some time for members of the public to accept female Mounties as legitimate figures of authority. Many of the first female Mounties recalled incidents when members of the community requested help from a male police officer rather than a female member. Denise Bell, who was stationed in a small town in the prairies in 1978, answered the detachment telephone on one occasion only to have someone ask to speak with a male police officer instead. Bell assured the caller that she was capable of helping with the query.[29] Trish O'Brien's community in the Maritimes had never seen a female Mountie before she arrived. She recalled that, initially, members of the public assumed that she was married to her male partner when they

---

27   Linden and Minch, *Women in Policing*, 112.

28   Donna Burns Morse, interview with author, April 20, 2010; also in Bonnie Reilly Schmidt, "Women on the Force," *Canada's History* (August/September 2011): 34–41.

29   Denise Bell, interview with author, April 19, 2008.

were spotted out on patrol together. O'Brien also found that civilians would invariably prefer to speak to the male officer during calls or would ask to speak to a man when they came to the detachment.[30] These accounts illustrate how the public initially lacked confidence in a woman's authority or her ability to do what was still considered to be a man's job.

Janice Murdoch recalled that in 1987, some in her first community thought she was not old enough to drive a vehicle, let alone enforce the law. Murdoch's ponytail and braces made her look younger than her twenty-one years. After a while, Murdoch noticed that if she was riding with a male auxiliary member, people would approach him first at a crime scene or during a call, making it necessary for her to step in and tell them that she was the police officer. Murdoch's husband, who was not a police officer, occasionally rode along with her as a volunteer during her shifts. On at least two occasions, witnesses turned to him for assistance instead of Murdoch, even though he was not wearing a police uniform. Even after nine years of service, Murdoch found that members of her community still preferred to speak with a man rather than a female police officer.[31]

The sight of a young woman in a uniform sometimes confused the public. Jane Hall, who looked like a teenager in 1978 even though she was twenty-three years old at the time, recalled responding to a routine call in North Vancouver, British Columbia. When she knocked on the door of a home, a "well-dressed woman in her mid-seventies" answered and "called to her husband, sitting on the couch behind her, 'Dear, the Girl Guides are here!'"[32] Cherise Marchand was the first woman to be posted to a detachment in a small city in western Canada. She recalled that she "just about caused a few accidents" when members of the public "did a double take" after seeing her on the street for the first time.[33] When Allison Palmer attended one accident scene, her presence created so many problems for investigators that they asked her to leave. Several passing motorists were so distracted

---

30   Trish O'Brien, telephone interview with author, November 13, 2008.

31   Janice Murdoch, interview with author, April 17, 2008.

32   Hall, *The Red Wall*, 73.

33   Cherise Marchand, interview with author, October 15, 2008.

by the sight of a female Mountie on the road that they almost caused another accident trying to get a second look at her.[34]

It was not long before female Mounties had to confront violence in their communities. Some men resisted the authority of female police officers by physically attacking them. It was one way they actively negotiated their masculine identity within their communities. Denise Bell recounted an incident in 1978 in which a man tackled her in a restaurant and tried to "put me through a wall" for no reason. Immediately, "before my feet even hit the ground someone grabbed the man and said, 'Don't you ever hit a woman!'" Bell then had to break the two men up after they entered into a fistfight over the incident.[35] Bell's experience illustrates the often contradictory responses women in the RCMP received from the public. While one man chose to react violently toward Bell as a figure of authority, the other reacted in a chivalrous manner to protect her from being attacked further.

Shelly Evans experienced high levels of violence from men at her first posting in 1988. She recollected that she seemed to be doing an inordinate amount of fighting there, in what she characterized as a "rough" community that included transient men working in the oil industry. Evans, who was just twenty-one years old at the time, remembered that there were always people who were surprised to see a woman responding to a police call. For Evans, gender was a factor in many of her dealings with the public, some of whom "had a real problem with a girl with a gun." One night she responded to a call about a bar fight, only to find that the bouncer at the bar resented her presence at the scene. In front of the bar's patrons, the bouncer slapped her across the face. "The next thing he knew he was picking himself up off the floor and he had a broken nose 'cause I laid him out," said Evans.[36] Whether or not the bouncer would have considered slapping a male police officer in the face is speculative. However, the bouncer clearly equated police authority, and his own, with masculinity and the use of force. On this occasion, Evans was unwilling to be humiliated in front of the bar's patrons. It was extremely important to her that

---

34   Allison Palmer, interview with author, June 11, 2008.

35   Denise Bell, interview with author, April 19, 2008.

36   Shelly Evans, interview with author, July 30, 2008.

she establish her authority as a police officer and remove any considerations of gender from future dealings with the public.

On another occasion, outside the same bar, Evans was attacked by
a university student whom she was attempting to arrest for impaired
driving. The student was "so scared at the thought of losing everything
and being impaired and going to jail" that he attempted to strangle
Evans by the side of the road. According to Evans, if she "had been able
to get to my gun I probably would have shot him. But I couldn't, and
I was, luckily, physically able to contain him until the backup troops
could arrive." Evans suffered a broken hand that required surgery.
She was then placed on light duties at the detachment for eight weeks
while she waited for it to heal. Nerve damage and arthritis in her hand
are her permanent reminders of the incident.[37]

Female Mounties were sometimes surprised by their own abilities. Louise Ferguson recalled her surprise at being able to physically
restrain an impaired driver who attempted to escape arrest. A "big
fight" took place when she tried to subdue him, but because she was
"a pretty good scrapper at the time" she made the arrest and took him
back to the detachment. When the breathalyzer operator finally arrived at the office, the suspect exclaimed, "Thank god you're here! She
already tried to kill me once!" Ferguson acknowledged that he was "a
little beat-up looking" after their fight.[38]

When Pam Osborne's authority was challenged by an older man
in her community, she responded to his gendered attitude toward
her with physical force. "I fought with this German farmer one night,
a grandfather ... We [the RCMP] were involved in an incident on the
block and he came up to it and I told him to get out of the way and
continue on. He refused. It was a definite 'I don't have to listen to you,
you're just a girl.'" Osborne ended up in a physical altercation with the
man, whom she arrested, took to jail, and charged with obstruction.[39]
The farmer's response to Osborne was informed by his belief that a

---

37   Ibid. The suspect was charged with impaired driving, resisting arrest, and
assault. He received one year of probation. Evans underwent a second surgery to remove the pins in her hand after they became infected. Evans, email communication to
author, August 29, 2008.

38   Louise Ferguson, interview with author, November 9, 2006.

39   Pam Osborne, interview with author, October 28, 2006.

woman did not have the authority to direct the activities of men in public spaces. Although female Mounties preferred to use negotiation rather than physical confrontation in their dealings with the public, they had little choice but to rely on their training to defend themselves when needed.

Donna Burns relied on her RCMP training to see her through her first life-threatening altercation, which took place just one week after her arrival in Port Alberni, British Columbia, in 1975. While attempting to question a suspect in a local restaurant, Burns touched the man lightly on the shoulder and asked him to step outside:

> [As] soon as I touched him, he went berserk. He got up, the table flew, he pushed me back over the counter and he starts choking me. And he's choking and nobody's coming to help me, of course ... But it was that Depot training, the ground fighting. [My hand] came up behind him, and like I said, he had that long blond hair and I just yanked it. And I got him off me and he's just going. And I don't remember how I got him from the fish and chip place to the car. But I remember ... I couldn't get cuffs on him ... I've got him in the back seat of the car, and he's just going wild ... But I'll never forget that he had his hands [on my neck] and I had bruises on my throat and he was choking me.[40]

Burns was so new to police work that she did not know how to turn on the police cruiser's siren as she made her way back to the detachment with the suspect.

When Burns returned to the detachment and her male colleagues saw who she had in the back of the police cruiser, she garnered their immediate respect. The suspect, who by this time was trying to kick out the windows of the cruiser, was well-known to the members of the Port Alberni detachment. "I couldn't do anything wrong" after that incident, said Burns. She knew that as a rookie police officer she needed to communicate to her male peers that she was not easily intimidated

---

40   Donna Burns Morse, interview with author, April 20, 2010. This incident is also recounted in Reilly Schmidt, "Women on the Force," 39.

or afraid to defend herself. And if members of the community who were watching the altercation in the restaurant had any questions about the ability of women to handle violent confrontations, their concerns were answered. The media eventually caught wind of the story about the assault on Burns and published an account of it in the local newspaper. Burns thought it was very fortunate that the incident happened so early on in her career since it gave her a lot of credibility, both with her peers and with members of the public.[41]

Louise Ferguson also gained credibility as a rookie police officer following a fortuitous altercation with an intoxicated man:

> The guy was quite combative, you know, pushing people and fighting. I just clicked into training mode, and of course at that time I was strong and still jogging every day. I got him in a choke hold and by the time the other member got there, I was just putting the cuffs on him and putting him in the car ... It was so easy, like it was really quite easy. But the next day it was all around ... that I'd been in this big fight and single-handedly took down this big huge logger guy. I mean, it wasn't even close to the truth.[42]

Not only did word about the altercation spread throughout her community, but neighbouring communities and detachments heard about it as well. Ferguson sensed that rumours about her encounter with the big logger would only help her credibility, so she did not dispute them.

Occasionally, male civilians came to the aid of female police officers. One day, Cherise Marchand's trainer decided to let her answer a call to pick up a man who was drunk and had passed out. Unbeknownst to Marchand, her trainer had already surmised who the man was, based on the location of the call. Marchand knew she had a problem when she arrived at the scene to find that the inebriated man was approximately six feet three and weighed well over two hundred

---

41 Donna Burns Morse, interview with author, April 20, 2010.

42 Louise Ferguson, interview with author, November 9, 2006.

pounds. As she was pulling the man down the driveway toward the police cruiser, an older man stopped his car, asked if she needed help, and gave her a hand in getting the man into the cruiser. Back at the detachment, when Marchand's trainer saw that she had successfully arrested the man, he responded, "That's not fair! I've been in the RCMP for six years and nobody's ever given me a hand for anything. This is the first time you go out by yourself, and you get somebody to help you put this drunk in your car?"[43] It was obvious to Marchand that her trainer believed he had set her up for failure. However, neither Marchand nor her trainer had anticipated that gentlemanly codes of conduct toward women sometimes resulted in successful outcomes to tough situations for female Mounties.

Understandings about gender worked in their favour in other ways. After Marianne Robson had arrested a male suspect at a local inn, he escaped from the back of her police cruiser. Robson chased him and caught him. The next day, word about their altercation spread through the community, including the fact that the suspect "got caught by the female Mountie." According to Robson, the man was so embarrassed about being chased and caught by a woman that he left town.[44] Carolyn Harper, a special constable stationed at a major Canadian airport, recalled that people actually thanked her when she wrote them a traffic ticket. "In 1975, they [would] thank you for writing a speeding ticket" because female Mounties were so novel. She remembered that they often exhibited a paternalistic attitude toward her by complimenting her for doing a good job. In her opinion, the fact that she was a female officer "contributed to a calmer situation," even when handing out tickets.[45]

Female Mounties were not above taking advantage of gendered attitudes to make their jobs easier. Jane Hall arrested an impaired driver in North Vancouver one night. After politely reading the breathalyzer demand to him and before he had time to think, she opened the back door of the police cruiser, slipped the handcuffs on him, and put him in

43   Cherise Marchand, interview with author, October 15, 2008.

44   Marianne Robson, interview with author, July 29, 2008.

45   Carolyn Harper, interview with author, June 28, 2010.

the back seat.[46] Unbeknownst to Hall, her suspect was one of the city's most notorious criminals and was under surveillance at the time by a member of the drug squad, who observed the entire arrest. The drug squad member later communicated a different version of events back at the detachment: "It was brutal … She must be a black belt or something; he never got a chance to even touch her," he recalled, marvelling at how easily Hall got the suspect into the cruiser. Many men, including RCMP officers, suspected that female police officers held some type of martial arts training. The suspicion was based on the assumption that the only way women could gain entrance to the RCMP in the first place was to possess specialized skills that could compensate for their weaker bodies. Few realized that most female Mounties did not possess martial arts skills apart from the arrest techniques they learned while at Depot. Despite the fact that the suspect was highly intoxicated and cooperated with Hall, even calling her "Ma'am" at one point, she allowed this version of events to circulate freely.[47]

Some male civilians preferred to be arrested by a female Mountie during tense situations. Pam Osborne remembered walking into a bar fight one night only to see that a suspect was "chest to chest and nose to nose with three male members around him, ready to go and fight." When Osborne arrived, the suspect decided to be arrested by her instead of fighting his way out with the three male Mounties. She walked him out of the bar without incident.[48] According to one study on policing, women were able to reduce violent situations because they had less to prove as far as their identity was concerned when they encountered hostile civilians.[49]

Louise Ferguson also thought that having a female presence at a bar fight tended to calm a potentially violent situation down significantly:

---

46   The breathalyzer demand is read to persons suspected of operating a motor vehicle while impaired. The demand requests that the suspect proceed to the detachment with the police officer to provide two breath samples to a qualified technician to determine the proportion of alcohol in their blood. Failure to comply with the breathalyzer demand is an indictable offense under Canada's *Criminal Code*, Section 235 (2).

47   Hall, *The Red Wall*, 77–79.

48   Pam Osborne, interview with author, October 28, 2006.

49   Herbert, "'Hard Charger' or 'Station Queen,'" 60.

Because there was less to prove from a male perspective, you know … you could see the guy thinking, "Number one, she's either got a black belt in karate and will beat the shit out of me and embarrass me in front of all my friends. Or, I will get the upper hand and all I've done is beaten up on some girl." If you're aware of that and play that you can defuse a lot of situations and offer someone the "out"—they don't have to find out one way or the other. You say, "Let's go to my police car and talk about it." They'll race you there. They want to get the situation resolved … In some cases, most people don't really want to have their friends see them beat up this lady cop.[50]

All of the female Mounties interviewed for this research utilized stereotypical understandings of femininity and masculinity at some point in their careers, not only to diffuse violent situations but to negotiate with suspects.

Gender stereotypes were often a double-edged sword for female police officers, though. Members of the public also used gendered approaches to female Mounties in an attempt to manipulate their way out of trouble. Shelly Evans cited several examples of men in the community who thought that they could get out of trouble by flirting with a female member. When their advances were rejected, they often characterized the female Mountie as "a bitch" who must be gay and circulated the information around the community.[51] Conversely, female civilians who relied on their femininity when dealing with male police officers were disappointed when they encountered a female Mountie. According to Carolyn Harper, women knew that "they had lost the little bit of an edge" when a female officer responded to a call.[52] Similarly, when Jane Hall responded to a call about a bar fight, one of the female combatants was disappointed to see her. The woman had grabbed one of the male constables as he struggled to arrest a suspect.

---

50   Louise Ferguson, interview with author, November 9, 2006.

51   Shelly Evans, interview with author, July 30, 2008.

52   Carolyn Harper, interview with author, June 28, 2010.

Hall remembered that up until that point the "female obviously felt untouchable," because she knew that if a male member grabbed her, the drunken onlookers would come to her rescue. "How unfortunate for her I was there, because the same social code that applied to her also applied to me," recounted Hall, who arrested the woman.[53]

Margaret Watson, who did not shy away from using physical force when necessary, found that women in her community were as dangerous as men at times. Watson cited domestic disputes as the type of incident in which women were more likely to be violent with police officers, male or female. But they were not the only calls in which she experienced violence from women. Watson remembered arresting a mentally unstable woman who dragged her down a flight of stairs and ripped her shirt off before she could restrain her.[54] Women in the community were sometimes as violent with female Mounties as men were, an indicator of the unpredictability of gender.

Some men assumed that they could outrun a woman and evade capture. Janice Murdoch found that men "might decide to fight or they might decide to run, but more often than not they will run, thinking I won't catch them."[55] Murdoch, a dog handler, recalled assisting in the apprehension of two men suspected of a violent assault. She tracked the suspects with her dog into an area of bush that was heavily wooded. Although she initially had backup officers aiding her in the search, they were soon left behind as Murdoch and her dog followed the suspects' trail. Even physically fit men found it difficult to track suspects for long periods of time without specialized training. Eventually, Murdoch located the two suspects and brought them out of the bush. On the way back to the detachment, one of the male officers asked the suspects why they had decided to run into the bush. They responded that when they saw the female police officer, they assumed that she would never catch them. Laughing, the male officers informed the suspects that Murdoch had just returned from running the Boston Marathon, so the chances of them outrunning her were slim.[56]

---

53   Hall, *The Red Wall*, 86.

54   Margaret Watson, interview with author, February 25, 2008.

55   Janice Murdoch, interview with author, April 17, 2008.

56   Janice Murdoch, interview with author, April 17, 2008.

Male members of the public, like the men in the RCMP, understood physicality and violence as manly characteristics. They also understood policing as masculine work in which the threat of force served as the definitive standard of police authority, even when they were on the receiving end of that force. These concepts were challenged when female Mounties met violence with violence, contrary to notions of the female body as an unlikely conduit of authority. Many female Mounties were willing to adopt the masculine standards they were trained to execute in order to reach their policing objectives, demonstrating that female Mounties were willing to break out of conventional constructions of gender to succeed.

At the same time, however, they resorted to understandings of difference to achieve their goals. Sometimes they relied on understandings of femininity to defuse dangerous situations and avoid physical confrontations. They also relied on their ability to talk their way out of tough situations, an alternative approach that ultimately differentiated the work of female Mounties from that of their male colleagues. As the justices of the Supreme Court of Canada wrote, "true equality requires differences to be accommodated," a concept that was gradually accepted by members of the communities where female Mounties policed.[57] Male Mounties, however, had greater difficulty relinquishing traditional standards of policing, and many refused to believe that alternative methods worked too.

---

57   Justice Beverley McLachlin quoted in Fudge and Lessard, "Challenging Norms and Creating Precedents," 341.

THE FIGHT FOR EQUALITY

I think we all expected a degree of resistance upon entering the
Force from our peers—however, the out-and-out bias and lack of
support from many Senior NCOs was a shock.

—Female RCMP Officer
Anonymous Survey Respondent, 1986

It was not long before female Mounties learned the extent to which
gendered attitudes operated within the RCMP. Many began to experience work environments that were often hostile to their presence. In
the 1970s and 1980s, the strongest opposition to women in the RCMP
came from non-commissioned officers (NCOs), the police force's middle managers.[1] Not all NCOs supported the RCMP's decision to open
up its ranks to women. Many were opposed to any renegotiation of
the masculine standards that were so foundational to the image of
the RCMP, and they worked to ensure that masculinity remained the
force's dominant feature.

This group of Mounties used their rank and position of power to
intimidate and marginalize the women of the RCMP. They relied on
the organizational structure of the RCMP to informally regulate them
and influence how they were received by their peers, commanding
officers, and members of the public. They also employed a number
of harassing techniques in an effort to force the women under their
command to ask for a transfer or resign. Their ability to freely harass junior officers without consequences signalled to members of
the rank-and-file that the practice of harassment was normative and
acceptable behaviour within RCMP culture. It was a situation that the

---

1   NCOs held the rank of corporal, sergeant, or staff sergeant.

RCMP refused to recognize or address, despite warnings that female Mounties were experiencing significant resistance from NCOs in the field.

THE RCMP STUDIES FEMALE MOUNTIES

In the 1980s, the RCMP noticed that attrition rates amongst female Mounties were high, and they commissioned a number of studies to investigate the reasons. In 1986, S/Sgt. S.E. Stark, at the behest of his commanding officers in "E" Division (BC/Yukon), undertook one of the largest studies of female Mounties ever conducted to that date.[2] *The Role of Female Constables in "E" Division* was initiated to identify and address some of the significant problems encountered by female Mounties across the division. Information was gathered through a questionnaire that was distributed to a select sample of members of the RCMP. Two questionnaires were developed—one for constables and one for supervisors—that asked questions about a variety of issues that female Mounties experienced, including training, the public, general duty work, violence, Mountie wives, social isolation, physical capabilities, and adaptation to the work.[3]

Stark's study was a significant document because it included direct quotes from the respondents who voluntarily and anonymously completed the survey. Their comments shed light on the gendered nature of RCMP culture ten years after women had joined the ranks. The comments made by supervisors were especially revealing. The study showed that NCOs often relied on conventional understandings of femininity in their assessments of female Mounties. According to one, "The Male member is physically more capable. Female members tend to be more of a social worker type, rather than enforcement minded. It is difficult for a woman to take charge of a situation involving men, unless of course it's marriage." Another commented, "Psychologically most women are not brought up to assume a position of authority, and their size, in most cases, does not exude the authority figure to the

---

2   "E" Division was the largest division in Canada in 1986. The survey sample size consisted of responses from 286 male constables, 109 junior NCOs, 75 senior NCOs, and 169 female Mounties, the entire population of women who were posted to the division at the time. Stark, *The Role of Female Constables*, 8.

3   Ibid. The questionnaires did not ask questions related to the issue of harassment.

general public,"[4] revealing that physical prowess was still considered a necessary component of police work.

Several NCOs referred to the unsuitability of women to perform general police duties; 85 percent viewed women as less able than men to provide adequate backup in potentially violent or physical confrontations.[5] Further, 88 percent of supervisors responded that they preferred to send men to assist with calls involving physical confrontation.[6] The assignment of certain tasks to female police officers by their supervisors soon emerged as a gendered division of labour within the RCMP. On a practical level, it denied women the opportunity to gain self-confidence and experience dealing with potentially violent civilians. On the other hand, by assigning women to tasks considered to be within their capabilities, supervisors aggravated the perception that they were receiving preferential treatment.

The more favourable treatment the women received from some NCOs did not go unnoticed by male constables. One observed that "females are, in some cases, directed away from violent and unsavory duties such as bar fights, drunken and wild parties, and situations that may require brute strength and fighting abilities." Another noted, "It is still habit to assign violent complaints to male members more frequently, or to ensure back-up more quickly if a female member is the first to receive the complaint."[7] An NCO's attitude frequently informed the attitudes of the men in the lower ranks, who soon adopted similar ideas about the physical limitations of women and their unsuitability for general-duty police work.

Some NCOs blamed the women themselves for fostering negative opinions about female members. According to one, "Most female members appear to have the opinion that they are something special and should not be required to perform the same duties as male members. This attitude often causes rifts in communication and subsequently a more difficult time for female members."[8] His observations indicated

---

4   Ibid., 147–48.

5   Ibid., 89.

6   Ibid., 90.

7   Ibid., 85.

8   Ibid., 65.

that some women expected, and received, preferential treatment while working general duties. These views were echoed by female Mounties as well. Margaret Watson, who joined in 1977, recalled that some women used their femininity as a reason not to back up a fellow officer or to avoid physical confrontations. Watson was offended by these women, whose behaviour and expectations complicated the working lives of all female Mounties. She maintained that "if you take the same pay, you have to be prepared to get physical."[9] Shelly Evans agreed, stating that women caused problems when they decided to "flirt and be some giddy little girl and leave all the dirty work to the boys." She observed that male police officers understandably resented having to carry a woman during the course of a shift.[10] As a result, many male Mounties assumed that all female Mounties, not just some, could not adequately meet the physical demands required for general policing duties. This earlier generation of women feared "group blame"—when the actions of one female police officer resulted in the categorization of all women as unequal to the job—and continued to work to gain credibility from their male peers by distancing themselves from what were perceived as feminist or feminine demands.

Trish O'Brien worked for an NCO who took a more traditional approach toward her as a police officer. O'Brien was twenty-two years old when she was stationed in eastern Canada in 1975. She recalled that the men she worked with treated her "like gold" and that her trainer did not afford her preferential treatment. But her supervisor had difficulty adjusting to having a woman on his watch for the first time:

> The boss struggled with it. He was the sergeant in charge and he was old school. And he was very reluctant about me out there. He was pushing for me, I was a little bit timid ... I needed to get out there and get more impaired drivers. That was his thing ... In one way he was a little protective, in another way he was pushing me to be more assertive and aggressive, and so on.[11]

---

9   Margaret Watson, interview with author, February 25, 2008.

10   Shelly Evans, interview with author, July 30, 2008.

11   Trish O'Brien, telephone interview with author, November 13, 2008.

O'Brien's supervisor had a tough time reconciling masculine standards of policing with his own ideas of femininity. Although he felt protective of her, he nonetheless attempted to instill in O'Brien the importance of adopting what were considered masculine characteristics. He left little room for O'Brien to develop alternative responses to general duty work.

Supervisors in charge of policing regions where individuals patrolled vast expanses of geographical space were also concerned with women working general police duties. Mark Baker, who was stationed as a corporal at a highway patrol unit in the Yukon, recalled that he and three constables were expected to patrol 3,400 miles of highway, an area that covered twelve detachments. Although he did not feel it necessary to check on his men regularly when they were out on patrol for a week or more at a time, he did check on his first female member on a daily basis:

> When I came into work in the morning I would check with Telecoms to see if they'd heard from her, and where she was and whether she'd [called] me for that morning yet, and when they last heard from her. If she went 10-7 [the Radio 10 code for "out of service"] to her residence at 11:30 at night and they hadn't heard from her by 8:00 o'clock in the morning, then I'd check at noon again ... Maybe [I] had a little less confidence in this person than I had in my male members, but I don't think it was gender specific ... She was not as assertive. I suppose that's the best way I could put it.[12]

For Baker, working with his first female Mountie challenged him to come to terms with his understanding that women were vulnerable and in need of protection. His reluctance to trust in the effectiveness of the self-defence training techniques women were taught in Depot was a common response for an older generation of men trying to adjust to women working as general-duty police officers.

---

12   Mark Baker, interview with author, February 10, 2009.

THE POWER OF NCOS

Since general duty work was highly visible to the Canadian public, it was one area where the image of Mounties as heroic crime fighters was more likely to be cultivated and reinforced. NCOs were the mediators of that image since commanding officers relied on them to assure the smooth running of the detachment, the cooperation of the public, and the effectiveness of the rank and file in the performance of their duties. NCOs were well positioned to either reinforce conventional relations of power between men and women or adapt to shifting understandings of masculine and feminine roles. Many chose the former course. They adhered to the paramilitary traditions of the RCMP in which lower-ranking police officers were trained not to question those in authority over them. It was this power structure that allowed NCOs to challenge the presence of women in the RCMP unimpeded.

NCOs who actively opposed the presence of female Mounties employed a number of strategies to justify their belief that women were unsuitable for policing. Many engaged in systematic harassment in an attempt to force a female member to resign or ask to be transferred. The experience of Shelly Evans illustrates the forms that the harassment often took. Evans was the first female Mountie to be posted to general duties at a small, five-member detachment in western Canada in the 1980s, where she encountered an NCO who "had a problem with women and made my life a living hell there for two years." Evans described the work, her roommates, and her male colleagues as "fabulous" at this posting. It was not long, however, before she became the object of the NCO's mentally and verbally abusive behaviour:

> You'd work all night [and he'd] be phoning you first thing in the morning [asking] "Where's this, where's that, why wasn't this written up? You put a claim in on my desk for overtime. I'm only giving you half." Verbally tell you to do stuff and then shit all over your files. Demeaning. Abusive. Rescheduling you so that you're working a month of nights. Stuff like that. Cancelling your leave. Very tormenting, very abusive.[13]

---

13   Shelly Evans, interview with author, July 30, 2008.

The situation with her NCO deteriorated to the point where Evans complained to the DSRR in her area, who offered to arrange for a transfer for her to another detachment. In response, Evans told the representative, "That's exactly what they want. I'm the first female at this posting and I'm not leaving until my time is done. Because it will ruin it and set the stage for any other females coming in here. I'm not doing it." Evans did tough it out for two more years before being transferred. She was eventually diagnosed with post-traumatic stress disorder (PTSD), "not from the situations I've been in, not the gore I've seen, the horrible situations, or anything like that." Instead, her diagnosis was the result of the harassment she experienced from her NCO.[14]

Rather than advocating for Evans and working on her behalf, the DSRR's solution to the problems being created by the NCO was to transfer her. Divisional representatives, although nominated and voted into their positions by the rank-and-file, were also NCOs and were often complicit in the systemic discrimination that the women faced. Although their rank was officially downplayed in an effort to project an image of advocacy for junior officers, some representatives hesitated, or even refused, to register a harassment complaint against a peer who held the same rank. The system of representation established in 1975 by Commissioner Maurice Nadon was failing the male and female police officers it was designed to serve. The failure of the DSRR system to adequately advocate on behalf of victims of abuse left them without recourse, contributing to the systemic nature of the problem. Indeed, Evans later learned that after she left the detachment, her former NCO transferred his abusive behaviour onto the male Aboriginal constable who was stationed there.[15] For this supervisor, anyone who was not a white, Anglo-Canadian male was a target for abuse. Harassment was an effective tool in removing unwanted members from under his command without consequences to his own career.

Mostly, the only alternatives for a female Mountie who was experiencing harassment in the 1970s and 1980s was to resign or request a transfer. In this way, the system disempowered the women who were often forced to choose between two undesirable alternatives. Receiving

14   Ibid.

15   Ibid.

a transfer did not eliminate unfair treatment, however, and often it was just the beginning of further harassment. The RCMP's culture was such that any female Mountie who reported harassment would be labelled a complainer, a reputation that would usually precede her to her next posting. It was one more way that the culture and organizational structure of the RCMP facilitated, rather than prevented, the harassment of female police officers.

Being labelled a complainer had serious consequences for female Mounties. The fear of retaliation meant that most women chose not to make a complaint. Shelly Evans described how one of her NCOs would get frustrated with her over the files she was working on, wanting her to process or conclude them quickly. Once, when she asked for more time to investigate, he vented his frustration toward her, saying, "Why can't you be like the other female members in this detachment and just be happy you have a job?"[16] Researchers categorize this type of remark by a supervisor as a form of gender harassment, since it conveys "direct rejection of non-traditional women and their right to work in higher paying fields."[17] When asked whether she complained about this NCO to senior officers, Evans commented, "You just rode it out, you wouldn't make a complaint. There was just no way. It's even dangerous to make complaints these days. It's just something that you don't do. There's always retaliation. Always."[18] Retaliation against female Mounties who lodged complaints was an indication of the extent of the power struggle that was taking place.

The fear of retaliation kept women in their place within the organization. Marianne Robson explained that a woman's job or a future promotion could be in jeopardy if she complained. A woman who spoke up was "seen as a whiner and complainer" who could not tolerate working in a male-dominated environment. "So, you know, you've gotta be like the boys and go along with what the boys want. Oh, no. Complaining? Absolutely not," observed Robson.[19] The threat of retaliation and labelling highlights the systemic nature of the problem

16   Ibid.

17   Andrews, *Stress in Women Police*, 5.

18   Shelly Evans, interview with author, July 30, 2000.

19   Marianne Robson, interview with author, July 29, 2008.

since the women had, but did not utilize, the complaint process that was available to them. Few were willing to risk the consequences if their complaint was ignored or the offending supervisor was not held to account for his actions. Without options to help them resolve the tensions that harassment created, it is not surprising that so many women felt they were under siege in the workplace.

The career prospects of female Mounties were particularly dependent on the goodwill of their NCOs who assessed their job performance. Consequently, keeping an NCO happy became essential if future opportunities to work in specialized fields such as forensics or plainclothes investigative work were to be realized. The annual performance evaluation system was the measuring stick used by the RCMP to determine the future career of every police officer. While performance ratings measured individual capability, they also had the potential for abuse. If female Mounties challenged abusive treatment, if their supervisors did not like the idea of women in the RCMP, or if women refused sexual advances from NCOs, they received lower marks on their performance evaluations, rendering them less competitive for advancement.[20]

The RCMP's performance evaluation system also influenced whether male police officers who witnessed a female Mountie being harassed spoke out about the abuse. They too were subject to retaliation by an unhappy NCO. Shelly Evans recalled that although she usually had the sympathy of her male peers, "They knew enough and they evaluated it enough to say, 'I can't step in and up for her, protect her, you know, show solidarity with her because then he'll turn on me.'" The sympathy of male colleagues only went so far.[21] The performance evaluation system was a powerful tool that bought the silence of anyone who was thinking of exposing the behaviour of an abusive NCO.

AFFIRMATIVE ACTION

The hiring of female Mounties was seen by many men in the RCMP as a politically correct initiative that was forced on the RCMP by the federal government in response to the demands being made by Canadian feminists. But employment equity policies were not just a political

20   Denise Bell, interview with author, April 19, 2008.

21   Shelly Evans, interview with author, July 30, 2008.

manoeuvre necessary to placate a vocal minority group. They were one way to ensure that the RCMP was more representative of the communities it policed.[22] The implementation of affirmative action policies was not a new practice in Canada. Similar programs dated back to World War II, when returning male war veterans were given preferential treatment for work in the public service as a gesture of gratitude by the Canadian government. Private industry also fired the women who had been working during the war to make room for returning servicemen. And when Prime Minister Pierre Trudeau initiated a policy to increase the number of francophone Canadians in the federal public service, he established an affirmative action program that promoted biculturalism.[23]

Legal scholars credit affirmative action initiatives as the "best known systemic remedy" to discriminatory treatment within organizations.[24] The RCMP implemented affirmative action initiatives because it believed that the attrition rates for women would decline if women were offered opportunities for advancement in sections that had traditionally remained closed to them. But some of the RCMP's commanding officers were still lukewarm to the policy. On June 25, 1986, D/Commr. T.S. Venner, in a memorandum to the commissioner, wrote:

> We seem to be always trying to rationalize our Recruiting/deployment of Female members up against urgent Federal government Affirmative Action programmes aimed at the employment of more women in the Public Service, equal pay for work of equal value, increases in the number of women at senior management levels, etc. That is all well and good; these are laudable objectives. But we must not lose sight of the unique role of the RCMP within that government framework and the simple fact that because of the nature of police duties it may never be possible to move as fast or as far as it is for other departments. I think

---

22 Solicitor General of Canada, "Women in Policing: Myths & Realities," (1993), RCMP file GM 448-36. Access to Information file GA-3951-3-03134/08.

23 Chabursky, "The Employment Equity Act," 321.

24 Ibid.

it is time we accepted that and defended it instead of hiding from and denying it.[25]

Venner's frustration over the timely implementation of affirmative action policies revealed that the highest levels of the RCMP continued to view police work as a masculine endeavour. His reasoning that the "nature of police duties" and the "unique role" of the RCMP made for slow progress spoke volumes about the RCMP's reluctance to fully integrate women into every aspect of police work.

Perhaps the deputy commissioner's exasperation was because he was already aware that women were resigning from the RCMP at double the rate of male Mounties. Years later, a Solicitor General's audit of the success rate of the RCMP's employment equity program between 1974 and 1985 found that of the 617 women who joined the RCMP, 43 percent left compared to 24 percent of the 5,149 men who joined during the same period.[26] The RCMP's affirmative action initiatives were effectively stalled by the time Venner was writing his memorandum. Although affirmative action created space for new opportunities for those women who stayed in the police force, harassment continued to disrupt the full integration of female Mounties. The RCMP remained focused on increasing the number of women being hired and on offering advancement opportunities to those who remained, rather than critically reviewing the structural processes that contributed to the steady stream of resignations.

Female RCMP officers resisted affirmative action policies, too, albeit for different reasons. Pam Osborne recalled that Commissioner Norman Inkster spoke to her troop at Depot in 1987, just before they graduated. The commissioner announced that female Mounties would be allowed to apply for positions as instructors at Depot for the first time in RCMP history. The positions were advertised within the RCMP as open only to women. It was a policy that was viewed as discriminatory toward male police officers and it was highly controversial within the police force at the time. Male members saw it

---

25   D/Commr. T.S. Venner to the Commr., memorandum, June 25, 1986. Author copy.

26   Solicitor General of Canada, "Women in Policing: Myths & Realities" (1993), RCMP file GM 448-36. Access to Information file GA-3951-3-03134/08.

as reverse discrimination. They were so incensed that a fund of more than seventeen thousand dollars was raised by members from across the country who sought a court injunction against the commissioner's plan.[27] Osborne and her troopmates had heard about the controversy and challenged the commissioner regarding the new policy: "We said, basically, thank you for making our lives worse because you've just re-iterated that women need special consideration" to get ahead. Osborne and her troopmates rightly believed that women should receive pro-motions based on their merit rather than their gender.[28] They failed to consider, however, that there were certain sections in the force at the time that remained closed to women no matter their seniority or merit. Further, the reality in the RCMP was that no matter how hard women worked or what their achievements were, they were still viewed as needing the assistance of men when it came to police work.

As women advanced up the chain of command within the RCMP, those who eventually received commissions often faced accusations of tokenism and preferential treatment. These women took exception to the argument that they were promoted because of their gender. Lou-ise Ferguson, who eventually received a commission during her long career with the RCMP, commented:

> I think it's one of the worst things we can do to one
> another, that affirmative-action stuff. Because we
> deserve these kinds of jobs and if you still continue
> to look for women in roles, then you take away their
> ability to totally own each one of those achievements
> they've had. Even at this stage of the game, I work hard.
> There are people that, I know when I meet them, they
> believe I'm the token female ... That bugs me because
> I don't think that's true. I worked really hard and I did
> good stuff, and still continue to do good stuff. I'm not say-
> ing I'm better than anyone else, but I'm totally qualified.

---

27   *The Windsor Star* (Ontario), "Mounties Adding Female Trainers," March 25, 1988. The plan called for the hiring of seven women at the rank of corporal to be instructors at the academy. At the time there were ninety instructors working at De-pot, none of which were female. *Windsor Star*, "Hiring Plan Angers Mounties," April 6, 1988.

28   Pam Osborne, interview with author, October 28, 2006.

I really resist pushing for employment equity and all of these things.[29]

For female Mounties, affirmative action was seen as a detriment because male police officers assumed that all women needed the initiatives to advance their careers. It was a critique that eliminated the agency of the women and minimized their achievements. Despite the successes of female Mounties, many men continued to view affirmative action as facilitating the promotion of unqualified women who were taking positions away from men. Affirmative action only reinforced arguments of difference rather than equality within police culture.

THE BATTLE FOR SURVIVAL

The slow implementation of employment equity policies in the 1970s and 1980s did little to help female Mounties in the field who were attempting to cope with the attitudes of their supervisors. Cherise Marchand's example is a case in point. Marchand, a French Canadian who did not have the benefit of language training following her time at Depot, was the first woman posted to a mid-sized detachment in an English-speaking community in the late 1970s.[30] The first few years were difficult for Marchand, who had to learn English in addition to adjusting to her new community and police work. Marchand recalled being told even before she entered the detachment that the supervisor did not want a female Mountie, let alone a French Canadian, working for him. Marchand had difficulty writing reports in English but she did not receive training to relieve the administrative problems she was having. Instead, her supervisor "took the red pen and just circled things they didn't like and shipped it back for me to rewrite it, without any guidance."[31]

After eight months, Marchand's NCO was transferred and a new supervisor arrived. He too harassed Marchand. She remembered that after a while, everything she did displeased him. If there was one

---

29   Louise Ferguson, interview with author, November 9, 2006.

30   It was not until after 1978 that French Canadians were sent to Ottawa for English-language instruction following Depot and prior to being posted to predominantly English-speaking communities.

31   Cherise Marchand, interview with author, October 15, 2008.

page number missing from a report, he would telephone her at home to come back to the detachment to fix it. At the time, Marchand was working twelve-hour shifts. She remembered, "I'd get home at 7:00 [a.m.] ... by the time I'd get to bed, probably 8:00, 8:30, well they'd call me at 9:00. Call me back to the office right there and then to put a page number when the other ones were numbered. I mean, if it was on the bottom right corner and it was on the top or something, that's not where they wanted it." She eventually learned that her supervisor was complaining about her work to commanding officers at subdivision headquarters. Her language barrier was being used to justify complaints about her inability to handle even the most routine police tasks. After four years of constant harassment, a male constable finally confided to Marchand, "You don't deserve this and I won't do anything to help them. But just so you know, they're out there to get you."[32] He was wary of retaliation from the NCO and the potential damage to his career if he advocated on her behalf.

Events suddenly took a fortuitous turn for Marchand just as she was on the verge of resigning. When investigators at subdivision headquarters required a French-speaking police officer to help them solve a major crime, Marchand was temporarily assigned to work on the investigation. According to Marchand, her NCO initially thought that officers at subdivision "would see that I was not worth anything and they would can me." After a month's time, however, she was still working on the file and there was no indication that her firing was imminent. The detachment NCO became impatient and wrote to commanding officers at subdivision, stating that Marchand should be fired. He claimed that she did not follow orders when he asked her to write traffic tickets. He insisted that she only wrote two tickets over an extended period of time, and since she was not much good for any other type of police work, she should lose her job.[33]

When officers at subdivision asked Marchand if the accusations about her work standards were true and whether she could disprove her NCO's claims, she took action. Marchand returned to her detachment that weekend when the NCO was not in the office. She opened the detachment's files and made copies of every single ticket she had

---

32   Ibid.

33   Ibid.

issued since being assigned to traffic duties. When Marchand produced the photocopies of almost two hundred tickets the following Monday, the commanding officer at subdivision arranged for an immediate personnel interview for her. By Friday of that week she was transferred to another detachment. For Marchand, the transfer was a "lifesaver."[34] Once again, however, the RCMP's solution was to move the victim rather than discipline the offending supervisor. Further, the commanding officers only believed Marchand's claims after she was able to prove that her NCO was lying. It was evidence of the strength of the paramilitary rank structure within the organization: the NCO did not suffer any consequences as a result of his behaviour toward Marchand and he remained at the detachment, where he continued to abuse junior police officers, male and female, for years afterward.

Abusive behaviour in the workplace included the use of verbal threats, focusing on negative aspects of work performance, setting up a person to fail, lying to an employee, manipulating or controlling an employee, making non-legitimate work requests, teasing, ridiculing, and name-calling, all of which are considered forms of harassment.[35] Based on this list, it is evident that Marchand was exposed to high levels of harassment. However, she was able to hang on and fight the pressure to resign. Today, she is still a member of the RCMP, a testament to her inner strength and determination to stick with the job under extremely adverse circumstances. She currently holds the rank of staff sergeant, an NCO.

Female Mounties had varying experiences in the workplace due to regional differences. Women stationed in small towns on the prairies often experienced a greater degree of discrimination and harassment than those who worked in larger urban centres. Cultural and social factors sometimes contributed to this treatment. For example, since the prairies were the site of the arrival of the first NWMP officers in 1874, the arrival of female Mounties disrupted the area's pride in its historical connection to the police force, which was still viewed as an iconic institution responsible for the taming of the west.[36] Not only

---

34   Ibid.

35   Andrews, *Stress in Women Police*, 6.

36   Hewitt, *Riding to the Rescue*, 4–7.

did smaller detachments have fewer women, but geographical space meant that the women were often separated by distance. Lorraine Gibson recognized these differences after she was transferred from a large urban area in British Columbia to a small detachment in Alberta. It was the first time she noticed that some female Mounties were not getting a lot of support. "I'd go to a call and they'd almost cling to me ... Like they were very supportive, wanted to hang out with you. I never realized how spoiled we were" at the larger centre where greater numbers of female members were stationed.[37]

It is little wonder that some female Mounties felt that they were in the midst of a battle for survival. Other women were forced to contend with similar situations. For example, Allison Palmer, a member of Troop 17, recalled that one supervisor would not talk to her during the entire first six months she was posted at the detachment. Several years later, Palmer had the opportunity to ask her former NCO why he hadn't spoken to her. He responded, "I couldn't, because if I paid attention to you, the guys would have got upset."[38] Although Palmer accepted his explanation, the refusal to speak to a junior female officer for extended periods of time illustrates the lengths some NCOs went to make female Mounties feel ostracized in the workplace. Palmer also worked with another supervisor who once questioned her about what she would do if she had to go to the bathroom while out on patrol. The implication was that since bathrooms were not always available in isolated locations, she would be unable to function while on duty. Palmer replied, "Squatter's rights!" to make the point that she did not necessarily need a bathroom.[39] The fact that the question was asked at all illustrates how male officers assumed that female biology made them poor police officers.

Palmer also endured continuous name-calling from her supervisor at her second posting. He persisted in calling her "Grandma" because her hair was starting to turn grey, even though she was still in her early thirties. Although younger constables sometimes called her "Mom" because she was older than they were, the NCO's demeaning

---

37   Lorraine Gibson, interview with author, May 16, 2008.

38   Allison Palmer, interview with author, June 11, 2008.

39   Ibid.

tone of voice, his continuous name-calling, and the fact that he did not refer to male members who were greying as "Grandpa" adversely affected Palmer. Further, she felt that she could not complain about the harassment because her supervisor was friendly with the commanding officer. Palmer turned to the DSRR, whom she asked to advocate on her behalf and help resolve the situation. But nothing came of her meetings with the representative, who found his own efforts were blocked because the NCO "had too many connections." She finally sought the advice of a psychologist, who helped her understand that the source of her stress was her supervisor's attitude toward women in policing.[40]

Palmer was not alone at this posting; in all, there were ten members, male and female, who transferred out of this detachment because of the NCO's harassment of junior police officers. It was an example of the power politics that enabled some supervisors to exert complete control over the men and women under their supervision. Further, commanding officers also worked to block complaints, probably in an effort to stem accusations about the failure of their own command. Since harassment was made possible by the hierarchical rank structure of the RCMP, few female Mounties expected the organization to defend or respect their workplace rights. Most of the women developed their own coping strategies to overcome the discrimination they were experiencing.

Supervisors' gendered attitudes toward female police officers were common in other Canadian police departments, demonstrating that the association of masculinity with police work was widespread. Municipal police officer Liz Davies recalled that her staff sergeant was "bound and determined" to get her to resign. She remembered that the detachment "had a coffee room downstairs, the constables' coffee room. The staff sergeant wouldn't let me in it. At first, when I was first hired, that was okay. I'd go down there, have my lunch, have my coffee. Then he decided, that's it, I wasn't gonna go in there anymore ... and I wasn't allowed to cross the threshold. Eventually, he had to give in because the union found out about this and they said, 'You know, you can't do this sort of thing.'" Although the union officially intervened on her behalf, the staff sergeant found alternative ways to pressure Davies. She recalled, "It was disgraceful, what they would do to me.

---

40   Ibid.

I don't know how, to this day, if I wasn't such a strong person, I wouldn't have been able to put up with it."[41]

The mayor of the city finally stepped in when he heard about the problems Davies was experiencing with her supervisor. He immediately took Davies over to his office, which was in the same building, and swore her in as a full-fledged constable after only five months of service, instead of waiting until the end of her six-month probationary period. Whether this mayor was an advocate for women's rights or whether his concern for Davies was motivated by paternalism is unclear. Nevertheless, he chose to make a positive statement regarding women in policing in his municipality by intervening on Davies's behalf in a very official and public way.

Of course, not all NCOs in the RCMP opposed the presence of women, and many adopted a paternalistic attitude toward those who were under their command. Several female Mounties recalled these men as very supportive and protective of them. Louise Ferguson's first staff sergeant was "an old dyed-in-the-wool, wonderful guy" who called her into his office just before she went to work her first graveyard shift. She had just eight months of service and he was nervous about her working alone. At the time, members of the RCMP did not carry portable radios while on patrol, contributing to the NCO's anxiety. He asked her if she was frightened. When she said "No!" he replied, "It scares the hell outta me!" He advised her not to be a hero and reminded her that "there isn't a guy here that wouldn't call for backup if they needed it. So don't think you're any different and don't be afraid to call for some help if you need it. If you can't get anybody else, you call me."[42] His words gave Ferguson confidence as a police officer and she felt accepted as a member of the RCMP.

Marianne Robson also remembered her first NCO and her male peers as "very, very protective because they didn't want me to get hurt ... I can say that throughout my whole career." Robson elaborated by saying that this was because "I kept my nose to the grindstone, I did what I was supposed to be doing, didn't raise a big fuss ... I just did my

---

41   Liz Davies, interview with author, July 17, 2008.

42   Louise Ferguson, interview with author, November 9, 2006.

job and kept my nose clean. Didn't try to raise any kind of issues."[43] Robson's comment, although a positive endorsement of the men she worked with, is revealing. She recognized that there was a professional cost for women who raised issues and questioned procedures. Her reluctance to create a "fuss" suggests that there was an unspoken understanding between her and her male colleagues that resulted in a more positive work experience for her, one that was paid for with her silence.

As women gained seniority in the RCMP, they eventually accessed NCO ranks. The first woman was promoted to the rank of corporal in 1981.[44] Shelly Evans was wary of her first female NCO because she did not have a "good reputation. The guys were always mumbling about her, this and that." Ironically, when the female NCO heard that Evans was being assigned to her watch, "She didn't want me either. She said, 'I don't want any more girls on my watch. One's enough, and it's me.'"[45] The response of both women to working with each other reveals the extent to which women sometimes adopted the gendered attitudes espoused by their male counterparts. But to their mutual surprise, their working relationship "just clicked." Not only did Evans gain the trust and support of her female NCO, but she learned something about her own attitudes toward women in the RCMP. According to Evans:

> Part of the reason why [the female NCO] had this bad reputation is because she wouldn't put up with crap. And I realized, I thought, here it is late in my career ... and I've just learned this lesson that I am part of the perpetuation of these stereotypes, not stereotypes, these labels. Oh, everybody says, "She's a disaster as a corporal. Can't believe she got the rank." ... [A]nd then you go there and you realize she's a damn good NCO. She's the first one to say, "I don't really know all the aspects of the job, so if I don't know something, then I'm

---

43   Marianne Robson, interview with author, July 29, 2008.

44   "First Female Milestones," http://www.rcmp-grc.gc.ca/rrecruiting-recrutement/fem/hist-eng.html (accessed March 21, 2012, now defunct).

45   Shelly Evans, interview with author, July 30, 2008.

gonna ask." She was an excellent people person. She's a manager. That's what an NCO should be.[46]

Evans was surprised to learn the degree to which female Mounties bought into ideas about the abilities of women in the RCMP. Despite their initial wariness, Evans and her NCO became friends. They are still friends today.

For the most part, female Mounties were unprepared for the level of opposition that characterized their daily working lives. Male supervisors did not wait for the women to prove themselves as police officers but began to exert pressure on them as soon as they arrived at their postings. Their tactics suggest that their opposition had more to do with gendered beliefs about women in policing than with the abilities of women to do the work. Many NCOs did not hesitate to capitalize on the power differentials they enjoyed to oppose women in the RCMP, and they emerged as the chief conveyors of discrimination. The consistency between accounts of harassment suggests that a culture of masculinity, rather than women's incompetency, was at the root of their difficulty in integrating. Nowhere was this more evident than when sexual harassment was used as a method of control.

---

46   Shelly Evans, interview with author, July 30, 2008.

SEXUAL HARASSMENT

Somewhere along the line, someone forgot to tell us in training that it wasn't the public we had to worry about; it was our own members we had to fear. If more of us knew then that we would not be greeted with "open arms" perhaps we'd have been more prepared.

—Female RCMP Officer
Anonymous Survey Respondent, 1986

The harassment of female Mounties took many forms in the RCMP, but the most common and pervasive form was sexual harassment. Power and control, and not sexual desire, were the prime motivations behind the sexual harassment of women in the RCMP. Sexual harassment neutralized the power and effectiveness of female Mounties, and it was the most effective means of forcing a woman's resignation in the 1970s and 1980s. When women were treated as sexual objects rather than professional colleagues, it drew attention to their biological difference from men and called into question their authority as police officers.

As with other forms of harassment, NCOs engaged in sexual harassment because they held considerable power over the junior officers under their command. But men from the lower ranks also sexually harassed female Mounties, through the use of crude jokes, sexually explicit comments, derogatory insults, and the display of pornography in the workplace. Sexual assault, sexual advances, and sexual touching also occurred. Commanding officers were complicit in perpetuating the problem through their failure to deal with women's complaints. As the RCMP's own studies demonstrated, the number of female Mounties who experienced sexual harassment was high. Yet commanding officers persisted in their refusal to see it as a systemic problem, offering other reasons for the high attrition rates of women such as marriage and motherhood.

Women were often punished by their peers for complaining to higher-ranking officers about the sexual harassment they received. And offenders were seldom held to account for their actions, which is why the RCMP's complaint system failed the police officers it was designed to protect. It was a no-win situation for female members who were told that harassment was simply a part of working in a male-dominated occupation. These tactics effectively silenced female Mounties, who resorted to their own informal coping methods, some verbal and others physical, when dealing with the men who sexually harassed them.

FEMALE SEXUALITY AND MALE MOUNTIES

Since female Mounties were still a novelty in the 1970s, their personal lives were constantly under scrutiny from both their colleagues and members of the public. In Canada, women who crossed the boundaries of appropriate feminine behaviour, by working in a male-dominated occupation, for example, were usually labelled as sexually immoral. A woman's sexuality was still seen as unpredictable, and women were viewed as irrational beings, especially during menstruation. Many in the RCMP understood women and their role in society in similar ways. As a result, female Mounties were often the subject of widespread gossip and speculation about their sexuality. "Female members must be more aware of their acquaintances. There is still a double standard in society today and no matter what the Charter of Rights states, female members will not be accepted by all male members," cautioned one survey respondent.[1]

Gossip was a powerful method of control that was used by men in the RCMP to discredit female Mounties. Those women who engaged in sexual relations with corporals at Depot, for example, put their reputations at risk even before they arrived at their first postings. According to Margaret Watson, "if you slept with one of the instructors at Depot, you might as well quit. Your reputation would already be out there. If there is one thing about male policemen, I would say that they are vicious gossips. The woman would be labelled a slut

---

1   Stark, *The Role of Female Constables*, 128–29.

for the rest of her service," a sexual double standard that excused the sexually provocative behaviour of the instructors, most of whom were married.[2]

Rumours about female recruits who were sleeping with male recruits quickly spread around Depot, too, and instructors were complicit in propagating the gossip. One incident in particular illustrates how corporals took the initiative to publicly shame female recruits who were sexually active. Jane Hall recalled a troopmate who was singled out for sleeping with her recruit boyfriend in an interview techniques class in 1977. During a role-play session following the lecture, the female recruit was selected to be the suspect and the instructor acted as the interrogator. He began his questioning by asking the woman how she spent her weekend. According to Hall, "We watched in shock as the instructor, who clearly knew every detail of her romantic escapade with a recruit boyfriend, reduced her to tears. Every detail of the weekend was exposed in what seemed like an endless and sadistic performance ... All the rest of us could do was to learn at the expense of my troopmate."[3] While it is unclear whether the woman's Mountie boyfriend was also publicly shamed, the message to the women in Hall's troop was clear: female Mounties had to control their sexuality.

A number of women interviewed for this study commented that they were concerned about their reputations once they began work in the field. As Pam Osborne explained, "Your reputation is everything in the RCMP and it goes places you have never been. Everybody knows everybody ... If you're a screw-up as a female, you're a lot more out there than if you're a screw-up as a guy."[4] Marianne Robson quickly learned that the men at her detachment loved to gossip too, and she was very careful about whom she associated with during her non-working hours. Robson recognized that if she wanted to keep her job, maintaining "a good reputation was part and parcel of that."[5] Leslie Clark was exasperated when she found that the sexual double standard was

---

2   Margaret Watson, interview with author, February 25, 2008.

3   Hall, *The Red Wall*, 54–55.

4   Pam Osborne, interview with author, October 28, 2006.

5   Marianne Robson, interview with author, July 29, 2008.

still in operation when she started work in the field in 1987. It was not something that she wanted to waste her time thinking about, but it was an issue that she was forced to consider. She remembered, "In the early days, women had to be careful. So I was careful. I didn't want to be branded a slut. So that was a bit of a pain. I mean, you know, god, I have to think about *this*?"[6] Similarly, Shelly Evans, who was hired in 1988, found that women were held to a higher moral standard than male police officers. Evans commented that the personal lives of single female members were more intensely scrutinized than those of male members. If a woman refused to "put out" when propositioned by a male member, she was branded as gay. At the same time, "If you did put out you were a slut ... Male member sleeps around, he's a man. Not the same for female members, who had to be way more careful and discreet."[7] It was a no-win situation for female Mounties.

As for dating civilian men in their communities, female Mounties often experienced tensions in trying to establish relationships. Their activities were monitored by their co-workers and by civilians. According to one study, meeting friends outside of police circles was almost impossible for those women who were posted to isolated or rural detachments.[8] One female Mountie commented, "In a small town everyone knows you. Females must really watch their reputation. It's OK for guys, not for the female."[9] Supervisors also noticed that women policing in small communities were required to be more circumspect in their personal lives because rumours travelled fast when a female Mountie was involved.[10] Allison Palmer concurred, recalling how quickly word spread when she dated a man from the small community she policed. Her date took her to the local bar: "Oh, god, the next day we were getting married ... and that was the first time we went out. We went out and had a drink."[11] Palmer's experience demonstrates that civilians often monitored

---

6   Leslie Clark, interview with author, October 9, 2008.

7   Shelly Evans, interview with author, July 30, 2008.

8   Linden and Minch, *Women in Policing*, 112.

9   Stark, *The Role of Female Constables*, 127.

10   Ibid., 129.

11   Allison Palmer, interview with author, June 11, 2008.

the off-duty activities of female Mounties, too. All of the attention was like "living in a fishbowl" in communities where female Mounties were still a novelty.[12]

Police work itself often interfered with Palmer's relationships with men. Shift work, long investigations, emergencies, and unpredictable hours, not to mention Palmer's love for the work, made it difficult for men to stay interested in pursuing a relationship with her. She explained that she would make plans to go to dinner or a dance only to have to cancel them later on so she could continue to work on a file. "Well, after a while people don't appreciate me not being available and so it was sort of a habit. As soon as you'd make big plans, there was always an investigation that came up. I didn't want to let go. Whether I maybe could have in some cases, maybe I could have. But, I mean, I worked forty-eight hours straight on one incident."[13] Palmer, who remained single throughout her long career, made a conscious decision to prioritize her work over dating or marriage.

THE LESBIAN MOUNTIE

The women of the RCMP were also monitored for heterosexual behaviour during a time when homosexuality was still considered a threat to state security. During the Cold War years, the image of the Mountie as a morally incorruptible agent of the state became extremely important as the police force began to monitor the sexual orientation of federal civil servants. Homosexuals who worked in the civil service were considered national security risks because they presumably feared the public exposure of their sexual orientation, making them susceptible to blackmail by foreign spies interested in obtaining government secrets. Between 1961 and 1962, the RCMP had identified 850 civil servants as suspected or confirmed homosexuals.[14] By 1967, the force had expanded their mandate beyond the civil service, compiling an index that contained over eight thousand names of Canadians

---

12   Stark, *The Role of Female Constables*, 126.

13   Allison Palmer, interview with author, June 11, 2008.

14   Gerry Kinsman and Patrizia Gentile, *The Canadian War on Queers: National Security as Sexual Regulation* (Vancouver: UBC Press, 2010), 4.

suspected of being homosexual.[15] The RCMP's investigations resulted in the firing of hundreds of people from their civil service jobs.

The project of regulating the sexuality of federal civil servants was massive in scope, and the RCMP's Security Service sought a quicker way of identifying homosexuals.[16] Psychological research being conducted by Carleton University professor Frank Wake in 1961 captured the RCMP's interest. Wake was developing a detecting device, dubbed the "fruit machine" by the RCMP, whereby suspected homosexuals were shown a series of hetero- and homoerotic pictures.[17] Their eye movements in response to the pictures were recorded to detect signs of sexual deviancy and determine their sexual orientation.[18] Between thirty and thirty-five people were actually tested on the machine by Wake, but with mixed findings. As a result, the fruit machine project folded in 1963 and it was never used in any official capacity by the RCMP.[19] The failure of the fruit machine did not deter the RCMP from its project of identifying homosexuals, however, and the police force had the full support of the federal government.[20] According to Prime Minister Pierre Elliot Trudeau, in a statement made in the House of Commons in 1973, homosexuals remained a security risk and would continue to be denied security clearances as federal employees.[21]

The fact that the RCMP was charged with regulating the sexual

---

15   Fewer than three thousand of the people on that list were actually working as civil servants. Reg Whitaker, Gregory S. Kealey, and Andrew Parnaby, *Secret Service: Political Policing in Canada From the Fenians to Fortress America* (Toronto: University of Toronto Press, 2012), 191. Also in Daniel J. Robinson and David Kimmel, "The Queer Career of Homosexual Security Vetting in Cold War Canada," *Canadian Historical Review* 75, no. 3 (1994): 320–21.

16   Kinsman and Gentile, *The Canadian War on Queers*, 167–69.

17   CBC, "RCMP Uses 'Fruit Machine' to Detect Gays," http://www.cbc.ca/archives/entry/rcmp-uses-fruit-machine-to-detect-gays.

18   Kinsman and Gentile, *The Canadian War on Queers*, 180–81.

19   Ibid., 188.

20   Gary Kinsman, "Constructing Gay Men and Lesbians as National Security Risks, 1950–70," *Whose National Security?: Canadian State Surveillance and the Creation of Enemies*, eds. Gary Kinsman, Dieter K. Buse, and Mercedes Steedman (Toronto: Between the Lines, 2000), 143–44.

21   Kinsman and Gentile, *The Canadian War on Queers*, 222.

morality of Canadians through the enforcement of laws governing sexual behaviour required that Mounties appear morally upright to ensure public trust and promote compliance. Marianne Robson remembered that in the 1970s, the possibility that a homosexual was employed by the RCMP was simply not discussed. It was assumed that there were no gay men, or later women, in the police force.[22] It is not surprising, then, that gay men and women working as Mounties concealed their sexual orientation from their colleagues during those years. Indeed, Margaret Watson commented that although there were three lesbians in her troop at Depot in 1977, it was not something she discovered until years later.[23]

The possibility that homosexuality existed within policing ranks remained a cause for concern. Sometimes male police officers became suspicious of a woman's sexual orientation if she developed a close friendship with another woman. Trish O'Brien discovered this firsthand after rumours began to circulate about her friendship with a woman she worked with at one posting:

> Rumour got out that we were gay. I didn't have a boyfriend and ... I think she might have been separated from her husband ... Anyway, at first we sort of laughed it off. But then it really started to get annoying. Jeez, if you can't have a friend, what business is it of theirs anyway? And I'm going back to the seventies now, the whole outlook on that was different than it is today. Then it was like, oh my god, people are gonna say that? Back then ... it was even used as blackmail at one time. I remember them [the RCMP] saying if you were involved in anything like that you were subject to blackmail.

The two women finally approached the NCO to complain about the gossip that was going around the office. Then one day, at the end of a detachment meeting, the NCO announced to everyone present, "Oh, and by the way, before we leave, someone's spreading the rumour

---

22   Marianne Robson, interview with author, July 29, 2008.

23   Margaret Watson, interview with author, February 25, 2008.

that Trish and Shirley are lesbians." O'Brien remembered being devastated by the NCO's actions because being gay in the RCMP was such a "big thing" in the 1970s.[24] Rather than confronting the gossips, the NCO chose to exert his power and control over the women by shaming them in front of their peers. The fact that the issue had to be addressed at all was a profoundly upsetting experience for O'Brien, even as she recalled it years later.

Women, like their male colleagues, were not above employing gossip to discourage the idea that all female Mounties were gay because they chose to work in a male-dominated occupation. Leslie Clark, who was in an all-female troop at Depot in 1987, remembered that one troopmate was suspected of being a lesbian and that it did cause some turmoil within the troop. The fact that the woman's sexual orientation was unclear was an issue for some because the woman's pit partner was heterosexual.[25] "But it was more like some people had this conspiracy theory that she was trying to convert [her pit partner]," said Clark. Although the gay member was not out at the time, speculation amongst the women about her orientation continued.[26] Their response suggests that the troop was eager to appear normal to stem gossip that the entire troop was gay.

It was not long before lesbian Mounties were resigning from the RCMP because they were being harassed for their sexual orientation. Kate Morton, who joined the RCMP in 1977, was gay but was not out when she went through training in Depot. According to her, there were at least three women in her troop who were gay: "In our troop it wasn't something anybody talked about. So I had no idea if anybody else in the troop knew ... Maybe some people did, but it wasn't anything that anyone discussed. It didn't seem to bother anybody. It wasn't like anybody was out. None of us were out." After Morton was posted to a rural detachment in eastern Canada in 1984, she began to experience harassment in the form of multiple transfers around the area. At the

---

24   Trish O'Brien, interview with author, November 13, 2008.

25   Some of the dormitories at Depot at the time were large rooms that housed an entire troop of thirty-two recruits. The space was divided up into groupings of two. Two recruits shared a clothes cupboard and desk area that was situated between their beds. This space was colloquially referred to as "the pit."

26   Leslie Clark, interview with author, October 9, 2008.

time, Morton was openly living with a woman, and rumours and gossip about their relationship were circulating around the detachment. Morton suspected that the transfers had a lot to do with her sexual orientation:

> I think that [being gay] was probably one of the reasons ... because it was after I decided that I was leaving, one of my buddies came and he said, "I'll be honest. There's this rumour going around, you know, we're here to support you, so you don't have to leave." I said, "No, I've already made up my mind. I'm going. I've had enough." ... But they weren't going to obviously force the issue [with me] because at least to that extent, you know, there's going to be a human rights issue here so we're not going to frig around with her. But, um, there was no exit interview. There was nothing like that.[27]

Morton's failure to embrace heterosexual norms clearly singled her out for harassment. In her case, commanding officers used their rank and the transfer system to wield their power over her career and pressure her to resign. They refused to openly acknowledge her sexual orientation or to even discuss it with her through an exit interview. Morton, who was relieved to leave the RCMP, did not pursue litigation against the police force.

SEXUAL HARASSMENT

Sexual harassment as a method of control was commonplace in most western police forces as a growing number of women entered the profession in the 1970s. Indeed, it was common in many male-dominated industries at the time, so much so that in 1978, Constance Backhouse and Leah Cohen conducted path-breaking research on the issue. Using a number of case studies to describe the range of behaviour that constituted sexual harassment, they defined it as "any repeated and unwanted sexual comments, looks, suggestions or physical contact that you find objectionable or offensive and causes you discomfort on the

---

27   Kate Morton, interview with author, February 26, 2008.

job."[28] They concluded that sexual harassment was not an expression of sexual desire but an assertion of power "expressed in a physical manner."[29]

It was not long afterwards that sexual harassment as a discriminatory act in the workplace began to be recognized by provincial and federal human rights tribunals in Canada. The first significant legal challenge in the development of sexual harassment case law took place in 1980 in Ontario and was adjudicated by a board of inquiry charged with enforcing the Ontario Human Rights Code. In *Bell v. The Flaming Steer Steakhouse*, Bell, one of two complainants in the case, alleged that the respondent had "subjected her to gender-based insults and taunting and propositioned her." Bell alleged that she had been fired for her failure to comply. However, the board of inquiry could not find proof that Bell had been discharged because she refused the sexual advances of her employer and dismissed the case.[30] Although Bell lost her case, the board's adjudicator did find that sexual harassment by an employer could amount to sex discrimination when it was found to be a condition of employment, opening the door for the development of case law on the issue.

In July 1983, the *Canadian Human Rights Act* was amended to include sexual harassment as "discrimination on the ground of sex."[31] The Canadian Human Rights Commission described sexual harassment as including verbal abuse or threats, unwelcome remarks, jokes, innuendos, or taunting; displaying of pornographic or other offensive or derogatory pictures; practical jokes which cause awkwardness or embarrassment; unwelcome invitations or requests, whether indirect or explicit or intimidation; leering or other gestures; unnecessary physical contact such as touching, patting, pinching, punching; or physical assault.[32] Sexual harassment was ruled as discriminatory

---

28   Constance Backhouse and Leah Cohen, *The Secret Oppression: Sexual Harassment of Working Women* (Toronto: Macmillan of Canada, 1978), 38.

29   Ibid., 42.

30   Deborah Ann Campbell, *The Evolution of Sexual Harassment Case Law in Canada* (Kingston: Industrial Relations Centre, Queen's University, 1992), 10.

31   Canadian Human Rights Commission, *Sexual Harassment Casebook, 1978-1984* (Ottawa, ON: Canadian Human Rights Commission, 1984), overleaf.

32   Campbell, *The Evolution of Sexual Harassment Case Law*, 10.

because it detrimentally affected the work environment and constituted a barrier to the employment of women.[33]

Since the Canadian Human Rights Act was not changed to include sexual harassment until 1983, female Mounties were working for the RCMP for nine years before they gained the legal grounds to contest sexual harassment through external avenues. In the 1970s and 1980s, the human rights of both male and female police officers were not generally regarded as a legitimate concern for the RCMP's commanding officers. When asked about the receptiveness of the RCMP to concepts of individual rights in the workplace, Marianne Robson laughed at the suggestion. In those days, the issue was just not addressed. Robson cited the RCMP's paramilitary background as one reason rights were not even on commanding officers' radar. "I mean, you had no rights. You were the property of the Mounted Police, almost," said Robson. She characterized the police force as a closed community where members were expected to do their job, keep their mouths shut, and not to ask questions.[34]

In the absence of case law and human rights codes in the 1970s, sexual harassment quickly became a systemic problem in the RCMP. All of the female RCMP officers who were interviewed for this research were subjected to some form of sexual harassment at some point in their careers, although one was reluctant to characterize it as such.[35] More recent studies have shown that while 50 to 58 percent of women in the broader workforce experienced some form of sexual harassment, the rate for women working in non-traditional occupations such as policing and firefighting was higher, at 69 to 77 percent. Further, women working in policing were less likely to identify harassing behaviours as such, even though they were more likely to be sexually harassed than women working in other occupations.[36]

---

33   Chabursky, "The Employment Equity Act," 353. At the time, the sexual harassment of men in the workplace was not a consideration and case law applied only to complaints made by women.

34   Marianne Robson, interview with author, July 29, 2008.

35   Louise Ferguson, interview with author, November 9, 2006.

36   Penny E. Harrington and Kimberly A. Lonsway, *Investigating Sexual Harassment in Law Enforcement and Nontraditional Fields for Women* (Upper Saddle River, NJ: Pearson/Prentice Hall, 2007), 11.

Lindsay Galloway's experience serves as an example of how sexual harassment could adversely affect a woman's career as a police officer. Galloway was twenty-three years old when she graduated from Depot in 1977. Her first posting was to a small city detachment in western Canada. There were other female RCMP officers working at the detachment at the time, and she recalled that members of the community, as well as her peers, respected her and were supportive of women in the RCMP. Galloway noticed, however, that higher-ranking older male officers working at the detachment thought that women did not belong in the RCMP. According to Galloway, "They were old-school and they didn't think that women were strong enough or big enough; they couldn't handle themselves in a bar fight, they would be afraid, the usual clichés about women not being tough enough."[37] Despite this opposition, Galloway did well on her watch, enjoyed the work, and was proud of her service as a Mountie.

That changed dramatically with the arrival of a new NCO, who was placed in charge of her watch. It was not long before the NCO began to sexually harass her. Within half an hour of the start of every graveyard shift (midnight to 8:00 a.m.), the NCO would call Galloway back to the detachment. He would get in the police cruiser with her and ride with her for the duration of her shift. Galloway described being in the police cruiser with the NCO in this way:

> I would be driving. Now he would do this every night. Every graveyard shift, he would do this. And he would say, "You know, if you're friendly, if you're good to me, I can help your career." And he would say, "Let's drive out to my place for coffee." ... He would actually say, "Don't answer any calls [on the police radio]. Don't take calls." It was awful ... I thought, if you even touch me, I swear I'm gonna kill you. And he didn't touch me. He knew I was revolted by him.[38]

Galloway reported the harassment to the OIC of the detachment, describing the unwanted advances being made by the NCO and the

---

37   Lindsay Galloway, interview with author, February 25, 2008.

38   Ibid.

fact that she no longer wanted to work with him. The OIC thought that the NCO was "just being friendly" and suggested that she was overreacting. Since she liked her OIC and respected his opinions, she decided that if she went outside of the detachment with her complaints, she would not be believed, or worse, she would be fired. Galloway approached other members of her watch, complaining about the NCO's advances: "I could see they were afraid because he was their supervisor too, and they were afraid that … if they intervened or went to him, that he would give them a bad assessment."[39]

Galloway, who says she became more and more depressed, continued to refuse the NCO's advances. Her worst fears materialized on the day that she received her annual performance evaluation. The NCO gave her a poor assessment, as promised. "And I quit, on the spot, that day. That would have been '79. I quit. I had been in two years. But that was my reason for quitting … I thought … I'm stuck with him, no one's gonna help me, and I was profoundly depressed at the time … I think they all thought that because he didn't touch me, I was overreacting. But it was really insidious." Galloway stated that in hindsight she did not have the right tools or information about the issue. She believed that she did the right thing by complaining to superior officers.[40] When her complaints were ignored, she felt she had few options but to resign.

Galloway's willingness to report the harassment to her commanding officers was unusual. Most of the sexual harassment in the RCMP in the 1970s and 1980s went unreported. "You didn't go and report [human rights violations] in 1975," explained Carolyn Harper. "Number one, you're battling a whole pile of things, including the fact that you're a woman in the force. You're trying to gain respect. The last thing you wanted to do was walk into a supervisor's door and start crying on his shoulder" and risk being labelled a complainer or a whiner.[41] Even after sexual harassment legislation came into being and the RCMP was moving toward instituting a zero-tolerance policy, female Mounties continued to employ a number of informal strategies to cope with the issue on their own. It was proof, according to two

---

39   Ibid.

40   Ibid.

41   Carolyn Harper, interview with author, June 28, 2010.

researchers studying women in the RCMP, that the RCMP's official policies and complaint mechanisms were a failure.[42]

COPING STRATEGIES

The coping strategies that female Mounties adopted were varied. Some women were not averse to employing physical force. One male Mountie remembered an incident when a woman on his watch responded violently to an inappropriate sexual comment a male colleague had made to her. She "turned around and cold-cocked him. He hit the floor flat on his back with his feet going. He was out. She was tough enough that she could do that. But it delivered a very strong message to the individual who shot his mouth off."[43] This female Mountie clearly adopted a masculine performance strategy to deal with harassing behaviour.

The use of physical force against a male member of the RCMP was unusual, however, and most female Mounties adopted strategies that were similar to the alternative approaches they utilized on the street when dealing with male civilians. Some were creative and utilized humour to defuse the unwanted sexual attention. Trish O'Brien recounted how a female friend once used humour to rebuff a sexual advance from her trainer, who carried a contraceptive in his wallet. One night when they were on patrol, he took the contraceptive out of his wallet and said to her "Look, I've got this French safe." "My god, that's been in your wallet there so long I can see the print in the leather!" she said. "So she shut him up," recalled O'Brien.[44]

Female Mounties also feigned ignorance when subjected to sexual advances. This was O'Brien's strategy during her first serious encounter with sexual harassment. She recalled being on patrol one night with a married man who held a more senior rank. He drove up to a cemetery where he parked the car and said, "You know, if we ever ... if we had sex here now, no one in the world would ever know about it." O'Brien remembered changing the topic and pretending not to understand what he was implying. She was very upset by this encounter, commenting

---

42   Kathryn Fitzgerald and Mike Clark, *Equality in Policing: A Focus on Gender at Burnaby Detachment of the RCMP*, undergraduate research paper, Simon Fraser University (April 5, 1994), 35.

43   Bill Jones, interview with author, October 3, 2011.

44   Trish O'Brien, telephone interview with author, November 13, 2008.

that the man was a well-respected, nice guy, and that "everybody liked him. And just the thought that he would try to take advantage like that, it really hurt me. And that lasted in my mind ... If I talk about it now I can relive that minute. It's almost like I got deceived by a friend."[45] Rather than complaining to commanding officers, she stayed silent, protecting the man whom everyone liked and respected at the detachment. Whether she decided no one would believe her, or whether she feared retaliation, was unclear. What was clear was her shock at being propositioned by a colleague whom she trusted. For O'Brien, it was not the actual harassment but the sense of betrayal that made the event a traumatic experience.

What did male Mounties think of their colleagues who engaged in sexual harassment? Many claimed that they did not see it taking place. According to Bill Jones, an NCO at the time women were first being admitted to the RCMP, "I didn't have direct knowledge because I'm the kind of guy that would have done something about it. But I did hear lots of stories."[46] Similarly, Cameron Montgomery, who was a commissioned officer in the 1970s and 1980s, did not directly witness sexual harassment but was "sure that it happened."[47] From these responses, it appears that rank sometimes played a role in concealing sexual harassment. In Jones's case, harassing behaviour was not likely to happen while he was present since he had the inclination, as well as the power, to take punitive action against anyone harassing a female co-worker. And senior officers like Montgomery were so far removed from the field that they did not witness it or have to deal with it directly.[48]

Darryl Butler, a commissioned officer who was stationed at an urban detachment, did act on complaints about sexual harassment when he received them from women under his command. Butler stated, "If you don't listen and do something you're crazy. Anybody that's in a supervisory position of some sort, if somebody comes to you and says, 'This is

---

45 Ibid.

46 Bill Jones, interview with author, October 3, 2011.

47 Cameron Montgomery, interview with author, May 24, 2007.

48 Researchers have found that men who sexually harass will only do so in certain situations, such as workplaces that tolerate the practice and in other places where those who sexually harass are not held accountable. Harrington and Lonsway, *Investigating Sexual Harassment in Law Enforcement*, 60.

going on,' you've got to do something. You cannot turn a blind eye to it."[49] He recollected specific situations when he counselled supervisors who were harassing junior women. He remembered seeing "staff sergeants, watch commanders, coming on to young female constables on their watch." Even after their advances were rebuffed, these men continued their harassing behaviour. He warned them that they were in danger of receiving a harassment complaint if they did not stop the practice.[50]

Further complicating the issue was the fact that some female Mounties were not above capitalizing on the issue in an attempt to garner preferential treatment. According to Butler, "Then of course ... if you're addressing performance issues and somebody's not performing as they should be, then all of a sudden that becomes harassment." Butler remembered dealing with situations in which supervisors were accused of harassment by junior female police officers because they did not like the performance evaluation that they received.[51] In those instances, the women in question contributed to gender-based antagonism within the RCMP and fostered group blame.

Many of the men who engaged in harassing behaviour were married, lending credence to wives' fears that the arrival of women in the RCMP posed a threat to their marriages. Cherise Marchand remembered being dropped off at home following a shift one morning by her sergeant who wanted to come into the house with her. When Marchand reminded him that he was married and she was dating someone, he encouraged her not to let those factors get in the way of what he wanted. She told him "What I think also matters. I don't want to have anything to do with you. Just leave me alone." Marchand did not file any type of harassment complaint against the NCO at the time. "Well, today I would. In those days, I was told I couldn't. There was nothing I could do," she remembered. Marchand was told by senior ranking officers at the detachment that "they had more important things to do than listen to me" and that she should just roll with the punches if she wanted to work in a man's world.[52]

---

49   Darryl Butler, interview with author, September 11, 2008.

50   Ibid.

51   Ibid.

52   Cherise Marchand, interview with author, October 15, 2008.

Male Mounties sometimes assumed female police officers would welcome their sexual advances. Marianne Robson recalled that at her first posting in 1975, the sexual advances she received were plentiful. She remembered that male members would show up at her apartment:

> Married members and single members. And I'd tell them to get lost. I think they thought it was their right. I made it clear it was not their right. Actually, I remember being at a promotion party ... probably one of my first ones I was at, and a fella from a neighbouring detachment ... he came up to me and grabbed my ass. I said, "Don't you ever put your fucking hands on me again." That was his right ... There were tons of advances.[53]

There is research that shows that the potential for a romantic relationship was one reason married men sexually harassed younger women in the workplace.[54] However, researchers have also learned that most cases of sexual harassment are not "to gain sexual favours" but are an attempt to humiliate or subordinate women, and to remind them they are not wanted in the workplace.[55] This was most likely the case for Robson. While she may have thought that her male co-workers viewed sex with her as their "right," there was more at play than an interest in a sexual relationship with her. Given the number of men who made advances toward her at this detachment, the issue was one of power and the exercise of masculine aggression toward a young woman.

JOKES, PORN, AND INAPPROPRIATE TOUCHING

Sexual harassment took many forms in the RCMP, but the most common were crude comments and sexual jokes. Trish O'Brien recalled that there were lots of sexist jokes and bad language being used. "Depending on the personality, we knew some of the members were pigs.

---

53   Marianne Robson, interview with author, July 29, 2008.

54   William E. Foote and Jane Goodman-Delahunty, *Evaluating Sexual Harassment: Psychological, Social, and Legal Considerations in Forensic Examinations* (Washington, DC: American Psychological Association, 2005), 117.

55   Harrington and Lonsway, "Investigating Sexual Harassment," 5.

And you just take them with a grain of salt, you know, the language and the comments," she said.[56] Shelly Evans commented that female Mounties often had to decide how much they were willing to tolerate. For Evans, "there always seemed to be that line and people definitely knew when they crossed it."[57] According to the authors of one study of the RCMP, a majority of the female respondents agreed with the statement that "office-room banter is sometimes offensive to female police officers." When male police officers were asked the same question, responses were equally divided between agreement and disagreement. These findings not only suggest that women found office banter more offensive, but that at least half of the male respondents knew it was offensive but engaged in the practice anyway. The authors also found that the male respondents disagreed that sexual harassment was commonplace in the RCMP.[58] Differences between male and female perceptions of what constituted sexual harassment clearly existed.

Janice Murdoch decided to file a formal complaint against one particular supervisor who had made derogatory comments about her at a public gathering where high-ranking commanding officers were present. She described the incident in this way:

> [H]e made a comment about my physical appearance and loud enough that everybody could hear ... The other police officers that I knew around me, they all joked and thought it was funny. I thought, you know, if I stood up and said, "Fuck you, you're an idiot!" then I would have been chastised. So I was in a position where he got away with it ... The people that were around me, they could have an effect on my career. They could be my next bosses ... So I was really backed in a corner ... He was being investigated for something else at the time of a sexual nature and he knew [that] I knew [about it]. And I think it was a way of keeping me in my place.[59]

---

56 Trish O'Brien, telephone interview with author, November 13, 2008.

57 Shelly Evans, interview with author, July 30, 2008.

58 Fitzgerald and Clark, *Equality in Policing*, 14–15.

59 Janice Murdoch, interview with author, April 17, 2008.

Murdoch remained silent at the time in the interests of her future career, filing a harassment complaint afterwards. But the derogatory comments about her body were one way this NCO drew attention to the unsuitability of women as police officers. They were also meant to remind Murdoch that she was excluded from the camaraderie that was taking place between the men at the social function.

Apart from sexist jokes and crude remarks, sexual harassment took more obvious physical forms. Shelly Evans recounted two instances of being sexually harassed by a co-worker. Although she attempted to handle the harassment on her own by challenging the man's behaviour, he persisted. On one occasion he slapped her "right on the ass in front of a prisoner." When she challenged him, she said that "he was just totally mystified why that would be a problem for me." He repeated the same behaviour on another occasion when he said to Evans, "'Yeah, I got this complaint where this woman is alleging that this guy did this,' which involved him again grabbing my butt." Public shaming was a powerful means of control for this man, who employed it a third time with Evans:

> We're at a detachment curling bonspiel ... My parents were there watching 'cause they lived close by. He was curling on the team with the detachment commander and he comes off the ice and I'm standing there, and he ends up putting his [curling] broom up between my legs and goosing me. And I turned around and shoved him, and I knocked him over two garbage pails and said, "Stop touching me!" And everybody was almost like, "Wow, I can't believe that you reacted that way." So, I mean, it's ignored. So you gotta deal with a lot of it yourself.[60]

Given that the men of the RCMP understood that female Mounties were trained in the use of force, it is somewhat surprising that they did not anticipate a physical response to harassing behaviour. The response of Evans's colleagues illustrates that the men who were present did not view inappropriate touching as meriting the level of

---

60   Shelly Evans, interview with author, July 30, 2008.

violence that Evans meted out. The incident confirms that many male police officers tended to downplay the significance of sexually aggressive physical contact, viewing it as natural behaviour toward women.

Male RCMP officers also used references to menstruation as a form of sexual harassment. Marianne Robson recalled working with a woman who arrived at her detachment six months after Robson. This woman experienced a level of sexual harassment that Robson described as "horrible." She remembered that there was one man in particular who "would leave Kotex pads in her [mail] slot at work." Robson counselled her female colleague to try not to react to his harassing tactics. But "everybody knew it was going on. I mean everybody, right up to the officers. They knew it was going on. Everybody thought it was a big joke. Right? But then it was only the two of us and again, if you start creating waves and ripples, I mean the force is a big, big organization."[61] Because the detachment's commanding officers and NCOs were cognizant of the harassment, and complicit in allowing it to continue, this female police officer had little recourse but to resign after a year and a half of service. Robson was very aware that if she chose to make waves and complain on behalf of her female colleague, she could also expect retaliation. Her experience illustrates how by harassing one woman, the men at this detachment effectively silenced both.

Menstruation figured prominently in arguments made by commanding officers in other jurisdictions as a central reason for excluding women from policing. In Philadelphia, Pennsylvania, in 1976, for example, the city's police commissioner stated in a deposition in a discrimination suit against the department that, due to "periods in their life when they are psychologically unbalanced because of physical problems that are occurring within them," women were unsuitable as police officers.[62] The argument that menstruation rendered women incapable of rational thought was grounded in social convention rather than scientific data. It was also adopted by the men of the RCMP as an informal means of resisting the presence of women, as Robson's example illustrates.

---

61   Marianne Robson, interview with author, July 29, 2008.

62   Joseph F. O'Neill, quoted in "Despite Some Gains, Female Cops Still Find Too Few Cracks in the Glass Ceiling," *Law Enforcement News* 26 (June 2000): 9.

Pornography was another form of sexual harassment that female Mounties experienced. Male Mounties used viewing pornography to reinforce heterosexuality as normative in police culture and masculinity as the dominant identity for police officers. In contrast, many women found pornographic photographs and videos of nude women or women engaged in sexual acts offensive and insulting—especially if they appeared in the workplace. This was due, in part, to a growing awareness of sexual harassment in Canadian society as women's rights activists "protested the sexual objectification and exploitation of women."[63] Yet in the RCMP, an environment where heterosexuality was valued as an expression of manliness, viewing pornography in the workplace was considered normative behaviour.

Leslie Clark recalled pornography on display at one posting where *Playboy* posters and nude calendars were visible in the squad room. "It was mostly personal calendars on someone's desk but of course, back then, we'd share desks," stated Clark. Although the images were not blatantly positioned, they were nonetheless there and noticeable to Clark. Sometimes, female Mounties were subjected to mindless insensitivity rather than overtly sexual harassment. The same could not be said for the time a hard-core pornographic film was being shown in the same squad room one night. Between fifteen and twenty men were watching the film, according to Clark, who "just didn't think it was appropriate to have, and you know, this is full-blown. This is not fake and [the actors are] going at it type of thing. And everyone is just sort of sitting around watching it." Clark wrestled with how she should react, whether to leave or stay. "At the time I didn't feel comfortable in going up and turning off the television set." Clark left the squad room instead.[64] While she found the film offensive, she feared retaliation if she vocalized her displeasure by turning the video off. In the end, it was the fear of being ostracized that silenced her.

The sexual objectification of women by male Mounties extended to female civilians as well. In particular, the men of the RCMP's Musical Ride participated in a sexualized ritual that reinforced their masculinity. Kate Morton was one of the first women selected to join the Musi-

---

63   Carrie N. Baker, *The Women's Movement Against Sexual Harassment* (New York: Cambridge University Press, 2008), 177.

64   Leslie Clark, interview with author, October 9, 2008.

cal Ride in 1980. But Morton turned the position down after hearing rumours about what went on during the Ride's national and international tours. She recalled learning that the men of the Musical Ride liked to hold "lawnmower competitions." The competition involved two members of the Ride who worked together to engage with a local woman from the community they were visiting. One Mountie would attempt to interest her in him romantically. A second Mountie would then try to steal her away from the first Mountie, or attempt to "mow" his grass. The competition was won if the second Mountie successfully stole the woman away from the first Mountie and engaged her in a sexual encounter. For Morton, rumours about lawnmower competitions were an ominous sign that she would be "given a rough time as a female" member of the Ride. She took the rumours so seriously that she decided to withdraw her application and stay in her current posting.[65]

CIVILIANS, FEMALE MOUNTIES, AND SEXUAL HARASSMENT

The women of the RCMP were also subjected to sexual harassment from male civilians who viewed female police officers as sexually transgressive and open to sexual overtures. Janet Porter's first visit to a prison took place in 1975, when she was a recruit just out of training. Porter, who was just nineteen at the time, responded with her partner to a call at a nearby penitentiary. Porter recollected, "That was a memorable experience. My partner and I went in and he said, 'You stay close to me.' And of course, all the guys came out of their prison cells. It was two storeys. And they were making all these rude noises. And, uh, that was scary. They were all looking at me like I was a piece of meat."[66] It was probable that the inmates had never seen a female Mountie before. To them, Porter was still a woman and fair game for sexual harassment, even though she was wearing a police uniform.

Pam Osborne experienced an especially graphic encounter with

---

65   Kate Morton, interview with author, February 26, 2008. In 2013, S/Sgt. Caroline O'Farrell filed a multi-million-dollar lawsuit against the RCMP for more than "100 substantiated incidents of assault or abuse that occurred" while she was a member of the Musical Ride in the 1980s. Andrew Seymour, "Mountie Sues RCMP, Senior Officers Over Alleged Abuse While She Was on Musical Ride Team," *Ottawa Citizen*, May 21, 2013.

66   Janet Porter, interview with author, October 20, 2008.

a member of the public. Osborne remembered receiving sexual comments "all the time from the public" and she was sometimes asked out on dates by the men she was arresting. She recalled one incident when she was booking a man she had just arrested into the cells at the detachment. "He showed me a picture of his brand new girlfriend, except it was her exposed vagina that was in the picture. But that was more for shock ... If I was shocked, then it was kind of like they won." Male civilians often retaliated for being placed under arrest by a woman by sexually harassing them.

Osborne recalled being harassed on another occasion when an older male prisoner taunted her sexually following his arrest. When she was booking him into the cells, the man began to grope himself. "A sixty-five-year-old grandfather groping himself, stripping in front of me, you know, flopping around, his penis in his hands, trying to whatever. Then he had the nerve to turn around and lay a complaint against me for the way he'd been handled [during the arrest]," said Osborne. The man claimed that he did not know why he was being placed under arrest, a serious violation of his rights. Fortunately for Osborne, male guards and sheriffs were also present in the cellblock and were witnesses to the man's behaviour. When her NCO was later contacted by the man's lawyer, "We responded to his lawyer that 'This was the circumstance. This was how his client was behaving. And by the way, did we mention that Cst. Osborne is a female?'" The complaint against Osborne was suddenly dropped.[67]

Members of the legal profession were not above sexually harassing female police officers either. Lawyers also relied on understandings of women working in a male-dominated organization as transgressive in efforts to manipulate them. Leslie Clark recalled one lawyer who attempted to have charges against his client dropped by appealing to what he perceived to be Clark's inability to control her natural sexual urges. Clark was investigating his client for passport fraud. She remembered that the "lawyer called up and he totally tried to schmooze me. It was disgusting. He was dripping. He was so obsequious ... What he said was ... 'You know, my client is a very handsome man and I'm sure if you saw him, this would all be dealt with' ... Implying that I would look at him and swoon and things would be done with."[68] The lawyer's effort

---

67   Pam Osborne, interview with author, October 28, 2006.

68   Leslie Clark, interview with author, October 9, 2008.

to proposition Clark on behalf of his client was an attempt to cloud her judgment and withdraw the investigation.

Some female police officers experienced a more serious form of sexual harassment: sexual assault. Female RCMP officers tended to handle sexual assaults in the same way they dealt with sexual harassment; most did not report the incident. Carolyn Harper was aware of one sexual assault of a female Mountie by a co-worker. "I know of a sexual assault. But that person never went forward ... And then when it did come out later on, [she] totally denied it. Like [she] just didn't want to have anything to do with it and still totally denied the fact that it happened." According to Harper, the male Mountie involved also denied that a sexual assault had taken place. The female police officer eventually resigned over the issue. Harper speculated that women in the RCMP resisted reporting a sexual assault for the same reasons female civilians refused to lodge a sexual assault complaint: they did not want others to know about the assault for fear of retaliation, or because they feared having their private lives opened to public scrutiny.[69]

THE PROBLEM EXPOSED

The extent of the sexual harassment of female Mounties was finally exposed in 1986, when the *Province* broke a story about rampant sexual harassment and sexism in the RCMP. Six female Mounties from British Columbia detachments made the claim that sexual harassment was the reason they and other female police officers were resigning in unprecedented numbers, at a rate that was five times higher than that of men.[70] According to Jane Hall, the article in the *Province* originated with some off-the-record comments made to a journalist during a social gathering.[71] The women subsequently agreed to be interviewed by the journalist on the condition that they, and their detachments, remain anonymous. The Canadian Press picked up the story, which garnered national and international attention:

---

69   Carolyn Harper, interview with author, June 28, 2010. Sherry Lee Benson-Podolchuk, in an autobiographical account of her tenure as an RCMP officer, described being sexually assaulted by a male Mountie while stationed in Selkirk, Manitoba, in 1993. See Sherry Lee Benson-Podolchuk, *Women Not Wanted* (Winnipeg, MB: Hignell Book Printing, 2007).

70   "Minister Wants Investigation," *Regina Leader-Post*, January 21, 1986.

71   Hall, *The Red Wall*, 238.

> [The women] told a Vancouver newspaper last week of
> corporals and sergeants who tried to coerce them into
> bed or played crude sex jokes on them. "I've had male
> members park outside my house so they could tell ev-
> erybody who I was dating and who stayed overnight"
> said one woman ... "I got tired of being propositioned
> by senior officers who thought you were a lesbian if
> you didn't or a slut if you did," said another woman in
> her late 20s. She quit the force after five years ... "When
> I complained, I was told I had an attitude problem."
> Wives of male officers made life difficult for a third
> policewoman until she got married. "The wives were
> unbelievable," said the woman, now 27. "They were
> all convinced you were sleeping with their husband.
> Some of the men even told their wives that to get more
> attention." ... RCMP records show that between Janu-
> ary, 1983 and January, 1985 the force hired 69 women.
> But during the same two-year span it lost 68 out of a
> total 458 women through resignations.[72]

The next day, Canada's Solicitor General Perrin Beatty issued a statement to the media. Beatty emphasized that the federal government would "not tolerate sexual harassment within the RCMP" and ordered Commissioner Robert Simmonds to investigate the claims made by the women in British Columbia.[73] The commissioner convened a hastily organized meeting of female Mounties in Burnaby and sent his representative from Ottawa to report back to him on the outcome. In addition to a discussion about sexual harassment, the female Mounties who were present also raised issues such as unpaid leave for family reasons and job-sharing. They also complained about the female uniform, particularly the pillbox hat and the regulation preventing women from wearing the same uniform as male officers, specifically

---

72   "Women Members of the RCMP Claim Sexual Harassment and Sexism," *Regina Leader-Post*, January 20, 1986. Also see "Across Canada Female Mounties Say Sexism is Rife," *Globe and Mail*, January 20, 1986; "Mounties Accused of Sexual Harassment," *Times* (London), January 21, 1986.

73   "Beatty Orders Probe of Sexism Charges by Female Mounties," *Globe and Mail*, January 21, 1986; "Minister Wants Investigation," *Regina Leader-Post*, January 21, 1986.

breeches and boots.[74] The women were fighting for equal rights as members of the RCMP across the board and were not just interested in resolving the issue of sexual harassment.

Despite the government's promises of swift action, however, sexual harassment continued in the RCMP. Alice Clark was "hounded, abused, and harassed" by her RCMP colleagues and supervisors at the detachment in Red Deer, Alberta, between 1981 and 1987. Clark, who was frequently referred to as a "bitch" and a "meter maid," was grabbed one day by a male police officer, who kissed her in the office. "He told me to call him when my husband was away if I wanted a real man." She also recalled male officers viewing pornographic videos at the office, despite protests from Clark and the other women working at the detachment. She resigned in 1987, and in 1993 she sued the RCMP for discrimination.[75]

The RCMP, perhaps sensing the possibility of future litigation problems, finally began to take notice of female attrition rates. As one media report quipped, "The Mounties may always get their man, it's the women they're having trouble with." A few months following the initial complaints made in British Columbia, the police force began to conduct audits of their policies and practices concerning female recruitment. The authors of one audit relied on RCMP statistics of women who had resigned from the police force between 1975 and 1985. They determined that 43 percent of women had resigned, compared with 24 percent of men who had joined the RCMP during the same period.[76]

Despite the concerns voiced by the women at the meeting in Burnaby, the problem of attrition was attributed to recruiting problems and the inability of women to meet physical fitness standards, rather than sexual harassment or discrimination. The report's authors claimed that "many women leave because they're more interested in raising a family while men quit out of job frustration."[77] The auditors sidestepped the issue of sexual harassment altogether. In fairness

---

74   Hall, *The Red Wall*, 237–38.

75   Alice Clark, quoted in Kerry Segrave, *Policewomen: A History* (London: McFarland & Company, 1995), 170.

76   "Female Mounties Quit at Twice the Rate of Men: Audit of the Force's Employment Equity Program Shows that Nearly Half of Female Applicants Fail Fitness Test," *Globe and Mail*, August 12, 1996.

77   Ibid.

to the auditors, they did recommend that the RCMP actually ask the women who were resigning for their reasons for doing so. However, this common-sense suggestion was "squashed by senior management unsure of the validity of the results or what reactions the question would evoke."[78] The persistent refusal of the police force's commanding officers to acknowledge or address the problem internally contributed to its systemic growth.

The RCMP was clearly aware that sexual harassment was a growing problem, evidenced by the number of internal studies that were under way by the 1990s. In 1996, the *Calgary Herald* obtained an RCMP study under the government's *Access to Information Act*. In that review, six out of ten female Mounties surveyed admitted to experiencing some form of sexual harassment on the job.[79] The public exposure of the extent of sexual harassment within the RCMP by the *Calgary Herald* pushed the police force to warn its members of a potential public backlash. In a pre-emptive strike against the news story that was scheduled to break on September 27, the RCMP's director of personnel, Asst. Commr. Dave Cleveland, issued a broadcast to all members of the RCMP on September 23 warning of "events that will unfold in the media over the next few days and weeks" regarding the issue. Cleveland assured members of the RCMP across Canada that the police force was taking measures to address sexual harassment, including "mandatory harassment awareness training courses for all employees and a review of the RCMP's transfer policy." He also announced that the RCMP had voluntarily entered into an employment equity agreement with the Canadian Human Rights Commission and was committed to ensuring that 32 percent of the cadets entering Regina for training were women.[80]

---

78   Ibid.

79   "Female RCMP Officers Sexually Harassed at Work: Six Out of 10 Surveyed Were Affected, Internal Study Says," *Globe and Mail*, September 27, 1996.

80   A/Commr. Dave Cleveland, "National Broadcast," September 23, 1996. Access to Information file GA-3951-3-03134/08. The RCMP honoured its commitment to hire more women; 32 percent of the cadets undergoing training in Regina in 1995–1996 were women. Corsianos, *Policing and Gendered Justice*, 34.

Whether or not the RCMP followed through on its promise to introduce mandatory harassment awareness training for all of its employees is unclear. What is known is that the sexual harassment of female Mounties continued.[81] Commanding officers' desire to protect the image of the RCMP as a Canadian icon contributed to the problem's persistence. By the time that Cleveland had broadcast his assurances, sexual harassment had become exceptionally effective in pressuring female Mounties to resign. Sexual harassment contributed to a toxic work environment for many of the women who were resigning from the RCMP in record numbers.

---

81   Four female RCMP officers sued the RCMP after being sexually assaulted by Sgt. Robert Blundell in Calgary between 1994 and 1997. The RCMP reached a settlement with the women out of court, and Blundell and the female police officers remained with the RCMP. See Joe Friesen and Andy Hoffman, "RCMP Reaches Settlement Over Sex-Assault Allegations," *Globe and Mail*, August 4, 2004.

VIRDEN, MANITOBA, 1978

I hesitated to shoot Archer because I'm human, not because I'm a
woman. But for the longest time I couldn't shake the feeling that I
kind of let my gender down.

—Candace Smith
RCMP Officer

onstable Candace Smith was a rookie police officer, just six weeks
out of training at the RCMP's academy in Regina, when she became
the first woman in the RCMP to be shot in the line of duty. Smith's
ordeal began in Virden, Manitoba, a small town located near the Saskatchewan border along the Trans-Canada Highway. Known as the
oil capital of Manitoba after its first successful oil well was drilled in
1951, Virden was also a popular nighttime stopping point for travel-
lers making their way across the country by car. From highway patrols
to checks of the community's businesses and hotels, keeping the peace
and enforcing the law as people passed through their community was
the responsibility of Virden's Mounties.

In the early morning hours of January 23, 1978, Constable Dennis Onofrey began a routine check of the vehicles in the parking lot of
Virden's Countryside Inn. His licence plate check revealed that a rental
van parked in front of room 20 was overdue from a company in Vancouver, British Columbia. He further learned that the man who had
rented the vehicle, Herbert Bruce Archer, and his companion Dorothy Lillian Malette, were wanted in connection with a series of violent
crimes in Vancouver and Calgary. Onofrey radioed to the three other
police officers on duty with him that night, requesting their assistance in questioning Archer and Malette at the motel. Corporal Russell Hornseth, who was in charge of the watch, and both members of
Virden's highway patrol, Constable John O'Ray and Constable Candace

Smith, responded. Smith and O'Ray served as backup for Hornseth and Onofrey, who approached the door of room 20.

When Hornseth knocked on the door, the lights inside the room went on and then off. In response, Onofrey drew his revolver and pointed it at the door. Hornseth called to the room's occupants several times, ordering them to open the door and step outside. When the door finally opened, Herbert Archer stood in the doorway with his right arm concealed behind the door frame. Archer noticed that Onofrey had assumed the combat firing position and that his service revolver was drawn and pointed at Malette inside the room. Suddenly, Archer stepped forward, raised the 20-gauge shotgun he held in his right hand, and fired at Onofrey, who was eight feet away. The shotgun blast hit the police officer directly in the chest, killing him instantly.

Chaos ensued as Hornseth ran for cover, shouting a warning to Smith and O'Ray, who also sought cover. Archer continued to fire, hitting Hornseth on the left side of his face and injuring his left eye. Despite his injury, Hornseth found cover behind one of the police cruisers and began to return Archer's fire. O'Ray ran for the cover of a house adjacent to the motel's parking lot, and Smith took cover behind a ten-inch-wide decorative abutment along the motel wall, just metres away from the door of room 20.

As Archer continued to fire, Hornseth, his eye bleeding profusely, and O'Ray managed to escape the gunfire and meet on the frontage road just north of the motel. Hornseth and O'Ray were unsure of the whereabouts or status of their colleagues. In 1978, members of the RCMP in Virden were not equipped with portable radios, and their only means of communication was via the radios in their police cruisers. Given that all four officers were out of their vehicles, Hornseth and O'Ray were unaware that Onofrey was dead. Both believed Smith to be safe, although neither knew exactly where she was. Hornseth directed O'Ray to return to the motel and keep Archer pinned inside the room and under fire until the detachment could send help. He then went to the nearby hospital for medical attention.

Smith remained pinned against the motel wall by Archer's gunfire. She did not realize that she was alone and without backup. Although she could see Onofrey's feet near Archer's van from her crouched position, she too did not realize that he was dead. The shooting finally stopped and things grew quiet. Smith was confused, wondering why the others had stopped shooting. She peered around the abutment to see Archer standing in the doorway with his back to her, looking around. He was unaware that she was there. Smith shouted, "Drop it!" and pointed her gun at him and fired, missing Archer as he ducked back into the room.

Archer, now aware of Smith's presence, began to fire along the hotel wall in her direction. Shotgun pellets hit Smith in the upper thigh and groin area, knocking her to the ground. In pain but still conscious, Smith continued to point her revolver at the door of room 20, pinning Archer inside by firing twice more when he reappeared. Archer then fired a .308 rifle out the door. The shot ricocheted off a downspout and tore into Smith's thigh before entering her abdomen. Smith stopped shooting and she began to lose consciousness. When the gunfire stopped, Archer left the safety of his room and checked Smith to see if she was dead. He took her service revolver from her hand. He then checked Onofrey's body, also removing the service revolver from his hand. The entire shooting had taken ten minutes.[1] Witnesses later described the gun battle as if a war was going on.

Archer and Malette fled the Countryside Inn, escaping in Hornseth's police cruiser. O'Ray, who by this time had returned to the scene, fired at the fleeing couple, wounding Malette in the ribs. O'Ray spotted Smith lying in front of the motel. She was unresponsive when he called her name. He also noticed Onofrey lying on the motel sidewalk. He radioed to the detachment, informing them of the shooting and the direction in which the escape vehicle was headed. He also reported that two officers were down and needed an ambulance. O'Ray gave chase to the fleeing Archer and Malette, but his cruiser was so damaged from the gunfire that he was forced to return to the Countryside Inn.

Archer and Malette travelled along the Trans-Canada Highway as far as the tiny community of Oak Lake, Manitoba, located one hour east of Virden. There, Archer embarked on a ninety-six-hour hostage taking in which three people, including the town's doctor, Markus Scherz, were taken captive. The RCMP's hostage negotiators were called in and the media descended on the small town. Recognizing that Malette

---

1   Many of the details of the Virden shooting related here were derived from the research of Robert Knuckle. See Robert Knuckle, *In the Line of Duty: The Honour Roll of the RCMP Since 1873* (Burnstown, Ontario: General Store Publishing, 1994), 385–86; Knuckle, *Beyond Reason*, 144–55.

required medical attention, and upon learning that the doctor was unable to treat her without hospitalization, Archer eventually released Malette following an agreement with hostage negotiators. Malette was taken to the hospital in Brandon, Manitoba. Archer finally gave himself up after hearing that she was alive and would survive her injuries. The hostages were released uninjured after their five-day ordeal.

Back at the Countryside Inn, Smith regained consciousness and, in intense pain and unaware that Archer and Malette had fled, began to drag herself along the sidewalk toward the safety of the motel's registration office. It was there that O'Ray found her. He put her in the back of his police cruiser and took her to the Virden hospital. Smith's injuries were life-threatening. She was later transferred by ambulance to the hospital in Brandon where Malette was also being treated. Smith's wounds were so serious that the doctors feared that she would not survive the lengthy ambulance trip to the larger trauma centre in Winnipeg. She underwent eight hours of surgery and spent six weeks in intensive care followed by three months of recovery in the hospital.

Following her surgery, Smith was placed in the bed next to the recovering Dorothy Malette in the Brandon hospital. Medical staff at the hospital were challenged by the task of treating two shooting victims at the same time. The decision to place Smith next to Malette, with only a curtain separating the two women, was made in the interests of efficient medical care. It was a decision that, as troopmate Jane Hall later recalled, prolonged "the psychological siege which had begun [for Smith] days earlier." Hall recognized that Smith needed psychological counselling to help her cope with the trauma. She broached the subject with the RCMP officer in charge of the investigation, who responded, "I spoke to her and I think she is handling it very well. She earned her spurs."[2] The commanding officer's dismissive attitude regarding Smith's psychological state reflected attitudes that were commonplace in many North American police departments at the time. Emotional detachment was often equated with professionalism in policing, and the RCMP simply assumed that its members did not require psychological help. The RCMP was also keen to downplay the physical and psychological dangers that the Mounties at Virden faced because they were inadequately armed and poorly equipped.

---

2   Hall, *The Red Wall*, 79.

It is not surprising, then, that the RCMP played a pivotal role in Smith's psychological stress following the shooting. To begin with, Smith, unlike the male officers who were involved with the shooting, was never debriefed about the crime because she was still in the hospital at the time. The only interview that RCMP investigators conducted with her lasted for ten minutes and took place while she was in intensive care. According to Smith, "They took a two-paragraph statement while I was drugged." Following her release from hospital, Smith was never interviewed about the shooting or given a chance to make an official statement. In fact, Smith was not aware of many of the details of the shooting but "picked them up here and there from comments made by others and during the trial and outside of the courtroom. I never knew the whole story."[3] Smith was left to piece together the events for herself.

Trauma counselling, a standard practice for police departments today, was not available for the members of the Virden detachment following Onofrey's murder. According to Smith, receiving counselling was considered a sign of mental weakness in the 1970s and "if you sought help from a psychologist, members [of the RCMP] wouldn't even want to work with you."[4] Seeking psychological help raised questions about whether or not a police officer was mentally capable of carrying out police duties. As a result, Smith did not seek professional counselling on her own initiative or push the issue with the RCMP. She loved police work and fully intended to return to active police duty as soon as she was physically capable of doing so.

The shooting at the Countryside Inn, and the ensuing hostage taking, was the focus of intensive national and international media coverage. Smith in particular received considerable attention as the first female Mountie to be shot in the line of duty. Canadians were emotionally moved by the attempted murder of Smith, who received cards, poems, letters, and flowers from people across the country. There were so many flowers that nurses distributed them throughout the hospital. So widespread was the media coverage that prosecutors and defence lawyers had difficulty in selecting jurors for Archer's trial. Seventy-three potential jurors were dismissed after admitting bias

---

3 Candace Smith, interview with author, April 19, 2008.

4 Ibid.

against the accused "on the basis of information they had heard or read on the case in the news media." Eventually, twelve jurors were selected and a date set for the trial.

The trial of Archer and Malette for the first-degree murder of Dennis Onofrey began on November 14, 1978, and Smith testified the next day. Journalists covering the trial reported that when Archer exited the motel room with his back to her, Smith had difficulty shooting him. For example, Brian Cole of the *Winnipeg Free Press* reported the following in the early edition of the newspaper:

> An RCMP constable, who had had only six weeks' field experience, testified Tuesday she had difficulty bringing herself to shoot at a man holding a shotgun during a gun battle last January at a Virden, Man., motel. With a quavering voice and appearing to fight back tears, Const. Candace Smith, 24, told a jury trial she had difficulty firing despite the knowledge that her life might depend on pulling the trigger.[5]

The final edition of the same newspaper, however, reprinted Cole's original story with a few amendments:

> Appearing to be holding back tears, Smith testified she had a hard time getting up the courage to shoot the man with her gun. She said she finally yelled, "Drop it!" and then fired at the man, but missed him. She then testified she waited about 90 seconds, knowing all the while that if the man came out of the room again he might shoot her. Twice more she fired at somebody peeking out from inside the suite, she said.[6]

Cole implied that Smith was indecisive and unable to accurately assess the level of violence she was facing. The media's coverage of

---

5   Brian Cole, "'I Couldn't Pull Trigger': Officer," *Winnipeg Free Press*, November 15, 1978.

6   Brian Cole, "I Knew I Had to Shoot, Policewoman Testifies," *Winnipeg Free Press Final*, November 15, 1978.

Smith's testimony was shaped by a gendered discourse that portrayed her, and, by corollary, all female Mounties, as too emotional to shoot a suspect during the commission of a violent crime.

Smith, who was surprised and angered by reports of her tearful testimony, had a different viewpoint. According to Smith, she was "on the stand for several hours" but "teared up for five seconds" when lawyers specifically asked her about seeing Onofrey's feet on the ground behind Archer's van. Smith's tearing up at that point was a compassionate and moral response to the death of a fellow police officer and the grief of his family and her co-workers. Today, studies on ethics and compassion describe the body's response to scenes of suffering as an ethical and humane response, rather than a sign of weakness.[7] But back in the 1970s, Smith's emotions on the witness stand were seen by journalists as evidence of emotional weakness. By focusing on Smith's perceived lack of emotional control instead of her bravery while wounded and under fire, they implied that Smith was unequal to the pressures of police work.

The jurors found Archer and Malette guilty of first-degree murder, and both were sentenced to life in prison. Archer, a diabetic, died as a result of gall-bladder surgery in 1991 while still incarcerated. Malette, after sixteen years in prison, applied for parole and was released in 1993. Russell Hornseth lost his left eye. Dennis Onofrey left behind a wife and two children. It would take Candace Smith three years to learn how to walk normally again.

Following the trial, the RCMP capitalized on the public's interest in Candace Smith and the Virden tragedy. A public relations representative of the police force fielded numerous requests to interview Smith and forwarded her contact information to several journalists. Smith thought it was part of her job as a member of the RCMP to grant media interviews. As a young and inexperienced police officer, she was too naive to realize that she had the freedom to turn down the media's requests. Smith began to feel used. She recalled that a journalist from *Reader's Digest* conducted a telephone interview with her but decided against publishing the story. Smith realized, "They wanted a Cinderella

---

7   Lauren Berlant, "Introduction," *Compassion: The Culture and Politics of an Emotion* (New York: Routledge, 2004), 6.

story, a happy ending story, but I don't have a happy ending story."[8] Eventually, she contacted the RCMP public relations person and asked that potential interviewers be screened before her contact information was released.

Smith eventually returned to active police duty at a rural posting in Manitoba after receiving medical clearance. Undertaking patrol work was something that Smith was proud of after months of pain and physical therapy. For Smith, "It was important to me to go and prove myself again. That took guts." Although she had healed physically, Smith continued to experience the mental and emotional effects of the shooting. To illustrate her struggle, Smith described her feelings as she approached the first few cars that she had pulled over following her return to duty: "I literally saw a shotgun coming out of those windows. I knew it wasn't there, but I still saw it and you still have to walk up to that car and say, 'Can I see your licence please?'"[9] Despite Smith's return to active duty, rumours began to circulate in the RCMP that Smith was working at a desk job. It was disturbing for Smith, who was proud of her recovery and eventual return to operational duties on the road. But rumours about her status on the job fed assumptions about work in the field as a masculine endeavour, in which only the physically and emotionally strong survived. Gossip that placed Smith and her damaged mind and body safely behind a desk was an indication of the privileged position work in the field occupied within police culture.

Many members of the RCMP were critical of Smith's actions at Virden. It was talk that began the day after Virden as word about the tragedy spread throughout the RCMP. Smith was frustrated that no one approached her directly with their questions or comments: "Being both female and a rookie, as well as having made errors of judgment in the split seconds involved, I was indeed an easy target [for my critics]. Especially for those who already had negative opinions about women in the force." This became particularly clear during a training course she was taking in Brandon, Manitoba, following her return to duty. The first morning of the course, she was advised that before class, instructors would be showing a slide presentation about the Virden shootings that had been developed by the RCMP. According to Smith,

---

8   Candace Smith, interview with author, April 19, 2008.

9   Ibid.

she had just half an hour to prepare herself for the presentation and the ensuing discussion with the forty to fifty male police officers who were also in attendance.

The slide presentation discussed the RCMP's investigation of Onofrey's murder. Smith's role in the Virden shootings was based on the two-paragraph statement that she had given to the RCMP while drugged and in intensive care. The RCMP police officers who developed the presentation did not ask Smith for her input during its creation. Smith recalled, "I watched this, and they were saying things like, 'This is where she took cover but she doesn't know why.' I had a reason for everything I did that day. I may have regretted not doing something else, but I had a reason for doing it that way ... [They] didn't even have enough respect to talk to me and ask me before they created this thing." Smith recounted her reaction to seeing this depiction of her for the first time:

> I sat there in disbelief that I was worth so little that I wasn't even worth talking to before they created this. And they were going across the country teaching this thing ... [O]bviously they were going to think women were assholes, because she ran around like a chicken with her head cut off, she didn't know why she did anything, like bullshit, I knew exactly what I was doing. I had a reason for everything I did that night. And then I got mad. I went back to the detachment and I was mad. They said, "She's emotional." ... To not even talk to you about it, you not only get shot but then you've got to be just discounted ... I still get choked.[10]

Smith's anger at seeing herself depicted in this way was further aggravated by her male colleagues at the detachment, who dismissed her anger by relying on conventional understandings of women as too emotional to deal with stressful events.

In contrast to the portrayal of her in the slide presentation, Smith's account of the shooting sheds light on her decisions while under fire:

---

10   Ibid.

Where I chose to take cover was closer than the alternative, which was much farther away. I decided to take the less attractive alternative because I knew I wouldn't make it across the open parking lot to be safer. I took cover behind a ten-inch wall that jutted out and I realized immediately that I was screwed. But you only have half a second to make a decision; you make that decision and then you're stuck with it.[11]

When asked about her failure to stop Archer by shooting him in the back, Smith recalled that she did pull the trigger:

He had his back to me and I was going to shoot him in the back. I thought I should warn him first, maybe I shouldn't have, and I regret it. And as I began to shout [in warning], he dove for the hotel room he had been staying in. Everything was hyperactive and my first shot missed. I was nervous. The next two shots I had just pinned him inside the room. I was just keeping him pinned and waiting for backup to arrive. I guess that meant that I shouldn't have warned him, and that is my big hate for myself. The other reason I hesitated for that fraction of a second to warn him was because when he stepped out of that room, no one else shot at him. I was alone there and did not know it.[12]

Smith's account contrasts significantly with the RCMP's version of the same events. Nevertheless, the video's subtext about female Mounties was conveyed to all RCMP officers who viewed the presentation as it travelled across Canada.

Today, Smith's account allows us to summarize the events of Virden in an alternative way. Smith and her colleagues at the motel were taken by surprise. They were outgunned by Archer. They were pinned down and unable to see each other. The officers did not have radio communication with each other or the detachment. Smith held her

---

11   Ibid.

12   Ibid.

ground and maintained sight of the door of room 20 during the exchange of gunfire. When the shooting stopped, she was unaware that Onofrey was dead or that Hornseth was seriously wounded. Smith, as a rookie police officer, was left alone at the scene. She was unaware that she was alone. Despite being struck by a shotgun blast that had knocked her to the ground, Smith held her position and kept her revolver trained on the door of room 20, firing twice more at Archer while he continued to fire at her. Smith single-handedly kept Archer and Malette pinned inside the hotel room while waiting for backup to arrive. It never came.

To be fair, Smith's actions at the Countryside Inn were not the only ones under scrutiny in the RCMP presentation. It was designed, after all, to teach other police officers how to make safe, sound, and split-second decisions under violent conditions. Smith remembered that Onofrey's choices were called into question, albeit more subtly, since he had lost his life. O'Ray was also judged for escaping the gunfire by running to nearby houses, although comments about his actions were also more indirect. None of the actions of the officers present at Virden escaped analysis in the slide presentation. However, viewers were never told that Smith's statement, on which her part in the presentation was based, was taken when she was in the hospital and under extreme physical duress and medicated. Instead, her supposed inability to clearly answer questions about the details of the shooting and the decisions she had made implied that she was too emotional to offer rational assessments of the crime.

Why were male RCMP officers interested in subjecting Smith to further psychological trauma by showing a flawed presentation about her actions at the shooting? Why would they develop and show a training presentation without her input or knowledge? And why would they surprise her with it? The fact that the subject of the training course was, according to Smith, unrelated to the Virden murder suggests that someone decided in advance to take advantage of Smith's presence to see what her reaction would be to the slides and the ensuing discussion. Surprising Smith at the last minute may have been an attempt to shame her for her perceived failure to live up to the values of bravery that were so deeply embedded in RCMP culture. But underlying the technical and highly dispassionate presentation was a subject that all police officers refuse to discuss: the fear of not returning home after the end of a shift. It was much easier to critique Smith and her co-survivors of Virden than engage with them on an emotional level about the life-and-death realities of police work.

The shooting took an emotional toll on Smith that continued for years. Smith struggled with guilt: "The guilt I felt was not so much, 'Yes, I should have shot him,' but Dennis [Onofrey] was obviously down. I didn't see his feet until a little later ... but my guilt was for the people [Archer] took hostage afterwards because I didn't shoot him. I did feel guilty about that." Smith also struggled with the feeling that she had somehow let women in the RCMP down. It was the group blame that most female Mounties feared. According to Smith, "I knew that even if I had done it perfectly, they still would have found something to complain about that they would have done differently. You never hear about the male member who missed the first shot, only the girl, the woman."[13]

Smith began to experience symptoms of post-traumatic stress disorder (PTSD) four years later while she was still working in the field. As current studies of PTSD demonstrate, the effects of the syndrome are often not evident until months or sometimes years afterward, and this was true in Smith's case. Smith's symptoms temporarily subsided when she left operational duties and was transferred to headquarters in Ottawa to work at a desk job. Smith was next transferred to an administrative position in Vancouver at "E" Division headquarters. While posted there, Smith did not receive an annual performance evaluation for three years. Although she continued to ask her supervisors for an assessment, no one complied with her requests. The absence of a performance rating meant that it was unlikely that she would be promoted or transferred to other units. Smith's supervisors' refusal to assess her performance was an indication that some members of the RCMP were working to force her to resign. This was confirmed by rumours Smith heard that they were trying to squeeze her out by transferring her back into the field after an eight-year absence. By this time in her career, both Smith and her supervisors knew that she would be unable psychologically to handle the strain of returning to general duties in the field. Employing gossip to force an unwanted police officer out of the RCMP was an informal exclusionary tactic used to exert pressure on a member who was perceived as weak.

---

13   Ibid.

Eventually, after years of sleeplessness, the strain became too much and Smith finally asked for a medical discharge. She had had enough of the rumours, uncertainty about her future position, and uncooperative supervisors. Smith finally received the trauma counselling that she should have had after Virden. A member of the RCMP's DSRR program advocated on her behalf and recommended that she receive professional counselling at the expense of the federal government. Veterans Affairs, the federal department in charge of health benefits for RCMP officers, paid for her treatment with a psychologist. Smith was officially diagnosed with PTSD and received a medical discharge from the RCMP in 1994.

When asked how she would like to be remembered as an RCMP officer, Smith commented: "That I cared and I really did try to help people. That really was my heart's desire. And I tried to treat people with respect. I do miss police work. I quite loved it. I hated the bureaucracy and the backstabbing ... but I loved the job itself."[14] It was a familiar refrain of female Mounties. Despite the level of harassment they received, their love of police work was reason enough to try to work around the gender conflicts that they faced.

Candace Smith's response during the gun battle emerged as the central focus of the arguments of those who were opposed to women as police officers. Despite the fact that male police officers were also injured or fatally wounded at Virden, it was the focus on Smith's actions that drew attention to the gendered divisions that existed within the RCMP. Smith's actions while under fire, her wounded body, her rehabilitation, and her return to active duty transcended understandings of women as the weaker sex. More importantly, her wounds called into question police work as a distinctly masculine occupation, since deadly violence against police officers was not gender specific. Her experiences were proof that a culture of masculinity, and not the inability of women to do the job, was at the root of the difficulties most women faced as they fought for full equality in the RCMP.

---

14   Ibid.

POST 1990:
BREAKING THE SILENCE

People [said] you couldn't send them here and there. What they
are talking about is muscle and muscle is only a small part of the
job. No one has ever questioned the courage of the female.

—Supt. William F. MacRae
Leader-Post (Regina), March 3, 1975

The fight for equality continued long after 1990 when Marianne
Robson placed a Stetson hat on her head for the first time. Issues
regarding the differences between male and female uniforms persisted. Although women could now wear the same review and service
order uniforms as their male colleagues, there were other orders of
dress that remained unchanged. The women's walking out order uniform for formal wear, which consisted of a long, navy-blue skirt and
black pumps, remained an official part of the female uniform. In January 2003, a female Mountie with seventeen years of service filed a
grievance with the RCMP's External Review Committee because she
was not allowed to wear the formal dress pants and congress boots
worn by men as part of her formal walking out order. The member
argued that the dress policy was discriminatory because it differentiated between male and female police officers.[1]

The RCMP denied her petition twice on the grounds that it was

---

1   Dene Moore, "Mandatory Skirts, Heels Scrapped for Female Mounties," Canadian Press, August 16, 2012. Congress boots are an ankle boot that has elastic gussets
on the sides. They were developed in the United States between 1840 and 1850 and
were so popular with politicians that they became known as "congress" boots. See
http://foottalk.blogspot.ca/2006/01/congress-boots.html.

force policy when she joined and she should have filed her grievance then. They also stated that one of the problems was that the pants and boots were expensive and difficult to source in women's sizes. It was not until 2012 that the RCMP relented, deciding that female Mounties who requested the formal pants and congress boots as part of their walking out order would be accommodated.[2] While some female Mounties enjoyed, even preferred, wearing the formal skirt, others decided that it was time that all orders of uniform and dress align with official RCMP employment equity policies. For these women, differences between male and female walking out orders were another visual inequality that called into question their credibility as police officers.

GENDER AND THE IMAGE OF THE RCMP

Female Mounties continued to be depicted in gendered ways well into the twenty-first century. In 2010, during the Vancouver Olympic Games, images of Canada formed a significant part of the event's closing ceremonies. Central to the program were a number of giant inflatable male Mountie figures. Dancing around these figures were numerous female dancers dressed in provocative, miniskirted Mountie costumes.[3] Many members of the RCMP took exception to the way female Mounties were portrayed during the program for an international audience. Female Mounties were no longer willing to remain silent about the sexualization of their image and voiced their complaints. The RCMP, who led security for the Olympic Games, protested to Vancouver Organizing Committee chairman John Furlong, who issued a public apology for the offence that was caused.[4] The sexualized portrayal of female Mounties during the closing ceremonies illustrates how gendered understandings of women persist across Canadian society.

Three years later, the RCMP Foundation, which owns the trademark to the RCMP's image, officially authorized the production of a Mountie Barbie doll. Mountie Barbie debuted in September 2013 to mark the 140th anniversary of the police force and to celebrate the

---

2   Moore, "Mandatory Skirts, Heels Scrapped for Female Mounties."

3   To view images of the women's costumes and the depiction of Mounties in the closing ceremonies, see http://www.vancouversun.com/news/canada/Photos+Olympic+closing+ceremony/4268769/story.html.

4   "Olympic Show Mini-Skirts Irk RCMP," *CBC News*, March 19, 2010.

upcoming fortieth anniversary of women in the RCMP.[5] The doll's packaging informed buyers that Mountie Barbie also came with "a pink passport for the perfect way for Barbie to travel across Canada, and the world, in style!"[6] Barbie dolls have long been criticized by consumer and parent groups in North America for idealizing an impossible body type for women and for conveying that message to children. Critics also take issue with the sexualization of the more than 135 different uniforms, most with pink accessories, worn by Barbie during the fifty-five years that she has been manufactured.[7] Mountie Barbie struck a negative chord with many female members of the RCMP who feared resurgence in the gendered attitudes toward them that they had fought so hard to overcome. Indeed, the name Barbie was sometimes used as a form of derision by the men of the RCMP when criticizing female Mounties. The appearance of Mountie Barbie, like the dancing female Mounties during the Olympics, did little to promote the respectability and credibility of women as figures of authority.

Scarlet fever, the sexual attraction women are said to experience when they see a male Mountie dressed in his red serge, appears to be thriving. This was very much in evidence in 2013 when Jenny Stewart, an eighty-eight-year-old hospice resident in Pt. Alberni, BC, met a Mountie for the first time. Jenny, who was raised in Scotland, saw her first Mountie as a ten-year-old child while on a school field trip to a British Empire exhibition. Next to a display of Canadian apples stood a handsome Mountie dressed in his red serge uniform. That image stayed with Stewart, who remembered thinking that one day she'd like to go to Canada and see a real Mountie again.

Part of Stewart's wish was realized when she immigrated to Canada as a war bride in 1946. The second part, however, remained elusive. For all of her years of living in Canada, she had never met a Mountie—that is,

5   "Mountie Barbie Sells Out in 48 Hours at RCMP Museum's Gift Shop," *Vancouver Sun*, September 25, 2013.

6   Emily Mertz, "Limited Edition RCMP Barbie for Sale," *Global News*, September 24, 2013. See http://globalnews.ca/news/860895/limited-edition-rcmp-barbie-for-sale/; also Michael Babad, "Meet RCMP Barbie (She always gets her man)," *Globe and Mail*, September 25, 2013.

7   Ashleigh Schmitz, "Why Is the Girl Scout Barbie Doll so Controversial?" *Community Table*, June 3, 2015, http://communitytable.com/318781/ashleighschmitz/why-is-the-girl-scout-barbie-doll-so-controversial/.

until a staff member at the hospice contacted the local detachment and Cst. Scott MacLeod arrived in his review order uniform for a surprise visit with Jenny. According to the hospice staff, Jenny was "starry-eyed" just to be in the same room with a Mountie.[8] We can only speculate about what Jenny's reaction might have been if a female Mountie had arrived for that visit instead. Her reaction to MacLeod suggests that she may have been quite disappointed. For many Canadians, young and old alike, it is still that handsome hero in his red serge uniform that remains the iconic symbol of Canada.

ONGOING STUDIES AND RCMP CULTURE

The RCMP continued to study female Mounties throughout the 1990s. In 1993, the RCMP's Personnel Directorate surveyed 525 members to determine why female, Aboriginal, and visible minority members continued to experience "apparent" higher attrition rates. The survey addressed issues of harassment, sexual harassment, morale, and job satisfaction. RCMP psychologist Dr. Glen Nosworthy, in the directorate's final report released in September 1996, found no evidence of "widespread ill-will toward designated group members in the RCMP." However, the report did conclude that "significant numbers of Caucasian Male members hold negative attitudes about the designated groups in certain areas." In particular, visible minorities were seen as "not respecting RCMP traditions" while Aboriginal and female members were "perceived as less committed to their careers." Further, white male Mounties felt that these groups desired preferential treatment and were prone to "imagining harassment and discrimination where they do not exist."[9] Another internal survey conducted in 1999 was so alarming that the RCMP's chief human resources officer, Garry Loeppky, issued "a force-wide alert" after the survey found that "60 per cent of female RCMP members reported being the victim of sexual harassment in the workplace." It was a number that was higher than the number of complaints that were being filed, a matter of "great concern" to Loeppky.[10]

---

8   Camille Bains, "Jenny Stewart's Mountie Dream Comes True 78 Years Later," *Canadian Press*, July 4, 2013.

9   Dr. Glen Nosworthy et al., *Report 3: Members' Views and Experiences of Harassment in the RCMP* (September 1996). Access to Information file GA-3951-3-03134/08.

10   Tonda MacCharles, "RCMP Watchdog Finds Glaring Gap in Tracking of Harassment Complaints," *Toronto Star*, February 14, 2013.

By the first decade of the twenty-first century, researchers began to pinpoint RCMP culture as a contributing factor to the problems women and minority groups in the police force were experiencing. In 2007, the RCMP commissioned an independent study to examine a number of workplace issues. Dr. Linda Duxbury studied the work environment and culture of the RCMP, concluding that "RCMP culture is not one that supports change." Her opinion was that the force may have been a victim of the "'success spiral' which occurs when an organization holds on too long to a culture in the belief that what has worked in the past will continue" to work in the future.[11]

Federal politicians began to conduct their own studies of RCMP culture. The Senate Standing Committee on National Security and Defence recommended in June 2013 that "meaningful cultural transformation and increased accountability" was needed in the RCMP.[12] By January 2014, the Honourable Judy Sgro and Senator Grant Mitchell were hosting roundtable events with female Mounties across the country to study a number of issues the women faced. Their final report, titled *Experts Summit on Challenges Facing the RCMP*, made thirteen recommendations including calls for cultural change within the RCMP.[13]

HARASSMENT

History continued to repeat itself as bullying, harassment, and sexual harassment remained a feature of RCMP culture. In 2012, yet another internal RCMP study revealed that female Mounties continued to be bullied and harassed by their colleagues and superiors. That study suggested that "gender-based harassment happened frequently," prompting D/Commr. Craig Callens to create a team of one hundred members to investigate harassment complaints.[14]

---

11   Dr. Linda Duxbury, *The RCMP Yesterday, Today and Tomorrow: An Independent Report Concerning Workplace Issues at the Royal Canadian Mounted Police* (November 2, 2007).

12   Senate Standing Committee on National Security and Defence, *Conduct Becoming: Why the Royal Canadian Mounted Police Must Transform its Culture* (June 18, 2013).

13   The Honourable Judy Sgro and Grant Mitchell, *Shattered Dreams: Addressing Harassment and Systemic Discontent Within the RCMP* (December 2014), i.

14   Andrea Woo, "Sexual-Harassment Claims Against RCMP Reach 336," *Globe and Mail*, July 18, 2014.

Many women in the RCMP were no longer willing to be silent about the harassment they were experiencing, and they began to turn to the court system to seek redress. Nancy Sulz, a former constable stationed in Merritt, BC, pursued financial compensation after being harassed by her NCO, whose actions, according to the trial judge, "were consistent with his experience of the paramilitary command structure of the RCMP." After ten years battling the RCMP in the courts, Sulz was awarded $950,000 in damages by the court in January 2006.[15] Thirty days later, the federal and provincial governments filed a notice of appeal, prolonging Sulz's legal battle and requiring her to prove, once again, that she had been harassed.[16]

In 2012, lawyers representing former and serving female Mounties, as well as female civilian employees, filed a class action lawsuit in BC Supreme Court alleging systemic discrimination by the RCMP.[17] The number of women joining the class action suit had reached 363 by the time of the hearing for certification in June 2015. One-third of the complainants were still working for the RCMP. Many of the women, representing nine provinces and all of the territories, characterized harassment and bullying as a widespread problem in the police force.[18] Those who were interviewed by the media stated that they hoped that the RCMP would recognize that harassing behaviour "has affected a lot of female members." They also commented that their motivation for coming forward and joining the lawsuit was to prevent the harassment of new women being hired. In response, the RCMP stated that it had repaired the problem of harassment by dealing with complaints quickly under its new harassment action plan.[19]

The RCMP is also adjusting its hiring practices. As of 2014, women

---

15   Gerry Bellett, "Ex-Mountie Wins Nearly $1M Harassment Suit," *National Post*, January 24, 2006.

16   Shannon Kari, "Ex-constable Must Again Prove RCMP Harassment," *Globe and Mail*, February 20, 2006.

17   Woo, "Sexual-Harassment Claims Against RCMP Reach 336."

18   Natalie Clancy, "More Women Alleging Harassment Want to Join Lawsuit Against RCMP," *CBC News*, May 31, 2015.

19   Simon Druker, "Lawyers for Hundreds of Female Mounties Hope to Convince a Judge to Certify Class-Action Suit," radio broadcast, *Vancouver News 1130*, June 1, 2015.

represented approximately 21 percent of members, a number the RCMP is working to increase to 30 percent by 2025. Citing a desire to be more representative of the communities it polices, the force has set a benchmark of recruiting 50 percent women in the 2014–2015 intake year, or half of the one thousand recruits they will send to Depot for training. The RCMP anticipates that it will achieve this number through advertising campaigns that target women, women-only recruiting presentations, an accelerated application process, and assisting female applicants to help them meet physical testing standards.[20] These initiatives suggest that the RCMP continues to believe that increasing the number of female police officers is the solution to the problem of discrimination against them.

History provides the context for understanding the persistence of the issues the RCMP is currently grappling with. The RCMP's systemic problems are deeply embedded in the nineteenth century and a reliance on a time when Mounties were cast as romantic and popular heroes who always got their man. The past shows us, however, that this heroic image was the creation of a number of historical figures who could not envision that one day women would be working alongside men in the daily operations of the police force. As a result, the RCMP's paramilitary system of operation, its rank structure, the geographical scope of its mandate, its centralized and hierarchical form of governance, its close ties to the history of Canada, its masculine and iconic image, and understandings of gender all contributed to a culture that was not receptive to the inclusion of women.

DANGER AND SACRIFICE

During the past forty years, the women of the RCMP have not hesitated to place their lives in danger for the sake of their communities. Five female Mounties have lost their lives in the line of duty. Special constable Nancy Marie Puttkemery, who joined the RCMP in 1975, was the first woman to join the RCMP's Air Services division as a pilot. She died when the RCMP aircraft she was piloting crashed during snowy and foggy conditions in 1989. Constable Della Sonya Beyak lost her life while on duty in 1989 as the result of a motor vehicle accident near

---

20   Douglas Quan, "RCMP Sets 'Ambitious' Recruitment Target: 50% Women," Postmedia News/Canada.com, October 19, 2014.

Assiniboia, Saskatchewan. Constable Christine Elizabeth Diotte died in 2002 when she was struck by a motor vehicle near Banff, Alberta. Constable Robin Cameron died from gunshot wounds she sustained while attending a domestic dispute in 2006. And Constable Chelsey Alice Robinson lost her life following a motor vehicle accident in Stony Plain, Alberta, in 2010.[21] Their examples demonstrate that a willingness to be placed in danger to protect others is gender neutral. Courage is not the sole preserve of men.

In 1998, Cst. Laurie White suffered a gunshot wound while attempting to serve a search warrant in Kitimat, BC. After eight hours of surgery, doctors were forced to amputate White's right leg below the knee. What appeared to be a career-ending event in the eyes of the RCMP was countered by White's fierce determination to meet the physical requirements necessary to return to active duty. It was just ten months later that White, fitted with her prosthesis, passed the RCMP's physical ability requirement evaluation test and returned to full, unrestricted, active duty.[22] She became the first amputee to serve as a member of the RCMP, demonstrating that women were more than equal to performing police duties on their own terms. White refused to remain silent about the shooting. She was awarded the Meritorious Service Medal by the Governor General of Canada on September 2, 2000, for her dedication to improving the lives of young Canadians with disabilities, notably for speaking publicly about her ordeal.[23] White is still a member of the RCMP today.

THE UNPAID MOUNTIE

The RCMP finally began to recognize the contributions of the Unpaid Mountie, or the Second Man, in 2010. The initiative was the result of a suggestion made to the commissioner by a member of the public. The RCMP's Honours and Recognition Directorate in conjunction with the Veterans' Association developed a "Second Man Commemorative

---

21   J.J. Healy, "RCMP Graves," http://www.rcmpgraves.com/forcefirsts/force-firsts.html.

22   Caroline Alphonso, "RCMP Corporal Laurie White Reflects on Shooting," *Globe and Mail*, November 7, 2007.

23   "Meritorious Service Decorations," *Canada Gazette* 134, no. 36 (September 2, 2000).

Brooch" in recognition of the service of Mountie wives to the RCMP. As of 2013, more than 470 women have received the brooch during official ceremonies held across the country.[24] Many Mountie wives are still active in the charity work of the Women's Auxiliary arm of the RCMP's Veterans' Associations across Canada.

TROOP 17 (1974/75)

As of 2015, all of the first female Mounties to be hired in 1974 have resigned or retired from the RCMP. Two of the women have passed away.

In 2006, Beverley Busson, a member of Troop 17, became the first female commissioner of the RCMP. Busson, who was preparing to retire at the time, accepted the post on an interim basis at the urging of the prime minister. Her tenure as commissioner ended in July 2007 when William Elliott, the force's first civilian commissioner, was appointed. Busson received a number of honours during the course of her long career with the RCMP, including being invested as a Commander of the Order of Merit and a recipient of the Order of British Columbia. She also holds an honorary doctorate.

Doris Toole retired from the Canadian Armed Forces in 1991 with the rank of colonel. She has kept in contact with members of Troop 17 and has attended anniversary events celebrating women in the RCMP as well as reunions organized by Troop 17. Toole has been recognized by the RCMP for her unique role as advisor to Troop 17 and has received commemorative medallions honouring the first women to join the force in 1974.

The women of Troop 17 were officially honoured by the RCMP in 2014 on the occasion of their fortieth anniversary. The RCMP's website featured articles about women in the RCMP and interviews with the first female Mounties. A commemorative medallion was struck in recognition of their hiring in 1974. In March 2015, the women received a second medallion in recognition of their graduation from Depot forty years earlier. Troop 17 continues to meet once every five years for a troop reunion, the most recent taking place in Las Vegas, Nevada, to celebrate their fortieth anniversary. They remain close friends.

---

24   James Murray, "RCMP Honour Wives of Early Officers," *Net News Ledger*, April 12, 2013, http://www.netnewsledger.com/2013/04/12/rcmp-honour-wives-of-early-officers/.

BIBLIOGRAPHY

PRIMARY SOURCES

RCMP Sources from the Period: Unpublished Documents, Studies, Speeches, and Correspondence

Andrews, Lynn. "Stress in Women Police." RCMP Health Services Directorate. December 1996. Access to Information file GA-3951-3-03134/08.

Baird, Sgt. D.R. *Policewomen in the R.C.M.P.* October 14, 1977. Access to Information file GA-3951-3-03134/08.

Bulletin. "Unisex Review Order—Female Members." RCMP file UDM 53. February 28, 1991; revised April 12, 1991.

Canadian Police Information Centre. Message to the Commissioner. August 30, 1974. RCMP file DPT-575 (17-74/75). Access to Information file GA-3951-3-03134/08.

———. Message to all divisions. September 13, 1974. RCMP file DPT-575 (17-74/75). Access to Information file GA-3951-3-03134/08.

Circular memorandum no. 229. The Commissioner to Officer Commanding. February 9, 1897. LAC RG-18-A-1, vol. 150, no. 211-98.

Circular memorandum no. 281. The Commissioner to Officer Commanding, all divisions. April 25, 1898. LAC RG-18-A-1, vol. 150, no. 211-98.

Cleveland, A/Commr. Dave. National broadcast. September 23, 1996. Access to Information file GA-3951-3-03134/08.

Department of Justice. Memorandum to NWMP. December 15, 1896. LAC RG-18-A-1, vol. 150, no. 211-98.

Graham, Cst. J.L. "Valedictory Address." Graduation dinner, Troop 17 (1974/75). March 3, 1975. RCMP Historical Collections Unit. Regina, Saskatchewan.

"Historical Evidence of A.M. Bulletin About Conversion of S/Csts. to Cst." RCMP file G524-17. November 24, 1992. Access to Information file GA-3951-3-03134/08.

Loo, Robert. *Interim Report: Stressors for Women in the Royal Canadian Mounted Police.* June 1984. Access to Information file GA-3951-3-03134/08.

Nadon, Commr. Maurice. Speech. Graduation parade ceremonies, Troop 17 (1974/75). March 3, 1975. Author copy.

———. Speech. "The Tenth Anniversary Dinner: Division Staff Relations Representatives." May 1984. Author copy.

NWMP. Memorandum to Deputy Minister of Justice. March 16, 1898. LAC RG-18-A-1, vol. 150, no. 211-98.

NWMP. Memorandum to the Commissioner. April 20, 1998. LAC RG-18-A-1, vol. 150, no. 211-98.

Pearson, L.B. "Announcement of Establishment of Royal Commission to Study Status." House of Commons Debates. February 3, 1967. 12613.

RCMP Memorandum. OIC Internal Affairs Branch to D.O.P. "Orders of Dress—Female Black Shoes (Pump)." RCMP file G 217 1 2. May 7, 1979. Access to Information file GA-3951-3-03134/08.

RCMP Memorandum. D/Commr. T.S. Venner to the Commr. RCMP file E330-2-99 (85/1). June 25, 1986.

Stark, S/Sgt. S.E. The Role of Female Constables in "E" Division. RCMP "E" Division Staffing and Personnel Branch. April 1986.

"Swearing in of Female Recruits." Press release. September 12, 1974.

Toole, Maj. D.E. Memorandum to the C.O., Depot Division. "Female Uniformed Member of the Force as Advisor." RCMP file DPT: 530-2-2. February 25, 1975. Author copy.

"Unisex Review Order—Female Members." Uniform and Dress Manual (12 April 1991). Access to Information file GA-3951-3-03134/08.

"Women Employed as Matrons—Not to be Taken on Strength of the Force." LAC, file RG 18-A-1, vol. 290, 702-04.

RCMP Publications

"A Guide to Success: Basic Recruit Training." RCMP Recruiting Guide. 1975.

"Canadian Chiefs of Police Conference." RCMP Quarterly 26, no. 3 (January 1961): 197–200.

Holm, E.A.F. "Police Image: A Paper Given at the Annual Dinner of the B.C. Provincial Police Held in Victoria on October 19, 1968." Scarlet and Gold, 50th Anniversary ed. (1968): 44–45.

Loates, Jean Alexandra. "Why I Joined the RCMP—Wives' Division." RCMP Quarterly 39, no. 2 (April 1974): 18–19.

Nowell, B.F. "Salute to the Wives." RCMP Quarterly 40, no. 4 (October 1975): 23.

"Policewomen, Why Not?" Royal Canadian Mounted Police Gazette 37, no. 7–8 (1975): 2–6.

"The First Troop." Royal Canadian Mounted Police Gazette 37, no. 7–8 (1975): 10–11.

Toole, Maj. D.E. "A View From the Sidelines." Royal Canadian Mounted Police Gazette 37, no. 7–8 (1975): 8–9.

Zanin, Brenda. "New Uniform Has Great Expectations." Pony Express (July/August 1998): 6.

———. "Police Women in the RCMP: In Touch With the RCMP's Feminine Side." Pony Express (October 1999).

RCMP Official Histories

Cooper, Monique, and Joel Walker. The Spirit of the Ride: The RCMP Musical Ride. Winnipeg: Heartland, 2007.

Horrall, S.W. The Pictorial History of the Royal Canadian Mounted Police. Toronto: McGraw-Hill Ryerson, 1973.

Sheehan, Dale, and Redd Oosten. Behind the Badge: History of the Royal Canadian Mounted Police "Depot" Division. Regina: Centax Books, 2006.

RCMP Popular Histories, Memoirs, and Autobiographies

Benson-Podolchuk, Sherry Lee. *Women Not Wanted: An Account of Workplace Conflict in the Male Dominated Bureaucracy of the RCMP*. Winnipeg: Hignell Book Printing, 2007.

Boulton, James J. *Uniforms of the Canadian Mounted Police*. North Battleford, Saskatchewan: Turner-Warwick Publications, 1990.

———. *Head-Dress of the Canadian Mounted Police*. Calgary: Bunker to Bunker Publishing, 2000.

Brennan, T. Ann. *The Real Klondike Kate*. Fredericton: Goose Lane Editions, 1990.

Brown, Lorne, and Caroline Brown. *An Unauthorized History of the RCMP*. Toronto: James Lorimer and Company, 1973.

Brunelle, Jacques. *The Royal Canadian Mounted Police in the 1990s: A Review of the Uniform, Dress and Kit of the RCMP*. Calgary: Bunker to Bunker Books, 1994.

Dobrowolsky, Helene. *Law of the Yukon: A Pictorial History of the Mounted Police in the Yukon*. Whitehorse: Lost Moose, 1995.

Duncan, Joy. *Red Serge Wives*. Alberta: Co-Op Press, 1974.

Hall, Jane. *The Red Wall: A Woman in the RCMP*. Renfrew, Ontario: General Store Publishing, 2007.

Haydon, A.L. *The Riders of the Plains: A Record of the Royal North-West Mounted Police of Canada, 1873–1918*. Toronto: The Copp Clark Co., 1919.

Knuckle, Robert. *In the Line of Duty: The Honour Roll of the RCMP Since 1873*. Burnstown, Ontario: General Store Publishing, 1994.

———. *Beyond Reason: The Murder of a Mountie*. Dundas, Ontario: Kayson Publishing, 1997.

Lee-Knight, Ruth. *When the Second Man Was a Woman*. Edited by Heather A. Punshon. Saskatoon: Imagine Publishing, 2004.

McKenzie, James. *Troop 17: The Making of Mounties*. Calgary: Detselig Enterprises, 1992.

Nicol, Eric, ed. *Dickens of the Mounted: The Astounding Long-Lost Letters of Inspector F. Dickens, NWMP, 1874–1886*. Toronto: McLelland & Stewart, 1989.

Paull, Dorothy Standish. *Scarlet Fever: A Story of Early Years in Banff and My Life as a Royal Canadian Mounted Policeman's Wife, 1914–1956*. Edited by Laura Chvojka. White Rock, BC: Self-published, 1993.

Sawatsky, John. *Men in the Shadows: The RCMP Security Service*. Toronto: Doubleday Canada, 1980.

Steele, Colonel S.B. *Forty Years in Canada: Reminiscences of the Great North-West with Some Account of His Service in South Africa*. New York: Dodd, Mead & Company, 1915.

"The Riders of the Plains," quoted in Andrew R. Graybill. *Policing the Great Plains: Rangers, Mounties, and the North American Frontier, 1875–1910*. Lincoln: University of Nebraska Press, 2007.

Treaty 7 Elders and Tribal Council et al. *The True Spirit and Original Intent of Treaty 7*. Montreal & Kingston: McGill-Queen's University Press, 1996.

Donny White. *In Search of Geraldine Moodie*. Regina: Canadian Plains Research Centre, University of Regina, 1998.

Other Published Manuscripts and Articles from the Period

Anderson, Doris. "The Strange Case of Policewoman Beckett." *Chatelaine* (April 1968): 3.

Gray, Charlotte. "Musical Riders: It Wasn't Easy Being the First Women on the RCMP Musical Ride." *Flare*, July 1982, 42–44.

LaMarsh, Judy. *Memoirs of a Bird in a Gilded Cage*. Toronto: McClelland & Stewart Limited, 1968.

Leighton, Tony. "Red Serge and High Spirits: Blood, Sweat and Fears: Life in the RCMP Training Depot." *Equinox* 22 (1985): 38–55.

MacLaren, Sherrill. *Braehead: Three Founding Families in Nineteenth Century Canada*. Toronto: McClelland & Stewart, 1986.

Melchionne, Theresa M. "Current Status and Problems of Women Police." *The Journal of Criminal Law, Criminology, and Police Science* 58, no. 2 (June 1967): 257–60.

Morris, Cerise. "'Determination and Thoroughness': The Movement for a Royal Commission on the Status of Women in Canada." *Atlantis* 5, no. 2 (Spring 1980): 1–21.

Newman, Christina. "What's so Funny About the Royal Commission on the Status of Women?" *Saturday Night* (January 1969): 21–26.

Ramsay, Jack. "My Case Against the RCMP." *Maclean's* (July 1972): 19–23; 58–74.

Government of Canada Sources

Canadian Human Rights Commission. *Sexual Harassment Casebook, 1978–1984*. Ottawa: Canadian Human Rights Commission, 1984.

Department of National Defense. "Bill C-90: An Act to Amend the National Defense Act." August 1, 1964.

Lalonde, Marc. *Status of Women in Canada: 1975*. Ottawa: Information Canada, 1975.

Munro, John C. *Status of Women in Canada: 1973*. Ottawa: Information Canada, 1973.

Pearson, Right Hon. L.B. "Announcement of Establishment of Royal Commission to Study Status of Women." House of Commons Debates. February 3, 1967. 12613. Order in Council PC 1967-312.

Report of the Royal Commission on the Status of Women in Canada. Ottawa: Information Canada, 1970.

Solicitor General of Canada. *Annual Report: 1974–1975*. Ottawa: Solicitor General of Canada, 1975.

———. *Women in Policing: Myths & Realities* (1993). RCMP file GM 448-36. Access to Information file GA-3951-3-03134/08.

Statistics Canada. Dunn, Sara. "Police Officers Murdered in the Line of Duty, 1961 to 2009." Fall 2010. http://www.statcan.gc.ca/pub/85-002-x/2010003/article/11354-eng.htm.

———. "Table 4: Police Officers by Sex, Canada, Selected Years." Police Administration Survey, Canadian Centre for Justice Statistics. http://www.statcan.gc.ca/pub/85-225-x/2010000/t005-eng.htm.

————. "Table 5: Male and Female Police Officers by Rank, Canada, 1986 to 2010." Police Administration Survey, Canadian Centre for Justice Statistics. http://www. statcan.gc.ca/pub/85-225-x/2010000/t006-eng.htm.

Douglas, T.C. "Request for Study of Status by Royal Commission." House of Commons Debates. January 10, 1967. 11587.

"Women in the RCMP." House of Commons Debates: Official Report, vol. III (1973), 2813; vol. V (1973), 4611.

Canadian Broadcasting Corporation Sources

Cross Country Checkup. "RCMP's Reputation Debated." CBC Radio. Originally aired June 10, 1973. http://www.cbc.ca/archives/entry/rcmps-reputation-debated.

The National. "Sikh Mounties Permitted to Wear Turbans." CBC Telvision. Originally aired March 15, 1990. http://www.cbc.ca/archives/entry/1990-sikh-mounties-permitted-to-wear-turbans.

The World at Six. "RCMP Welcomes First Female Officers." CBC Radio. Originally aired September 16, 1974. http://www.cbc.ca/archives/entry/1974-rcmp-wel-comes-first-female-officers.

Other Primary Sources on Policing

Anderson, Sgt. Mary A. Women in Law Enforcement: A Primer for Policewomen. Portland, Oregon: Metropolitan Press, 1973.

Boles, Sheldon, ed. "Old Surrey Boys." Veterans' Update. 2nd ed. Vancouver: RCMP Veterans' Association, 2012.

Brown, Jennifer M. "Sex Discrimination and Sexual Harassment in the Police: A UK Perspective." International Conference of Women Police. November 1993. Speaking notes. Access to Information file GA-3951-3-03134/08.

Edmunds, William Lewis. "The Woman Called Klondike Kate: One of the First Few Women to Enter the Klondike in the Trying Years of '98: A Hint of the Varied Experiences in Her Eventful Life." Maclean's, (December 15, 1922): 64–65.

Fitzgerald, Kathryn, and Mike Clark. "Equality in Policing: A Focus on Gender at Burnaby Detachment of the RCMP." Undergraduate research paper, Simon Fraser University, 1994.

Hamilton, Mary E. The Policewoman: Her Service and Ideals. New York: Frederick A. Stokes Company, 1924.

Lazar, Jonathan M. "Female Police Officers: Their Past, Present and Future." Undergraduate research paper, March 1993. Access to Information file GA-3951-3-03134/08.

Linden, Rick and Candice Minch. "Women in Policing: A Review." Working paper submitted to the Ministry of the Solicitor General of Canada. Winnipeg: Institute for Social and Economic Research, University of Manitoba, 1982.

Owens, Nancy J., ed. "Proceedings of the Annual Meeting of the International Textile and Apparel Association, Inc." November 1998, 18–21.

Owings, Chloe. Women Police: A Study of the Development and Status of the Women Police Movement. Montclair, NJ: Patterson Smith, 1925 & 1969.

"Rose Fortune." Association of Black Law Enforcers. http://www.ableorg.ca/pdf/fortunebutler.pdf.

Slaughter, Sgt. Cory. "Women's Journey into Policing." Unpublished paper. Ottawa Police Service, 2003, 1–5.

Toronto Police Service. "Herstory: Milestones in the History of the Toronto Police Service." http://www.torontopolice.on.ca/museum/herstory milestones_in_the_history of tps women.pdf.

United Nations General Assembly Resolution #3275 (XXIX). "International Women's Year." December 10, 1974. http://www.un-documents.net/a29r3275.htm.

Secondary Sources

Books

Bacchi, Carol Lee. *Liberation Deferred?: The Ideas of the English-Canadian Suffragists, 1877–1918*. Toronto: University of Toronto Press, 1983.

Backhouse, Constance, and Leah Cohen. *The Secret Oppression: Sexual Harassment of Working Women*. Toronto: Macmillan of Canada, 1978.

Berlant, Lauren. *Compassion: The Culture and Politics of an Emotion*. New York: Routledge, 2004.

Burke, Kathy, and Neal Hirschfeld. *Detective: The Inspirational Story of the Trailblazing Woman Cop Who Wouldn't Quit*. New York: Scribner, 2006.

Burton, Pierre. *The Klondike Quest: A Photographic Essay, 1897–1899*. Erin, ON: Boston Mills Press, 2005.

Carter, Sarah. *The Importance of Being Monogamous: Marriage and Nation Building in Western Canada to 1915*. Edmonton: University of Alberta Press; Athabasca: Athabasca University Press, 2008.

Corsianos, Marilyn. *Policing and Gendered Justice: Examining the Possibilities*. Toronto: University of Toronto Press, 2009.

Dashuk, James. *Clearing the Plains: Disease, Politics of Starvation, and the Loss of Aboriginal Life*. Regina: University of Regina Press, 2013.

Dawson, Michael. *The Mountie: From Dime Novel to Disney*. Toronto: Between the Lines, 1998.

Dyhouse, Carol. *Feminism and the Family in England, 1880–1939*. Oxford: Blackwell, 1989.

Eisenberg, Adam. *A Different Shade of Blue: How Women Changed the Face of Police Work*. Lake Forest, CA: Behler Press, 2009.

Foote, William E., and Jane Goodman-Delahunty. *Evaluating Sexual Harassment: Psychological, Social, and Legal Considerations in Forensic Examinations*. Washington, DC: American Psychological Association, 2005.

Fudge, Judy, and Hester Lessard. "Challenging Norms and Creating Precedents: The Tale of a Woman Firefighter in the Forests of British Columbia." In *Work on Trial: Canadian Labour Law Struggles*, edited by Judy Fudge and Eric Tucker, 315–53. Toronto: The Osgoode Society for Canadian Legal History, 2010.

Gentile, Patrizia. "'Government Girls' and 'Ottawa Men': Cold War Management of Gender Relations in the Civil Service." In *Whose National Security?: Canadian State Surveillance and the Creation of Enemies*, edited by Gary Kinsman, Dieter K. Buse, and Mercedes Steedman, 130–41. Toronto: Between the Lines, 2000.

Gwyn, Sandra. *The Private Capital: Ambition and Love in the Age of Macdonald and Laurier*. Toronto: McClelland & Stewart, 1985.

Harrington, Penny E., and Kimberly A. Lonsway. *Investigating Sexual Harassment in Law Enforcement and Nontraditional Fields for Women*. Upper Saddle River, NJ: Pearson/Prentice Hall, 2007.

Hewitt, Steve. *Riding to the Rescue: The Transformation of the RCMP in Alberta and Saskatchewan, 1914–1939*. Toronto: University of Toronto Press, 2006.

Horrall, S.W. "The Royal North-West Mounted Police and Labour Unrest in Western Canada, 1919." In *Lawful Authority: Readings on the History of Criminal Justice in Canada*, edited by R.C. Macleod, 18–33. Toronto: Copp Clark Pitman, 1988.

Kinsman, Gary. "Constructing Gay Men and Lesbians as National Security Risks, 1950–70." In *Whose National Security?: Canadian State Surveillance and the Creation of Enemies*, edited by Gary Kinsman, Dieter K. Buse, and Mercedes Steedman, 143–53. Toronto: Between the Lines, 2000.

Kinsman, Gary, and Patrizia Gentile. *The Canadian War on Queers: National Security as Sexual Regulation*. Vancouver: UBC Press, 2010.

MacDonald, Robert H. *Sons of the Empire: The Frontier and the Boy Scout Movement, 1890–1918*. Toronto: University of Toronto Press, 1993.

Macleod, R.C. *The NWMP and Law Enforcement, 1873–1905*. Toronto: University of Toronto Press, 1976.

Marquis, Greg. *Policing Canada's Century: A History of the Canadian Association of Chiefs of Police*. Toronto: University of Toronto Press, 1993.

———. "Policing Two Imperial Frontiers: The Royal Irish Constabulary and the North-West Mounted Police." In *Laws and Societies in the Canadian Prairie West, 1670–1940*, edited by Louis A. Knafla and Jonathan Swainger, 185–210. Vancouver: UBC Press, 2005.

Mawby, Rob C. *Policing Images: Policing, Communication and Legitimacy*. Portland, OR: Willan Publishing, 2002.

McPherson, Kathryn. "'The Case of the Kissing Nurse': Femininity, Sexuality, and Canadian Nursing, 1900–1970." In *Gendered Pasts: Historical Essays in Femininity and Masculinity in Canada*, edited by Kathryn McPherson, Cecilia Morgan, and Nancy M. Forestell, 179–98. Toronto: University of Toronto Press, 2003.

Pierson, Ruth Roach. *"They're Still Women After All": The Second World War and Canadian Womanhood*. Toronto: McClelland & Stewart, 1986.

Raibmon, Paige. *Authentic Indians: Episodes of Encounter from the Late-Nineteenth-Century Northwest Coast*. Durham and London: Duke University Press, 2005.

Reiner, Robert. *The Politics of the Police*. 3rd ed. New York: Oxford University Press, 2000.

Sangster, Joan. *Transforming Labour: Women and Work in Postwar Canada*. Toronto: University of Toronto Press, 2010.

———. "Debating Maternity Rights: Pacific Western Airlines and Flight Attendants' Struggle to 'Fly Pregnant' in the 1970s." In *Work on Trial: Canadian Labour Law Struggles*, edited by Judy Fudge and Eric Tucker, 283–313. Toronto: The Osgood Society for Canadian Legal History, 2010.

Schmidt, Bonnie Reilly. "Contesting a Canadian Icon: Female Police Bodies and the Challenge to the Masculine Image of the Royal Canadian Mounted Police in the 1970s." In *Contesting Bodies and Nation in Canadian History*, edited by Patrizia Gentile and Jane Nicholas, 368–85. Toronto: University of Toronto Press, 2013.

Schulz, Dorothy Moses. "Policewomen in the 1950s: Paving the Way for Patrol." In *Women Police*, edited by Mangai Natarajan, 37–62. Hants, UK: Ashgate, 2005.

———. *From Social Worker to Crimefighter: Women in United States Municipal Policing*. Westport, CT: Praeger, 1995.

Townsey, Roi D. "Female Patrol Officers: A Review of the Physical Capability Issue." In *The Criminal Justice System and Women: Women Offenders, Victims, Workers*, edited by Barbara Raffel Price and Natalie J. Sokoloff, 413–25. New York: Clark Boardman Company, 1982.

Waddington, P.A.J. *Policing Citizens: Authority and Rights*. Philadelphia: UCL Press, 1999.

Walden, Keith. *Visions of Order: The Canadian Mounties in Symbol and Myth*. Toronto: Butterworth & Co., 1982.

Watts, Sarah. *Rough Rider in the White House: Theodore Roosevelt and the Politics of Desire*. Chicago: University of Chicago Press, 2003.

Whitaker, Reg, Gregory S. Kealey, and Andrew Parnaby. *Secret Service: Political Policing in Canada from the Fenians to Fortress America*. Toronto: University of Toronto Press, 2012.

Articles

Baker, Carrie N. "Race, Class, and Sexual Harassment in the 1970s." *Feminist Studies* 30, no. 1 (Spring 2004): 7–27.

Bell, Daniel J. "Policewomen: Myths and Reality." *Journal of Police Science and Administration* 10, no. 1 (1982): 112–20.

Chabursky, Lubomyr. "The Employment Equity Act: An Examination of Its Development and Direction." *Ottawa Law Review* 24: 305–61.

Clément, Dominique. "The October Crisis of 1970: Human Rights Abuses under the War Measures Act." *Journal of Canadian Studies* 42, no. 2 (Spring 2008): 160 86.

Craik, Jennifer. "The Cultural Politics of the Uniform." *Fashion Theory* 7, no. 2 (2003): 127–47.

Dawson, Michael. "'That Nice Red Coat Goes to My Head Like Champagne': Gender, Antimodernism and the Mountie Image, 1880–1960." *Journal of Canadian Studies* 32, no. 3 (1997): 119–39.

"Despite Some Gains, Female Cops Still Find Too Few Cracks in the Glass Ceiling." *Law Enforcement News* 26 (June 2000): 9–10.

"Dr. Kenneth Cooper." Cooper 40 Aerobics. http://www.cooperacrobics.com.

Garcia, Venessa. "'Difference' in the Police Department: Women, Policing, and 'Doing Gender.'" *Journal of Contemporary Criminal Justice* 19 (2003): 330–44.

Gutek, Barbara A. "Sexual Harassment: Rights and Responsibilities." *Employee Responsibilities and Rights Journal* 6, no. 4 (1993): 325–40.

Herbert, Steve. "'Hard Charger' or 'Station Queen': Policing and the Masculinist State." *Gender, Place & Culture: A Journal of Feminist Geography* 8, no. 1 (2001): 55–71.

Hewitt, Steve. "The Masculine Mountie: The Royal Canadian Mounted Police as a Male Institution, 1914–1939." *Journal of the Canadian Historical Association* 7 n.s. (1996): 153–74.

Horrall, S.W. "Sir John A. Macdonald and the Mounted Police Force for the Northwest Territories." *Canadian Historical Review* 53, no. 2 (June 1972): 179–200.

Kurtz, Don L. "Controlled Burn: The Gendering of Stress and Burnout in Modern Policing." *Feminist Criminology* 3, no. 3 (2008): 216–38.

Levine, Philippa. "'Walking the Streets in a Way No Decent Woman Should': Women Police in World War I." *Journal of Modern History* 66, no. 1 (March 1994): 34–78.

Lonsway, Kimberly A. "Tearing Down the Wall: Problems with Consistency, Validity, and Adverse Impact of Physical Agility Testing in Police Selection." *Police Quarterly* 6, no. 3 (September 2003): 237–77.

Morton, Desmond. "Cavalry or Police: Keeping the Peace on Two Adjacent Frontiers, 1870–1900." *Journal of Canadian Studies* 12, no. 2 (1977): 27–37.

Myers, Tamara. "Women Policing Women: A Patrol Woman in Montreal in the 1910s." *Journal of the Canadian Historical Association* 4, no. 1 (1993): 229–45.

Robinson, Daniel J., and David Kimmel. "The Queer Career of Homosexual Security Vetting in Cold War Canada." *Canadian Historical Review* 75, no. 3 (1994): 319–45.

Robinson, Marcus. "Fashion: Mounted Police." *Saturday Night*, October 1996, 28.

Schmidt, Bonnie Reilly. "Women on the Force." *Canada's History* (August–September 2011): 34–41.

———. "'The Greatest Man-Catcher of All': The First Female Mounties, the Media, and the Royal Canadian Mounted Police." *Journal of the Canadian Historical Association* 22, no. 1 (2011): 200–42.

Schulz, Dorothy Moses. "From Policewoman to Police Officer: An Unfinished Revolution." *Police Studies* 16, no. 3 (Fall 1993): 90.

Sethna, Christabelle, and Steve Hewitt. "Clandestine Operations: The Vancouver Women's Caucus, the Abortion Caravan, and the RCMP." *The Canadian Historical Review* 90, no. 3 (September 2009): 463–95.

Stone, Rebecca. "Sam Browne and Beyond: A Look at Duty Belts." *Police: The Law Enforcement Magazine* (November 2000): unnumbered.

Wickens, Barbara. "Dressing the Part." *Maclean's* (May 6, 1996): 11.

Winslow, Donna, and Jason Dunn. "Women in the Canadian Forces: Between Legal and Social Integration." *Current Sociology* 50 (2002): 641–67.

INDEX